Praise for

Using the Power of Hope to Cope with Dying

"This potent and inspiring message is highly recommended for both the professional and the nonprofessional end-of-life caregiver."
—Dolores Krieger, Ph.D., R.N., author of *Therapeutic Touch as Transpersonal Healing*

"When a person is dying, the sense of having lost all hope is often worse than the prospect of death; this book is an antidote to hopelessness."
—Ira Byock, M.D., palliative care physician; author of *Dying Well* and *The Four Things That Matter Most*

"Hope is necessary for survival. It is not about statistics and there is no false hope. This book gives the reader an excellent perspective about the role hope can play in one's life while confronting one's mortality. You can learn to live until you die rather than be dying."
—Bernie Siegel, M.D., author of *Love, Medicine & Miracles* and *Help Me to Heal*

"I have just finished reading your manuscript.... It is an interesting and moving contribution to the huge literature on death."
—Elisabeth Kübler-Ross, M.D., author of *On Death and Dying*, who got a chance to read the working manuscript for this book prior to her own death in 2004.

"Rabindranath Tagore, the great Indian poet, said, 'Hope is the bird that sings before the dawn.' In this wonderful book, Cathleen Fanslow-Brunjes helps us recognize this song so we can harmonize with it. It is when the darkness is the most profound that hope emerges as the true reality. She gives us tools which we can use to create the music of love which each soul needs."
—Gladys Taylor McGarey, M.D., M.D.(H)., Founder and Past President of the American Holistic Medical Association

To my father,
without whom I would not be who I am,
and to my three teachers:
Dolores Krieger, Ph.D., R.N.;
Elisabeth Kübler-Ross M.D.;
and Dora Kunz

USING THE POWER OF HOPE TO COPE WITH DYING

The Four Stages of Hope

CATHLEEN FANSLOW-BRUNJES, M.A., R.N.

Fresno, California

Printed in the United States of America.

Published by
Quill Driver Books, an imprint of Linden Publishing
2006 S. Mary, Fresno, CA 93721
559-233-6633 / 800-345-4447
QuillDriverBooks.com

Quill Driver Books' titles may be purchased for educational, fund-raising, business or promotional use. Please contact Special Markets, Quill Driver Books, at the above address or phone numbers.

Quill Driver Books Project Cadre:
Doris Hall, Christine Hernandez, Dave Marion,
Stephen Blake Mettee, Cassandra Williams

First Printing

ISBN 978-1-610350-24-2

To order a copy of this book, please call
1-800-345-4447.

Library of Congress Cataloging-in-Publication Data

Fanslow-Brunjes, Cathleen, 1939-
Using the power of hope to cope with dying : the four stages of hope / by Cathleen Fanslow-Brunjes.
p. cm.
ISBN 978-1-610350-24-2
1. Death—Psychological aspects. 2. Hope—Psychological aspects. I. Title.
HQ1073.F36 2008
155.9'37—dc22

2008003483

Mixed Sources
Product group from well-managed
forests and other controlled sources
www.fsc.org Cert no. SW-COC-002283
© 1996 Forest Stewardship Council
FSC

Contents

Hope is the thing with feathers
that perches in the soul
and sings the tune without the words
and never stops at all...

—Emily Dickinson

Foreword

*H*ope is a powerful word. It is a word used by all of us in many different ways and with many different meanings. The *American Heritage College Dictionary* defines *hope* in one way as "to wish for something with expectation of its fulfillment, to expect and desire." But hope is different from wishing for something or being positive about events in your life, whatever form those events may take.

Hope is everywhere. Think about your family and your friends. Recall the way in which each one has dealt with life's experiences. Every one of us has our own way...a story about how we hope and what hope means to us. Hope is an integral part of our life and follows us as we experience life and death. It gives us a way to deal with what has happened to us.

This book, authored by my longtime friend and colleague, Cathleen Fanslow, is about helping those facing death, something many fear and do not wish to think about. It provides a powerful tool to help the dying and their family and loved ones cope with the inevitable act of dying. Those of us who began our careers in the early sixties and continue to practice today have seen many changes in the way health care is practiced and death is addressed.

This book about using the power of hope to cope with dying evolved from the author's many years of personal experiences caring for the sick and terminally ill. It draws on both what patients taught a young practitioner before the days of hospice care and on the approaches to terminal care available today. What better way to help each of us as we experience the loss of our loved ones and address our own mortality?

This book is about hope and how it will help you to confront the reality that death will eventually occur to all of us. It provides a meaningful and simple approach to the experience of dying.

Carol Reed Ash, Ed.D., R.N., FAAN
Professor Emeritus, University of Florida
Editor, *Cancer Nursing*

Acknowledgments

I would like to thank Candace Lyle Hogan who inspired me initially and helped me hear my voice in writing and Lester Hoffman whose help in refining the proposal and sample chapters was invaluable. I would also like to thank Janet Macrae, my faithful friend, who encouraged and supported me every step of the way; Kate Poss whose typing and editing skills made it come together; and Steve Mettee and his staff at Quill Driver Books whose remarkable skill at editing and refining my work made this dream become a reality.

For so many years my family, friends, colleagues, and above all my students, have been asking me to please finish my book, constantly saying, "We need it." I thank you for all your patience and support and I hope that this is just what you have been hoping for. Finally I want to thank all the patients and their loved ones who have been my teachers and my inspiration.

Introduction
The Meaning of Hope

When I became a registered nurse in 1964, before the era of hospice and patient-centered care, those with a terminal illness eked out their last days largely forgotten within a hospital's cold walls. These were the days before Elisabeth Kübler-Ross's landmark book, *On Death and Dying*, brought them out of the darkness; the days when the dying person was placed in a room at the end of the hall like an unmentionable, rarely referred to by name—it was always "the cancer in room 44" or "the heart attack in 27."

Because we in the medical profession could not cure them, the fact that they continued to die flew in the face of our thinking that we should be able to control everything. So it was, *If I can't cure you, I'm going to put you at that end room....* I can't tell you how many fights I had during that time, when doctors talked about, "Oh, the bladder cancer in room 306"— no name, no person, just a diagnosis and a room number. I wondered, *what does that do to the person?* Terminal illness had robbed them of a well-functioning body, and now the doctor strips them of their selfhood and identity. Early on, I saw how the abandonment of the dying begins.

And I can't tell you how many altercations I had over it. I'll never forget this one young doctor whom I heard talking this way. I was still in my floor-length white nun's habit (with the under cap and bonnet that allowed for absolutely no peripheral vision), the old kind that came out of the laundry starched out to *here!* So there I was in my thick white belt and cuff links with a silver cross, but that didn't stop me from acting out my rowdy nature. I'm from Brooklyn, after all, and I fancied myself a champion of the underdog, so when I heard this doctor talking as if a dying patient were not a person, I came bustling down the hall at him like a white hot fury. I stepped on his foot and grabbed his tie, and said, "How dare you! That is not just simply a diagnosis or a room number, that's a person—and what is that person's name?"

What Elisabeth Kübler-Ross, who was a psychiatrist and a doctor (and also my teacher when I began), brought into the medically dominated, cure-oriented world of that time was a new framework of thinking about the dying. She insisted on acknowledging what the terminally ill were going through psychologically. But she, as well as I, always sensed that there was something more going on than psychology, something deeper, but we weren't able to name it then.

Kübler-Ross attempted to give patients some kind of control over their fate by helping them understand the psychodynamic shifts they were going through. By classifying these shifts—naming them "the stages of grief"—she identified the psychological behaviors of the dying person and the coping mechanisms they used from diagnosis through death.

Her first stage is *Denial*: *No, no, not me.* Then *Anger* comes in: *Why me?* The anger stage is followed by the *Bargaining* stage: *Yes me, but...* The next stage is *Depression*: *Oh my god, I'm going to die.* And finally, *Acceptance*, the final stage: *I'm going to die, and somehow it's all right.* What she did was identify behaviors, and, thankfully, that alone sparked a revolution in how we thought about the process of death and how people in the medical profession treated the dying. But we both realized, as revolutionary as this was, it was just a start.

The psychodynamics reflect only a part of the dying person's experience. What was left was unearthing their own hope system, where they really live.

I knew there was something different than just this set of psychodynamics, something else going on at a deeper level than the psychological, something even more dynamic and powerful than psychological theories could explain. Eventually, over years of observation and being at the bedside, I was able to give it a name: *Hope*, a term not unfamiliar to the medical establishment even then, and a concept that has come to intrigue the academics more and more in the context of end-of-life care.

Hope is universally understood to mean something more profound than simply a wish or a goal. But it's not a loaded word so far, since it has escaped religious or spiritual connotations, and therefore people can consider it regardless of their belief system. I found that by addressing hope as the key underlying dynamic within each person that it really is , I could facilitate a dying person's entree into the powerful force of healing that was already within them. Time and again, I saw hope operating in a variety of people in the same ways. To enable people to use this pattern as a helping tool, I named it, quantified it, and taught it in workshops: *The Hope System.* By recognizing each person's hope system, I could connect with the dying where they really live.

But first I had to understand where I really lived, what really moved and motivated me at the core. I had to unearth my own hope system, just as in this book readers will be asked to do, before being able to walk with the dying on their final journey.

I started out my life's work tending to the dying, which has turned out to be my true calling, getting the best education possible at that time for this type of work by joining a convent. The religious community that I entered at age seventeen was a rather unusual one for the time, the late 1950s, and it was this difference from other teaching orders of nuns that attracted me. This congregation was called Nursing Sisters of the Sick Poor, which described its mission: the care of the sick poor in their own homes. The Sisters seemed to be more compassionate and kind to the people and patients with whom they worked. They were freer than other medical professionals and assisted and communicated with people in a very real and special way that appealed to me.

In 1961, I was sent forth to become a nurse. I came into nursing in a way that is now almost extinct, through a diploma school of nursing that combined intense class work with working on the units actually caring for patients. In effect, nursing students staffed the hospital, working all three shifts—days, evenings, and nights. For various reasons (mostly as punishment for some infraction or another), I seemed to always be working the night shift, but that turned out to be a gift. It is a well-known fact that most people die at night, usually between 2 A.M. and 4 A.M. So it was from the dying themselves that I learned my most valuable lessons early on.

Although I was just twenty-one and only a student nurse, I always had a sense of comfort with the dying, and I was never anxious or afraid of the experience in any way. Well, my hands never shook, anyway, but you never saw my knees—because of the habit. I realize now that it was a preparation for the rest of my life.

In the early 1960s we were still in the old full habit, with only our face visible (for "custody of the eyes") and dressed completely in white from head to toe when we worked in the hospital. Many patients, especially the dying, would call us angels and our very presence seemed to calm them as death came near. Because we were Sisters, they thought we had an inside track on helping people as they came to the end of their lives.

When we were sent out to care for people in their homes, we were not allowed to receive gifts, of course, and neither could we take anything with us except a sandwich and a tea bag. I remember the first day after graduating as a nurse—July 7, 1964. As part of the Nursing Sisters of the Sick Poor, I was dropped off at the subway station in Jamaica, Queens, to begin making my rounds. There I was in my full black habit (a nun's street wear), a rather medieval sight in gabardine—cincture (belt) gripping my waist as if girding me before battle—my nursing bag, along with my sandwich and tea bag in hand, when my long rosary caught in the subway door! Good thing I was young and could run to keep up with the train, and that the rosary was on an elastic cord with a Velcro closure.

We took a sandwich and a tea bag for our lunch, because the only thing we could take from the poor was water. There was tremendous freedom in being able to care for patients in such a pure way, asking nothing from them, requiring nothing from them but the privilege and opportunity to care for them at life's end. I now realize that it was this freedom to be able to be with patients and their families in such an extraordinary way that kept me in religious life for so long.

I did home nursing for the majority of the sixteen years I was a nun. This time afforded me the opportunity to accompany literally hundreds of dying persons on their final journey. We would take care of them during the day, return to the convent to say our prayers, eat dinner, and often go back out and stay with them throughout the night until they died, caring for them and supporting the family.

In subsequent years, I have worked pretty much nonstop with the terminally ill and their caregivers and grieving families, primarily in home care and in all types of institutions—hospitals, hospices, nursing homes—performing jobs on all levels, including managerial positions and as director of nursing. Concurrently, beginning early in my career, I developed workshops on grief and The Hope System for both professionals and laypeople, learning much, in turn, from the 40,000 students I've taught throughout the United States, Canada, and in Europe. My work has been recognized as pioneering the improvement of end-of-life care and I am frequently sought out to describe it, on television, the radio, and through other media outlets.

Beginning in the early 1970s, I also participated in the beginning of Therapeutic Touch, with Dolores Krieger, Ph.D., R.N., and Dora Kunz, the science-based healing art that is used in more hospitals in the United States than any other complementary therapy or form of energy work. I also teach it, and developed a technique based on its principals, which many people feel comfortable employing with the dying, called The Hand-Heart Connection (see Chapter 9).

My early life choices, and all those that have followed in the last forty years, gave me the opportunity to become the ultimate companion many times, placing me on the receiving end of the gift of insight. There have been so many journeys, each made in his or her own way, yet each and every person so generous in sharing their wisdom. We have much to learn from the dying. It is my privilege to share what they have taught me.

Facing death may be life's most difficult challenge, an inner journey. But, in this book, as a I did when a member of the Nursing Sisters of the Sick Poor, I use a gentle way of moving readers through the process of dying, increasing their awareness of life and living as much as of the process of death and dying.

I believe this book is timely enough to meet the needs of the baby-boomer generation, and it can be seen as the helpmate that helpmates have been waiting for: a systematic guidebook for how to navigate this voyage into the unknown, by conquering fear with compassion.

Offering practical advice in a way readers will be able to use, regardless of their beliefs, The Hope System addresses all levels of the experience—physical, emotional, psychological, and spiritual—within the embrace of that thing called "hope," just as the dying do. Hope is the foundation of the dying person's world. By systematically learning how to recognize and honor a dying person's hopes, anyone can support him or her from first diagnosis to last breath in a way that is healing for all.

What is hope? Hope is many things, with as many responses as there are people to whom one asks the question. Hope is like a diamond, being multifaceted; often clear and sparkling, sometimes a bit cloudy with a hint of yellow; or perhaps it appears dull and lifeless.

At other times it's vibrant, blue-white beauty dazzles the eye. Yet the diamond, despite its various appearances, remains true to its essence, the highest and most perfect crystal.

Hope within the human being, like the diamond, has its myriad of facets and manifestations. Hope is the essence of the person, an integral part of each individual's life matrix. It has many names in a variety of cultures and languages. I have also defined and redefined it in this book to describe its ever-changing role within our human lives.

I named hope our primary motivator, that fundamental life force that moves and directs us throughout our journey called life. Others have defined hope as energy of specific and exquisite dimensions and intricacies. Still, others hold it a theological virtue, which, with faith and charity, forms the foundation of Christian belief. Some have likened it to goals, as things of great importance yet to be accomplished.

I like to teach people things and give them tools that are simple and that work. But first I had to learn myself. Fortunately, many people helped me do that along the way. In particular, I remember John, a man who exemplified to me how useful and effective The Hope System could be in facilitating understanding and communication between everyone involved—patient, family, and professional caregivers alike. The story of this remarkable man appears in Chapter 1.

More than a *wish*, of deeper origin than a *goal*, that thing called *hope* is actually what drives the process of change, whether the transition is into death, or into a different way of living. There is a reason for the maxim, "hope springs eternal." Hope is the feeling that makes it possible to imagine how something good might come of death, the most dramatic change of all.

Simple and utilitarian, The Hope System works great at cutting through the patient-role garbage to return an individual to personhood—in their eyes and in the eyes of others. Realizing the power of this simple, yet profound, tool has changed the quality and effectiveness of my interactions with dying people and their loved ones ever since. I know it will help you as it has helped me, and many others, to accompany the dying in a real and connected way.

Chapter 1

The Power of Hope in Living & Dying

Being there when it counts means being compassionately present in the moment with a person in crisis, being a *listening presence*. You don't have to be there physically; you can be present over the phone or in a letter or via e-mail, as long as you compassionately focus on the needs of the moment.

You also need to be gentle and compassionate with yourself and that begins with self-understanding. You must recognize "what's yours" before you can distinguish "what's theirs" in this intense world of feeling.

Exploring Your Own Feelings Toward Death

First, I will take you through an exercise designed to unearth your own attitude towards death and loss. This awareness will enable you to find your way beyond pity, sympathy, and even empathy, to true *compassion*, that transpersonal state where caregivers can offer the most support and healthy connections to the dying.

This gentle and effective lesson called "The Five Columns" is practiced in my workshops. Before I relate my experiences with it, try it yourself. Properly done, it requires a bit of self-exploration, a necessary prerequisite to becoming a compassionate presence for the dying.

Using a blank sheet of paper, draw five columns. Across the top of the page, title them:

- Life
- Death

- Death of the person closest to me
- Parts of my body or my life most difficult for me to lose
- My own death

Write down the first words or phrases that come to mind under each of these columns. Don't worry about spelling or grammar, just write.

Have an internal dialog about your responses. Mentally walk in the footsteps of the terminally ill, exploring your feelings as you do so. If you take a minute to do this exercise before reading on, it will allow you to compare what you write with what others have written without being influenced by what they wrote. Each of us have our own unique way to respond to these questions. There are no right or wrong responses; each response is "normal" for you. By doing this exercise you will learn from the "laboratory of the self" some of what the dying may experience from the moment of the life-changing diagnosis to the moment of death, as well as your own feelings about death and the dying.

Five Columns Workshops

I have tested this approach with thousands of workshop students—health-care professionals, laypeople, and the dying themselves.

As my workshops begin, I ask participants to turn off their cell phones and consciously let go of all the busyness, responsibilities, and demands of their lives and to take an inward journey with me.

Column One

We start with the life column. Underneath that word I ask that they write whatever "falls out of their mind onto the paper." I tell them not to worry about spelling or grammar, but to just let the words flow onto the paper, inspired by the word *Life*.

When they have finished writing, I ask them to call out words from their individual columns, which I write on a white board to make a composite column for the group to see and reflect upon.

The responses from the life column usually flow easily and sometimes I have to slow the participants down in order to get all the answers on the board. For the most part the responses are light, easily shared, and quickly fill the column. Frequently the patterns that emerge have to do with daily life, work responsibility, relationships, love, joy, family, and children. Faith and God come in. Words and phrases that are recurrent in this column include *beach, water, trees, hiking, picnics, taking walks, the color green, blue skies, sunsets, sunrises,* and *vacations.* Difficult subjects such as *money, not enough time, too much work, loss,* and *death* usually don't come up until the end of the column.

We talk for a few minutes about what these terms mean to us. At this juncture I start using the phrase *normal and unique* to describe for them their particular response to this word *Life.* I explain that each response is unique to them and their personal life experiences, and, if they are caring for a dying person, unique to the bond between that person and themselves. Each response is normal as well, in that it is normal for them to feel as they do. Guilt and self-recrimination should be left at the door.

At the end of our discussion, I ask that they count the number of responses in their life column. Their entries often exceed twenty. Subsequent columns usually have considerably fewer.

As you read this, have you been able to see similar words and patterns in your own response? Do you think your responses are normal? Can you see how they would be unique to you and your particular life experiences?

Column Two

At the top of the next column I ask students to write the word *Death* and to again write their responses. When the group has finished writing, I ask, "Is there a change in the room? Has something happened here?"

Often I sense my asking these questions brings a feeling of relief. I hear sighs and comments such as, "It *is* darker now." The terms *heavy, sad,* and *quieter* often come up. Some people express that they feel uncomfortable or that they felt a pall come over the group.

The students are always interested, as you may be, about a phenomenon I have repeatedly observed with this *Death* column. It is my experience that people's handwriting changes somewhat when writing in this column. People are often surprised to find they have written their responses smaller, bigger, printed instead of using cursive, or different in another way when compared to their life column.

In order to help the participants go deeper into themselves I ask the question, "If there was not such a noticeable change in atmosphere in a group of health and hospice caregivers, should I be concerned? Why might that happen?"

Some of the answers heard most frequently are: "They are in denial" and "They have become hardened or burned out."

In addition to the above, I usually add that the health caregivers may not have personally experienced death, so it is not real to them. It is not part of their consciousness.

I then discuss a common, unexplored motivation—often existing on an unconscious level—that I have found to exist in groups of people drawn to work with the dying. They may have experienced the death of someone close to them at an early age (birth to toddler) or at a developmentally fragile time, such as when they were a teenager, and it has left a deep imprint on them; a mark that has not been uncovered or dealt with in their life thus far. Many people recognize this in themselves for the first time during my workshops, as others share similar early death, loss, and separation experiences they have endured.

I also have observed that the entries in the *Life* and *Death* columns often contain similar responses regarding the "grounders" or stabilizers inherent in peoples' lives. These include family, friends, and other support people, and transcendent elements, such as faith, God, and a belief in an afterlife.

Column Three

When we are done discussing this column I write: "Death of the person closest to me" at the top of the third column on the white board. As I do this, I often begin to feel a change in the room. When I finish writing, I turn in anticipation of their question. I say, "It may be someone who has died or someone who is still alive, whatever comes to your mind first, just go with it, and let the words flow out onto your paper."

As I wait for them to write in their own column, I frequently observe behaviors different than I did when assigning the first two columns. There are more tears and expressions of sadness and discomfort in the group. Many people sit and stare, cross their arms and glare at me, or look away. Some begin writing furiously, while others need to go to the restroom or leave the room for awhile.

I sense when the group has had enough time and begin the dialog by asking, "What happened here?"

Some of the responses I have heard repeatedly are:

"You brought it all back."

"Awful."

"I refuse."

"Everything went black."

"Tears and sadness."

"I'll never get over it."

Others are:

"I was surprised by who came up as the closest."

"It was hard to choose who was the closest; I had more than one."

"I remembered what she was to me."

"I lost the love of my life."

"Memories are a great gift."

I can feel their eyes on me as I record on the white board the generally heavy emotions felt and expressed quickly and clearly by the group. I push them a bit, sharing that, "I feel another strong emotion, that none of you have mentioned. What do you think it is?"

Silence usually prevails so I answer my own question: "I feel anger, strong anger, mostly aimed at me." At this moment I again stress that all their feelings are normal and unique to their life experiences and the relationship they had with the people who died. "Why wouldn't you feel angry?" I ask. "How dare I make you think about this and feel this way?" They often say something like, "Boy, Cathy, you have a lot of nerve," or, "Yes, why?" Again I stress the importance of lessons learned in the laboratory of the self.

Perhaps you had similar feelings and responses as you wrote under column three.

My next question to the group is, "Was there anyone who was not able to write in this column?" Usually there is at least one. "Was everyone able to choose someone who was the closest to them? How many of you could not respond or write initially? You needed to wait, push the paper away, but then after awhile were able to respond?"

I tell them that those who reacted in this manner demonstrated in a profound way what people are going through when they are faced with the possibility of the death of the person closest to them. It is a common first response to deny the likelihood of death, push it away, run from it, because it is too painful to even consider that the person they love and need, by whom they are defined in so many ways, will die and leave them.

Next I ask how many of the students put a relationship such as mother, father, or spouse at the top of the column. (My personal definition of closest, which is the presence of both a love bond and a need bond in defining the relationship, is a concept further explored in Chapter 6.)

Many respond in the affirmative and a dialog ensues. Then I ask if anyone wrote a name at the top of their column. Rarely in my workshops, does someone do this. For the most part students say something like, "It makes it too real if I put a name." Another response is, "I wouldn't put his name down because then it might happen, or come true. I don't want to jinx anyone I love."

I ask how many of the class thought about someone who had already died. I ask how long ago. The answers range widely, from a few months to thirty years. Then I ask, "How did writing about it feel to you?" The answers may be:

"It felt like yesterday."

"I saw her face again."

"It helped to remember."

"You made me miss her again."

"I can't believe it's been twenty years."

I use their responses to bring out another gift of this column, that even though time has passed since a death, the memory of it can bring on brand-new feelings. This demonstrates that grief has no timetable and that lingering or latent negative feelings from the past can be reexamined and reconciled in the present. This may be done by talking it over with someone or saying things previously left unsaid in a letter to the deceased or in a journal. Other rituals of remembrance and release may be employed as well. Catholics often have masses said for loved ones who have died.

All of this demonstrates that the grief process is often quite difficult and prolonged. It may require outside help and assistance to cope with it and live on.

In my experience, denial and anger are the two strongest feelings in response to this column. So, why do I do it? Why do I push my students? Because I am asking them to explore and understand what they themselves are experiencing. This helps them to understand not only themselves, but, in their role as caregivers, it helps them understand what those closest to the dying go through.

This is a good time to break and have refreshments, and to walk about. Often students will come up and share more with me at this time. If someone has had an intense and emotional response and has left the room, either I seek them out, or if they have come with someone, I send their companion to find them. I ask if I am needed to intervene; if more time is needed.

I then continue and students return when they feel ready. It is interesting to note that among the thousands of people who have come through my workshops, I have only had one woman who was not able to return. She realized that it was too soon after her mother's death to attend something as intense as my presentation.

Column Four

At the top of the next column, I ask the students to write, "Parts of my body or my life most difficult for me to lose." I encourage them to choose parts of their body first and then they can choose any other aspect of life that comes to mind.

Again, I sense a change in the room's atmosphere. Initially it is lighter, then it seems to darken a bit. My first question when students have finished writing is to ask how many chose a part of their body. Most hands pop up. When I ask, what they chose, "My eyesight" is always the most frequent response. This is followed by loss of hearing, mobility, independence, hands, legs, and almost universally, loss of mind.

As I continue to talk with the group I will hear the words *breast* and *uterus* come forth, usually expressed in a tentative voice. If I do not hear or see any of these personal responses, I suggest them. What comes out is the deeply hidden fear that loss of the parts that define one as a man or woman is just too scary to verbalize or put into words. In all my years of doing these workshops, only once did a man mention prostrate in the group setting, and never was the word *penis* spoken.

As I mentioned earlier, the change in atmosphere is again different for this column. People respond slower and more thoughtfully. When questioned about their responses, I get comments such as, "I thought column three was the worst, but this surprised me in its intensity and was harder than I thought it would be," and, "It came too close; it was not someone else." Many relate that it is difficult for them to make such choices.

The primary theme that emerges is that losing a part of oneself is actually perceived as a "little death." Suddenly, one is vulnerable to death itself.

Following this, interesting dialog begins and I hear sighs of relief as the group shares things other than their body that would be most difficult for them to lose. *Children, spouse, partner, companion,* and *lover* usually top the list. *Faith, independence, energy, God, the ability to love and be loved, a sense of humor,* and *the ability to think* frequently appear. *Joy, hope,* and *nature* are also mentioned regularly.

These responses flood out of participants' mouths, and column four begins to overflow, a virtual inventory of the most important things for them to hold onto, those attributes which, on many levels, mean the value of life itself, not just survival.

One important result of this column is that it helps participants understand more deeply why the dying often became very pensive or quiet prior to death. They are mourning the past loss of parts of themselves and preparing to lose all they have known.

What were your responses? Did you write similar words or expressions as the groups had or did you write something different? Remember do not judge. Yours and their answers are normal and unique. There are no wrong answers.

Column Five

Usually I ask the group what they think column five will be. Suggestions pop out and finally I hear, "Our own death." So, on the top of the fifth column, I ask students to write "My own death." To make it more personal and revealing, I tell them to imagine how they want to die. Where? Alone? If not, with whom?

Almost universally I hear:

"No pain. I cannot bear too much."

"I want to be alert and pain-free."

"Finish my business."

"Say good-byes."

"Make amends."

"Be right with God."

"See loved ones again."

Since there are always many who mention pain I ask, "How many of you want your death to be quick and painless?"

Many respond affirmatively. Then I hear:

"Not too fast or sudden."

"I want enough time to say good-bye"

"...time to finish my business."

"Not too much time! I don't want to suffer."

"I don't want to have my death prolonged."

"I want to live, not just survive."

"Not yet, I'm not ready."

The absence of pain on the physical level is the highest priority in all my workshops, followed by absence of pain on emotional, mental, and spiritual levels. Quality of life issues come to the fore in this column. What is universally shared is that the absence of pain on many levels is what brings about a peaceful death.

I push the class to write everything they want for their death in this column.

"I want a party."

"Please celebrate my life."

"No tears."

"Leave with a job well-done."

"I want to die after seeing my children's children, until the fourth generation."

"I don't want to be put in the ground. Cremation is the best."

"Bury me in my pink dress."

"No wake or funeral."

As you can imagine I've heard practically every kind of way to die imaginable.

"I want white satin sheets."

"Out under the stars."

"Surrounded by family."

"In the arms of my husband."

"Cryogenics for me."

"In my sleep."

"No machines, just let me go—let nature take its course."

"At home."

"Not in the hospital."

When we have filled this column to overflowing with their wants, I encourage the students to go home and share their thoughts with their loved ones so their wishes may be honored. It never ceases to amaze me how many people, even among caregivers to the dying, do not have wills or other pre-death and post-death arrangements made for their families.

In summary I ask the group, "Why did I ask you to do this on this lovely warm day?"

I may hear:

"To help us understand what both the dying and their families go through, to resensitize us, to help us 'feel.'"

"To learn what to hold onto and what to let go of."

"What is really important to me in both life and death?"

"Dying is not an easy process."

"How to be there with family and patient because I walked in their footsteps here today."

I tell the students that all of their responses are right on, but ask them to go a little deeper into themselves and ask what they saw when comparing their own column with the group's column. They answer that they had very similar responses as the group's.

I explain that I have done this exercise with groups across the United States and internationally. I have done it with preschool kids with leukemia using finger paints for their columns; with school-age kids using drawings, clay, and oral stories; with teenagers using their favorite songs; with adults stricken with cancer and AIDS; and with the families and friends of all these people. "If I place their five columns on top of your five columns, what would we see?"

Students answer:

"The same responses."

"Similar words or expressions."

"Even without words, their pictures would tell the same story."

Then I ask what this means to them. And I hear:

"We are all the same."

"We are all connected."

"Working with the dying is learned by experience, not from books."

"The dying have all the answers if we listen and ask the right questions."

Finally I ask, "What have you learned and experienced today? What do you think is the greatest gift we have to give the dying?"

Responses are:

"Compassion."

"Listen, look, and learn."

"Greater understanding of what they may be experiencing."

"We are all normal and unique."

"The dying are our greatest teachers."

I close by telling the class that the greatest gift we have to share with the dying person and those who love them is our humanity, as death is part of life; the two are intermingled realities, each with its own perspective.

If our humanity is the most important gift we have to share with the dying, how do we, who are so much a part of the living, share this gift with those who are on their last journey as a living person?

Let's build upon some of the lessons of the Five Columns exercise:

- That death is a part of life.
- That we too will die.
- That we all have a fear of death.

These general principles—the three assumptions underlying my clinical approach to dying persons and their loved ones—can become your own touchstone in your effort to be present for the dying. Having looked inward to deepen awareness of your own feelings about death, you are now prepared to look beyond yourself, to better understand the needs and behaviors of those actually confronting death.

This is also the first step in exercising true compassion. And compassion, as distinguished from sympathy, and, even empathy, is the engine that drives the healing gift of humanity from one person to another.

Three Parts of the Fear of Death

We learn to become a listening presence (how to *be there* when it counts) first by listening to self (through the Five Columns exercise), and next, by learning to *hear* what the dying fear in death. The following examples from my own experience with the dying demonstrate how to discern which of the three parts of the fear of death a person may be focused on. Is it:

- fear of the process,
- fear of the moment of death, or
- fear of the hereafter?

By knowing what the dying fear in death, we can intervene more realistically and help them to have a death that is peaceful. I have found that asking a patient, "What do you fear in death?" is definitely *not* the way to elicit this information. And, for the most part, we don't need to use such a direct approach. What I have learned over the years is if we listen carefully to a person's words and actions, we hear and see what they most fear.

Fear of the Process

As an example of the fear of the process, my patient Joe, at first, appeared to be focused on his treatment. Then I began to hear a change in him: "Cathy, my aunt died of cancer and what I remember about it was that she suffered a lot." Clearly, Joe "told" me that his prevalent fear was fear of the process: "Will it be painful? You don't have too much pain with my problem, do you, Cathy?"

Armed with this knowledge, the care team knew they must really help him manage his pain and provide relief for his symptoms during every step of his journey to a peaceful death. "What I remember is that she really suffered. I hope this medicine keeps working like the Energizer Bunny," Joe said.

Fear of the Moment

Fear of the moment of death is expressed in a variety of ways. I have seen patients turn day into night, sleeping all day and lying awake all night. Still others want the lights left on and need reassurance that "someone will be here all night." For those with this fear, we need to have family members or other caregivers stay with them at night to decrease their fear. Darkness and death often become synonymous in the mind of the dying as they feel their end coming closer.

"Death comes like a thief in the night." "He slipped away in the middle of the night." These thoughts aren't totally irrational; as I mentioned, most patients die between 2 A.M. and 4 A.M.

Leaving lights on, playing the radio or TV, bringing the patient out to the nurse's station, moving him nearer to where people and activity are, along with administering mild antianxiety medications, palliation (pain relief/comfort care), and the listening presence of another all help to dispel the fear of the moment when life meets death.

We may do all the above to help the dying have a peaceful passage, but as we will learn in Chapter 6, the choice of the when, how, where, and with whom the patient chooses to die, is always up to them, as it will be our choice when our time comes.

Fear of the Hereafter

From my expereince, fear of the hereafter, manifested as a fear of the unknown or of possible judgment, is the third most prevalent fear the dying have. Frequently this fear is raised in a most interesting way. I've been asked the question: "You've been with a lot of people who have died, haven't you, Cathy?" After I answer in the affirmative, they query, "Do you think there is anything after death? Where do you think we go after...? Do you believe in heaven or hell? What if I can't forgive someone?" I share my thoughts and beliefs with them and ask if they need to speak to someone more "in that business" than I am. Often they do, but are reluctant to come right out and ask.

I have found that the fear of judgment and the need for reconciliation on the spiritual level increases as death nears.

At this point the caregiver's mediator or messenger role comes into play. Patients have said, "I haven't seen my brother in over twenty years. We had a fight and I don't even remember what we fought about." Many times their spouse or kids are angry as well. Here, I ask the question, "How may I help you?" knowing that their statement is a plea for help to come to peace and/or reconciliation in this matter. Then I or another team member, pastoral care or social worker, will make the call or write the letter to get this person's message to the loved one, thus providing help in "mending fences." Being able to reconcile with family or others can decrease the fear of judgment after death and decrease the physical, mental, emotional, and spiritual pain prior to death.

Listening and hearing what the dying fear most in death enables us to help them achieve the peaceful death they are hoping for.

What are You Hoping for?

As you read this, you may wonder how I came to this way of relating to both the dying person and their loved ones. The answer is quite simple: The dying themselves have been my teachers in the forty years I have been assisting them. They taught me how to enter their private world. How did I get them to teach me? Simply by asking them the question, "What are you hoping for?" and then allowing their answers to guide me in *how to be there* with them on their final journey.

John

In particular, one patient of mine illustrates how effective this question can be in facilitating understanding and communication between everyone involved: patient, family, and professional caregivers alike.

Years ago, as part of my role as a clinical nurse specialist in oncology, I was asked by the staff of a medical oncology unit to see a man named John. They said that he seemed a bit down, and maybe needed someone to talk to. A former policeman, he was a perfect example of the strong, silent type, but the staff had sensed sadness in him recently. In my visit with him, we got to know each other some. He spoke openly about his diagnosis and prognosis, and lovingly about his wife of fifty years and his family.

During our conversation I asked him, "What are you hoping for?" He replied quickly, "I hope the Mets win." So we both smiled and exchanged baseball stories. After chatting a bit more, I told him I would return to see him again and then I left, understanding from his response that John did not want to explore anything more deeply with me at that time. This simple question drew John out of his medically defined role of the compliant patient, and gave him the opportunity to regain his sense of self as the full person he was before his diagnosis, not simply as a cancer patient.

Several days later, as I was walking down the hall, I heard my name called, and turned to see John walking toward me with his ever-present IV pole. He was accompanied by four men, each one taller and bigger than he. These were his four sons: two policemen, a fireman, and a detective.

"Cathy, I want to talk to you," John said. "Remember the question you asked me the other day? I want you to ask me it again."

By this time, John and his giant sons had surrounded me—I felt like a small sapling gazing up at giant redwoods—and I responded dutifully, "I asked your father what he was hoping for."

Looking directly at me, John gave his real answer: "I hope my sons will understand that I don't want any more chemotherapy. I want to go home and be with their mother and see my grandchildren, without vomiting my guts out, for as long as I have left to be with them."

The sons looked at him and then at me and I can assure you there was not a dry eye among us.

John went home that very day. He spent quality time with his wife, his children, and his grandchildren, just as he hoped he would. And then he died peacefully at home, his wife and his sons beside him, assisted by a local hospice team.

Perhaps the most important lesson that John taught me early on in my career, one that has remained and grows stronger to this day, is to always remember how difficult it is for families to let go of their loved ones, and how much of a struggle it is for the patient to leave those he loves as well. But in patient-centered care, it's the person who is ill who has the final say in how he lives or dies.

Being asked, "What are you hoping for?" brought John back to his personhood, because the ability to have hope is the core of the self—the essence of what it is to be human. As long as you're alive, you have hope. And sometimes hope is the only grasp you have on being true to yourself. Reconnecting with his own personal hope system empowered John to change the course of his life. He could then decide how he would live out his death. He could derive the peace that comes from making the choices that reflected his deeper hopes for himself and his family.

As a result, John was able to live and die as he hoped he would. In addition, his sons would live on after his death knowing that they truly listened to their father and chose to honor and respect his wishes as he was dying, just as they had done in life.

As I mentioned, I like to give people tools that are simple and that work. As you can see from John's story, learning about and showing simple consideration for what a person is hoping for is great at cutting through the patient-role limitations to return an individual to full personhood in their own eyes and in the eyes of everyone who is relating to them.

Realizing the power of this simple, yet profound, question has changed the quality and effectiveness of my interactions with dying persons and their loved ones ever since I met John. I know it will help you, as it has helped me and many others, to accompany the dying in a fully human manner.

The Power of Hope

Here I would like to introduce the concept of "the power of hope." Hope is an interior force, a powerful, usually conscious, but sometimes unconscious, motivator.

Hope existed before we were born in the utterances and desires (hope systems) of our parents and grandparents:

"I hope it's a boy to carry on the name."

"I hope it's a girl after three boys!"

"I don't care as long as the baby is healthy."

Hope is a current flowing through life, guiding and directing us, changing in strength as we need it. It stretches from the mundane to crises large and small:

"I hope to ride my two wheeler without the training wheels by my birthday."

"I hope I get on the little league team."

"Mom's sick; I hope she doesn't die."

"I hope I get my license."

"I hope I get invited to the prom."

"I hope to become an architect."

"To graduate summa cum laude is my hope."

"I sure hope she says yes!"

And of course the hope of every beauty queen: "I hope for world peace!"

Hope is such an integral part of our lives that, like breath, we could not live without it. And, like our breath, hope adapts to the many changes and crises we face in life, and provides us with the internal strength to cope with and live through even the most devastating, life-threatening situations. Hope is the belief that potentials may be fulfilled. And, just as hope is apparent throughout our lives, it is never more apparent than when we are staring death in the face.

Since hope is an energy manifestation of the human essence, it is useful as a therapeutic modality. Hope is an integrator of all life's processes, the interweaving thread that binds those processes together, making a cohesive design, creating a unique pattern that becomes the hope system of each individual. Hope alters or affects our perceptions, enabling us to be open and increasing our realm of possibilities.

We are confronted with the power of hope as an internal motivation force. Let us consider the wellspring of hope, rising from within the person, empowering the person to behave in ways that achieve self-fulfillment. Hope facilitates the true development of the potential of each human. (It is only in death that our full potential is realized.)

The power of hope is a premise on which The Hope System was developed and the ensuing chapters are based. The Hope System emphasizes how much of an advocate within us hope truly is. This can't be emphasized enough, because traditionally the concept of hope has been relegated to the sidelines, like an unreasonably avid, blindly-optimistic fan.

Too often we use phrases like, "hoping against hope," or "hopelessly unrealistic," to describe a positive attitude that flies in the face of negative odds, whereas, for a person face-to-face with death, hope functions as the most genuine guide of all. In my experience of observing and communicating with the dying, the role that hope serves in the transitional process could almost be described as that of a hormone. Indeed, the most current research on hope is in the biological sciences, as if hope were a part of our endocrine system, possibly no less vital than other hormones.

Jerome Groopman, M.D., in his book *The Anatomy of Hope*, writes, "Researchers are learning that a change in mind-set has the power to alter neurochemistry. Belief and expectations—the key elements of hope—can block pain by releasing the brain's endorphins and enkephalins, mimicking the effects of morphine. In some cases, hope can also have important effects on fundamental physiological processes like respiration, circulation, and motor function."

A remarkable insight is that *the basic needs of the dying are also those of the living*. The three basic needs of the dying are:

- The need to know they will not be abandoned,
- The need for self-expression, and
- The need for hope.

Through examples in the following chapters you will learn ways in which hope itself gives us a rationale for feeling hopeful when nothing else does. Even when circumstances seem to give us no grounds for hope, the act of hoping itself establishes its own rationality. Recognizing the power of hope is important for several reasons:

- In acknowledging hope as a positive force, caregivers strengthen the dying person's strongest inner advocate, which promotes healing.
- In listening without judgment, caregivers support fulfillment of the dying person's second basic need: the need for self-expression.
- From birth to death, hope enables us to shape and reshape our concept of self-identity so that we can thrive in alien territory, even against the seemingly insurmountable odds of terminal illness.
- Hope is an integral part of the life-death process; it is the mechanism by which we gain access to the reservoir of our own (and the universal) intrinsic life force.
- In accepting the expressed hopes of the dying, caregivers support the quality of life for the dying, which often enables them to outlive their prognosis.

The hope system within each of us is that from which we draw the strength to face and deal with life's challenges and struggles; the courage to face change, from birth to death, with equanimity. This is apparent throughout our lives, but it is all-pervasive as we proceed on our journey toward death, the final stage of human growth.

In this chapter, you've examined your own attitudes toward death and have gained an understanding that, in general, the basic needs of the dying are also those of the living. With this accumulated awareness of how alike we all are, while still acknowledging the importance of respecting individual differences, you are ready to focus on what distinguishes those facing imminent death from the rest of us, as we'll do in the next chapter, "The Four Stages of Hope."

Chapter 2

The Four Stages of Hope

Elisabeth Kübler-Ross, a renowned psychiatrist—and also my teacher when I began my work with the dying—brought into the medically dominated, cure-oriented world of the 1970s, a new framework of thinking about the dying. She insisted that families, friends, and professional caregivers must all acknowledge what the terminally ill were going through psychologically. And, in its time, this was indeed revolutionary. But she, as well as I, always sensed that there was something more going on than psychology, something deeper—but we were not able to name it then.

The Five Stages of Grief

Kübler-Ross attempted to give patients some kind of control over their fate by helping them understand the psychodynamic shifts they were going through. By classifying these shifts—naming them "the five stages of grief"—she identified the psychological behaviors of the dying person and the coping mechanisms they used from diagnosis through death.

Her first stage is *Denial*: "No, no not me."

Then *Anger* comes in: "Why me?"

Anger is followed by the *Bargaining* stage: "Yes me, but..."

The next stage is *Depression*: "Oh my God, I'm going to die."

And the final stage is *Acceptance*: "I'm going to die, and somehow it's all right."

What Kübler-Ross did was identify behaviors and coping mechanisms. And this was a monumental advance in its time. By itself, it sparked a revolution in how we all think about the process of death—and a revolution in how the medical profession treated the dying.

But both Kübler-Ross and I realized that, revolutionary as her five stages were for that time, they were only a start. Why did we think that? We felt that way because the psychodynamics of this scheme reflected *only a part* of the dying person's experience. As time went on, her five stages turned into a set of rigid boxes, with people artificially trying to move the dying from one stage to another ("Okay, let's move him out of his denial now.").

Doing this in such a rigid manner carries with it the danger of reducing the dying person to some fragment of his whole self. As I mentioned, this was much more common than you'd want to believe—doctors or nurses talking about "the cancer in Room 30" or "the heart attack at the end of the hall." Again we were restoring the old impersonal, purely clinical habit of viewing the dying person as nothing more than their medical or psychological status.

I realized that we needed to view the patient *as a whole person*, rather than as a disease or as being at a certain psychological stage in the dying process.

Taking up where Kübler-Ross left off, and with her blessing to take the next step beyond her approach, I developed a unique framework for understanding the dying person and responding to what they are *experiencing internally as a whole human being*. My approach, which I introduce in this chapter, expands and deepens Kübler-Ross's stages, which are solely from a psychodynamic perspective. It keeps the patient's family and the caregivers focused on the dying patient as a whole person, fully present on all levels—physical, emotional, mental, and spiritual. And when we relate to the dying person in this way, we are being a fully-aware person ourselves, rather than the unaware, fearful person so many of us become around a dying person.

The Hope System

I named my approach "The Hope System"—which prompted Kübler-Ross to call me "The Hope Lady." My approach enables the caregiver and the family to understand that *the dying person's hopes are* central to his or her wholeness, and must be respected fully—rather than reducing the person to a reflection of the psychological stage they are going through at the moment. Thus, The Hope System goes well beyond both Kübler-Ross's psychodynamic approach and the medical model, by bringing back the concept of the whole person as the focus of how we think about and relate to the dying patient.

The four stages of hope are:

- *Hope for Cure:* "I'm gonna beat this thing!"
- *Hope for Treatment*: "I hope I'm in the 29 percent that chemo helps!"
- *Hope for Prolongation of Life*: "I hope to walk my daughter down the aisle."
- *Hope for a Peaceful Death*: "I hope I die pain-free and alert."

These four stages of hope alert the caregiver and the family to what is going on in the inner world of the dying person, as their hopes change in the face of impending death.

In this book, I provide you with practical, time-tested tips for how to relate to the dying patient as a whole person. You will learn new ways of *being with* those who are dying, ways that are effective in meeting their needs. I will show you why, when we put the concept of hope and The Hope System at the center of how we relate to the dying, we are not just honoring the whole person in the dying individual, but are also honoring the whole person in ourselves. After all, if we fall into the trap of reducing the dying to nothing more than a disease, a diagnosis, or a stage in a psychological framework, we are also failing to honor our own wholeness as a person.

The Dignity of the Dying

My approach is intended to restore the dignity that has so often been lost due to the "medicalization" of death—the twentieth-century trend of people no longer dying at home but rather dying in an impersonal, cold hospital room at the end of the hall. The Hope System helps family and professional caregiver alike to recreate how people were routinely treated when they died at home, as fully human until their last moment—and never as merely "the cancer in Room 32."

In addition, as we honor the dying in this humane manner, we learn to assist them on their final journey. Guiding them in this manner teaches us how to live our own lives more fully each day.

It is crucial to realize that when we support a patient's hopes in this manner, we meet the three basic inner needs of the dying, as mentioned in Chapter 1:

- the need to not feel abandoned,
- the need for self-expression, and
- the need for hope.

Four Journeys

Now at this juncture, I invite you to walk with me in the footsteps of four of my most memorable patients as they make the four stages of hope come alive. As I share their stories it will become apparent that from diagnosis until death there is continuous movement back and forth, between and among the four types of hope.

Martha

First, let's meet Martha, the wife and caregiver of a hospice patient of mine, living in a fifth floor walk-up tenement apartment building in a South Bronx neighborhood. On one of my visits, she had shared with me that she noticed "something" in her breast in the shower, and she asked me to look at it. I immediately encouraged her to see her physician, who upon examination sent her to a surgeon for evaluation.

Listen with me now as she tells me what she heard the doctor say: "When I went to the doctor about the lump in my breast, he said, he could cut it out and then everything would be all right." Her words clearly tell us that her predominant hope is hope for cure.

We may never know what the doctor actually said to Martha, but what she heard was very much determined by what she was hoping for in regard to her condition.

Another important fact in her hope for cure was that her husband was terminally ill, and he needed her to be cured so she could take care of him. In fact, she refused postoperative chemotherapy and radiation and is fine to this day, still living in the same neighborhood and taking care of her grandchildren.

Charlie

Our second story takes us to Long Island and the radiation therapy department of a large hospital. In my role as a clinical nurse specialist in oncology, I sat in on all the initial interviews with the radiologists, to discuss the treatment plan with each new patient. In one such interview, I was drawn from the first moment to a big, loud, tough teddy bear of a man named Charlie. Charlie had the thickest Brooklyn accent I'd ever heard—and being Brooklyn-born myself, I'd certainly heard many people who spoke "Brooklynese."

One afternoon when I returned from lunch, I literally bumped into Charlie as he exited the treatment room. Greeting me with a big smile and booming voice, he pointed at his large protruding abdomen, swollen from a big tumor, and said, "See this tumor, Cathy? Between me and the cobalt, it doesn't have a chance!" We were attempting to shrink the large tumor so that surgery could be performed to remove it.

There were many strikes against Charlie: He was obese, he was a heavy smoker and drinker, and he'd already had heart surgery for a triple bypass. However, armed with the power stemming from his predominant hope for treatment, "me and the cobalt" and his underlying hope for cure, "it doesn't have a chance," Charlie's response to treatment was amazing in view of his type of tumor and his medical problems. As a matter of fact, we were actually able to shrink the tumor so that almost all of it could be removed, and he outlived his initial prognosis of three to six months by living two and one-half comfortable years—until his heart disease took its toll on him.

Jane

Next, come with me to sunny California where Jane and her husband are still reeling from the news they heard that morning at the doctor's office: "There is nothing more we can do for you, Jane," their doctor had said.

"When he mentioned hospice, we wanted to know what to expect—does that mean I have to be dead in six months?" Jane asked. After I assured her that she didn't have to die within six months to come into hospice, she said, "Oh, I'm so relieved to hear that! You see, my daughter is two months pregnant and I hope to be here for the birth and be able to hold my first grandchild." Jane's husband and I heard her words of hope loud and clear: Her predominant hope was hope for prolongation of life, since she knew there was no more treatment for her.

And her hope for prolongation of life was not simply about how long she would live, it was about the quality of the life she would lead during that time. She felt that by coming into the hospice now, we would help her control the symptoms when her condition worsened, and help her remain comfortable so that she could be at the birth and be able to hold her grandchild "even for a little while." With the help of the hospice team—and empowered by her own hope system—Jane was able to be there at the birth and hold her grandson. Indeed, she almost made it to his first Christmas, outliving the one to three month estimate the doctor had written on the original referral for hospice care.

Frank

Crossing the country, let's return to the East Coast and visit Frank, a gentleman I had the privilege to accompany for several years on his journey with head and neck cancer. Like his disease process, Frank's journey took many twists and turns, as did his almost continually changing hope system. This was due to the many and various treatments he tried that he hoped would lead to a cure. Frank had endured radical surgery twice to remove the original tumor that had spread to his tongue, then experimental chemotherapy and, finally, a long course of radiation therapy.

I have chosen to share Frank's story with you not just because I knew him for such a long time, but because he taught me so much about the importance of listening to, and trusting, the inner wisdom that I have found is so strong within people with an incurable disease. Walking with him, we traveled from hope for cure, to hope for treatment, and back again a number of times—with hope for prolongation of life popping up to enable him to live through all the treatments he had successfully endured. My companions on Frank's journeys of hope hither and yonder were his wonderful wife and children.

After Frank's last surgery and his discharge, I received a note from his wife telling me that he had been able to go see his mother, finish his business with her, and finally tell her he loved her and said good-bye face-to-face, which brought him the peace and reconciliation he had hoped for since childhood.

Several months passed, and one day I received the phone call that I had been, both waiting for and dreading: I heard the head nurse on the medical floor, not the surgical floor, say, "Hi, Cathy, Frank's back and he's asking for you." This time I knew what to expect and I also knew we were both hoping for the same thing. As I entered the room, Frank's blue eyes twinkled and his warm smile greeted me. Then slowly I saw how thin and weak his body had become. As his wife came to greet me and we held each other, I saw the tears in her eyes. Frank handed me his ever-present yellow pad on which he had written so many changing hopes over the years, then he took my free hand and held it tight, looking me straight in the eye as I read what he had written. "Cathy. Do you think the medicine will keep me comfortable until…?"

"Yes, Frank, we will keep you comfortable until…" I answered, with our eyes still locked in place. He smiled his thanks for my reassuring words. Over the next three days, I witnessed his hope for a peaceful death become stronger and stronger until he died peacefully in the arms of his loving wife. He had left me one more message on the yellow pad before he died. It read: "Cathy, I hope you can continue to be there for my wife. Thanks for everything. Frank." I still have all of Frank's messages written on those yellow pads. Each time we move, my husband holds them up and I say, "Put them back in my special box; I don't care how ragged they are, they are still precious to me."

These stories illustrate how The Hope System connects us to the humanity of the dying. This tool enables both professional caregivers, as well as the patients' loved ones, to constantly relate to and connect with the dying person as a whole person.

What I have learned over the years is that there is a special "body wisdom"—almost instinctual in nature—that is triggered in those with a terminal illness, as the disease progresses within them. Thus, each stage of The Hope System is activated by the progressive physiological changes caused by the terminal illness itself, and each provides an opportunity for the caregiver to seek out the needs that are specific to the individual at that moment, in order to understand what to do or say or not do or say.

James

For example, when my patient James felt that his treatment was doing nothing but causing more pain and weakness, he stopped saying "I hope this treatment works," and asked me, "If I stop radiation now, will I be able to walk or sit in a wheelchair by June?" If all treatments have been exhausted, this question becomes the cue for the most helpful response, which is not blurting out, "You can't stop radiation now!" but rather asking a question: "How is that month significant for you?" or "What's happening in June?" The answer might be, "My daughter's graduation."

The caregiver's next question, "What are you hoping for?" might be answered with "I'd like to be able to see my daughter graduate."

In this scenario, James is telling us that his hope system has shifted from hope for treatment to hope for prolongation of life. That stage of hope usually indicates that a person has accepted that medical treatment cannot affect a cure and that now he or she is hoping for medical intervention that promotes quality of life for the time they have left, such as an adjustment in their pain medication.

This latter stage of hope can be difficult for a loved one to accept; yet it's important to acknowledge what is heard and alert the medical staff to this change. (Chapters 7 and 8 provide practical advice on how family members and health-care professionals can best handle such scenarios.)

Patient-Driven Care Through Listening

The ideal, based on all my work with the dying, is for long-term care and end-of-life care to be *patient-driven*. There is a wisdom in the dying that drives the transitional process from within—a wisdom that they first feel, and then express, *in their hopes*.

Once caregivers and loved ones *really listen to* and acknowledge where the patient is in their hope system, they often find that:

- We activate great reserves of strength even in the most
    physically incapacitated patient.
- We bring them great relief and open the door to further
    and deeper communication.

- Talking with patients about their hopes makes it easier for
the caregiver to understand what the dying person needs.
- Being in sync with the patient's hope system allows the
patient and loved ones more quality time together, for
mending fences, expressing love, and for all those things
that provide the best chance for a peaceful death.
- Caregivers and loved ones are prepared for a healthier
grieving process, one without remorse or regret,
knowing they have treated the dying patient as a
person, not just as a diagnosis or a disease entity.
- There is no such thing as a person without some type of
hope—no one can live or die, for even a moment,
without hope.

If we acknowledge that, at a core level, the patient himself is hope itself, we can see why hope is where we need to center our expectations, both as family members and professional caregivers. As the terminal illness progresses, hope actually comes closer to the surface than ever before. When a person is presented with a terminal diagnosis, hope begins to rise from the inner depths, on call now, on guard, our corporeal sentinel and guide. Spend one day with someone recently diagnosed with a terminal illness and you will understand the power of hope.

The Hope System helps the patient, the caregivers, and the families in two different ways. First, it is a tool that immediately reveals what's happening within the dying; second, it helps us learn what they need from us, based on their expressed hopes, and tells us what we need to do. Through its four stages, The Hope System provides a model that anyone can use to support the person's predominant hope at each moment on the deepest level, as they care for him. Understanding the four stages of hope alerts the caregiver to what's going on in the patient, as his primary hope stage changes in the face of impending death.

Being Present

As I've learned from the journeys of my patients, very few of the dying move through the four stages of The Hope System in a predictable and orderly fashion from stage one to stage four. During such an intense time, their hopes change in more of a back-and-forth zigzagging pattern than a linear continuum. But the patient and their family may be experiencing different fluctuations and be out of sync with each other.

The most important lesson of all is that when you acknowledge whatever stage of hope the dying person is currently going through, you are being there for them when it counts; you are serving as a listening presence.

By learning to track which stage of The Hope System the dying person is going through over time—what their specific hopes are and how they are changing—you become able to engage with them on the deepest level, on a continuing and ongoing basis. In becoming aware of the changing hopes of the dying patient, and resonating with these hopes, we avoid the trap of projecting our own hope system onto them. We actually hear what it is *they* are hoping for, instead of hearing what *we* imagine they are hoping for, or what we think they should be hoping for.

Making such a meaningful human connection—by asking the one simple question, "What are you hoping for?"—is healthy for all concerned. It is sure to foster clearer communication, a vital factor in ensuring appropriate medical treatment and patient-directed care from the moment of diagnosis all the way to the moment of death.

That this approach should be as effective as I've found it to be in thousands of patients and their families isn't all that difficult to understand: After all, we are what we hope—the dying as well as the living. And, as we learned earlier in this chapter, our own humanity and wholeness are enlarged by asking this critical question, and listening to the answer. By acknowledging *their* hopes at every stage, we are more in touch with our *own* hopes, both before and after our loved one or our patient has died—and are more fully able, as survivors, to live our own lives without regret or guilt.

Chapter 3

The Patient's Journey

No matter how we define this somewhat mysterious and fascinating four-letter word, we probably agree that *hope* is not passive; it has an intrinsic energy within it that seems to direct, guide, move, and change people through their life situations. Never is this dynamic force more apparent than when one is confronted with the reality that one's own life is limited and will, in a certain matter of time, come to an end, that moment when we face our own death.

Having been involved with dying persons and their families in an intense way for the past forty years, I have become acutely aware of this deep, intrinsic force within each human being, and have studied it at great length. The cornerstone of my own approach to dying persons and their families begins with the following sentence, which introduces the inner world in each of us where hope lives and moves and waits to be addressed:

> *All of us can live with the knowledge that we have an incurable disease, but none of us can live with the thought that we are hopeless.*

Let us examine this phrase that plays such a key role in describing what follows. The patient's acknowledgment of having an incurable disease, "something fatal, which will ultimately take my life," occurs first on the intellectual level. Then, in time, this knowledge of incurability slowly filters through the mental, emotional, physical, and spiritual levels and certainly has a deep effect. Faced with this devastating knowledge, this person can still live out and complete life. One knows it is possible to live even with the slow progression of disease robbing vitality until death arrives.

Hope Is Essential

None of us can exist in this world with the thought of hopelessness, for hope is an integral part of all levels and aspects of each individual. Could you live with the essential condemnation of you as a person, of your very essence, who you really are? Being labeled hopeless is like being declared a non-being, an object, not a human being, with all that entails—no history, no present, no future—truly a death sentence far more devastating and destructive than the disease that may be spreading unmercifully throughout your body.

We humans, when devoid of our hopes, feel robbed of the essence that defines us on all levels.

Surely none of us would want to be thought of as "Room 308—just a hopeless case." This type of insensitive statement demonstrates a somewhat prevalent attitude still among some health-care providers today: "Since there is nothing I can do for the patients, since I am not able to cure them of their diseases, why stay involved with them at all?" Thus, the abandonment of the dying subtly begins.

People need to die as they live, with their intrinsic life force, their individual hope system, in place. If we want to relate to the dying as human beings, we must not deal with them as hopeless cases, but rather direct our energies to accompanying them on their final journey. In order to do this, we must be willing to help them unearth their own hope systems.

Everyone's hope system can enable them to live each day until they die as the whole person they want to be, no matter what the depth or extent of the physical disease they are enduring. Despite all their suffering on a physical or emotional level, hope opens for them the possibility of realizing their full human potential. Indeed, the crisis of impending death can create tremendous opportunities for growth in many dimensions of who we are as humans.

It is deep interior hopes that enable the dying to live each day in the face of incurable disease, until they are ready and able to let go and face death.

The Hope System approach to the dying reaches into and relates to each person's intrinsic hopes, for we are what we hope. In order to understand the key concept of The Hope System, it is necessary to emphasize that hope, our interior life force, is merely changing. It is never destroyed. Hope is always present with each person experiencing the final life-into-death passage, and it motivates each one to live through the dying process from the moment of the fatal disease or condition's diagnosis, until death.

Imaginary Journey

In order to present The Hope System in a more real and meaningful way, I ask you to take an imaginary journey with me—the same journey that all patients take from the moment they are diagnosed with a fatal disease until they confront death. Here the four tenets of The Hope System are: Hope for cure; hope for treatment; hope for prolongation of life; and hope for a peaceful death are presented as the actual dying person may experience them.

Let us pretend that you have not been feeling well, simply not yourself, more fatigued than usual, without any specific reason you can attribute to this change. Perhaps you might have noticed a small swelling in the glands of your neck or underarm, or a lump that does not go away, or a persistent cough, or painless bleeding.

You, like all patients before you, go to the doctor and he validates that indeed you are looking a little tired and pale. He wants to take some blood, or upon examining the swelling states that he will biopsy that enlarged gland or lump. What would you, as every person before you, hope for at that moment? Some responses from actual patients have been, "Please let the blood work show only a strep throat, mononucleosis, or even hepatitis, but *don't* let it be leukemia or any kind of cancer or AIDS. Whatever the diagnosis is, please let me have something that can be cured!" Thus, you arrive at the first step of The Hope System, which is hope for cure.

Let us continue on our imaginary journey. The doctor, upon receiving your blood work, says, "I don't like the looks of this report. I'd like to put you in the hospital for more tests." Perhaps, after reviewing the test results, he states, "I'll have to cut that out, but I'm sure I can get it all. Perhaps you may need some radiation to the area, but after that everything will be okay." While we are still primarily hoping for a cure, another factor has been introduced, i.e. various treatments to effect a cure. We now put our hope into the treatment modalities to bring a cure. Thus, the second stage of The Hope System comes into being, hope for treatment.

The Hope for Treatment

The hope for treatment phase is the focusing of hope as a life force, or empowerment, into the treatments. This strengthens the patients, enabling them to endure the pain and discomfort created by modern curative approaches such as chemotherapy, disfiguring surgery, radiation therapy, or experimental medications and protocols. The strength or power of our hope system is apparent throughout this period, and it becomes a driving force that empowers us to get through the treatment. This interior source, which I call the power of hope, enables most patients to withstand not only the application of their therapies, but the side effects that are often more uncomfortable and debilitating than the treatments.

The hope for cure and hope for treatment stages are often quite prolonged, due to the variety and intensity of treatment approaches that our modern-day technology has produced. In addition, within this phase the cure may have many faces and wear different hats. Cure may mean hoping for temporary cessation of the spread of cancer or hope to control symptoms or bothersome side effects of experimental protocols as is often the case with people with AIDS or other chronic terminal illnesses.

There are variations in the intensity of individual hope systems noted during this time, no matter its length, depending on the effectiveness of a treatment modality at any given time. For example, shrinking a tumor through the use of radiation or chemotherapy for a certain period of time may bring relief. Utilizing radiation therapy to control or decrease bone pain, thereby increasing comfort, movement, and function may definitely affect both the intensity and duration of hope within this phase.

Changes in the intensity and length of The Hope System may also stem from the medical world's ability to effectively control the side effects from disease progression or the treatment modalities themselves. Health providers now have a large variety of medications and alternative or complementary approaches to control nausea, vomiting, and diarrhea. Steroids and nonsteroidal anti-inflammatory drugs are also useful to reduce inflammation or swelling, thereby controlling nerve and bone pain.

The time period marked by hope for cure and hope for treatment varies with each individual, and depends on all the factors of disease progression, available therapies, and the patient's response to treatment modalities, plus the various side effects caused by treatment approaches. Medications or treatments with possible cure potential, such as protease inhibitors in the cocktail for persons with AIDS, also directly affect the length of time of both these phases of The Hope System.

All these combined factors, as well as the emotional, psychological, and social interplays within and external to the patient at any given time, contribute to variations with the patient's hope system. Each factor appears to play a role in igniting an inner reality, or interior knowing, moving a person from within—from a primary hope for cure to a more specific hope for treatment that will effect a cure at this time.

However long or short this time sequence is, it does come to an end. It is put on hold or pushed into the background. This shift in hope is triggered when at some point in time, the medical world says to the patient and family, "There is nothing more that we can do for you. We have exhausted our armamentarium of treatment approaches for your disease," or, "Surgery is no longer an option for you now." They may state, "At this time, chemotherapy would be ineffective," or make a similar comment.

The Hope for Prolongation of Life

The patient's individual hope system is quite unique at this time, and the patient often responds in a most remarkable way when confronted with this information. These words speak of death, since those whom we saw as having the power to save us are no longer able to do so. Rather than being totally crushed by this life-threatening message, almost immediately an amazing change takes effect. Our intrinsic life force is actually enlivened, not destroyed, by these statements. The ill seem to be able to reach down into their inner core of hope and summon up the strength they need to live out their lives for as long as they hope to live. I call this stage hope for prolongation of life.

There are myriad manifestations of the hope for prolongation of life in the many levels within the terminally ill, each expressed in distinct ways. Some will state that they hope for a miracle. Others say that they hope for time, because "In time, if I live long enough, they will find the cure and miraculously, I will be saved; that is, I will be cured."

Kübler-Ross' stage of bargaining is frequently heard within this phase of The Hope System. Bargaining enables both patient and family to acknowledge the reality of the possibility of death, but it also brings in hope to hold death at a safe distance. Frequently they say, "I want to see my daughter graduate," or "I want to be able to hold my grandchild." Obviously one has to be alive to both see and hold. So, while the major hope is no longer for cure or treatment, it is certainly for life, not just for survival.

It is in this phase that the quality-of-life issues become paramount. During this stage, the importance of the control of pain and symptoms that are robbing patients of the quality of their remaining time must be dealt with effectively, competently, and compassionately so that their hopes are respected and affirmed.

Some might say that hope for prolongation of life is synonymous with the will to live. However one may choose to define this very real time period, I have been amazed over and over again by the strength and tenacity seen in the dying at this time. For example, I have seen patients who have agreed with their physicians to stop IV and tube feedings, who are unable to eat or drink, and live not only for days, but weeks. In fact, one patient (who you will read about in Chapter 5) lived on literally nothing for weeks in a comatose state, unable to discern night from day or mark the passage of time. Defying all the rules, he lived until his birthday so that his wife would be able to receive his Social Security and pension benefits.

Perhaps in your own life you have experienced a loved one or a patient "hanging onto life by a thread." Frequently we see the dying wait for their favorite child or special nurse to be with them at the moment of death. I have seen patients hold on or wait until after a major holiday like Thanksgiving, Christmas, or a birthday so that time of happiness and celebration is not marred by their death.

The power of this phase enables many people to outlive their prognoses. The capacity to hope for and experience life to the fullest does determine the individual's ability to participate fully and knowingly to achieve his or her highest potential. It is the difference between truly being alive and living fully, and just surviving. It has to do with the quality of life, not just the fact of life or simply existing. The hope for prolongation of life means, "I choose to live fully alive in the face of a terminal illness and hope that I am given the control I need to live out my life in the manner I choose."

The Hope for a Peaceful Death

When the fundamental hope is no longer for cure, treatment, or prolongation of life, there are significant behaviors that indicate that the primary hope is for a peaceful death. These are so significant that they are discussed in detail in Chapter 4. These behaviors are all indicative of the person shifting his focus from the things of life and all that life has meant to centering on his own death. Becoming quiet, withdrawn, refusing to eat or take medications—all life affirming behaviors—to actually turning their backs on the world and the significant people in their primary worlds are all indicators of the fourth and final stage, the hope for a peaceful death.

As we examine this hope, we note that the hope is not simply for death but death that is peaceful. The important question is, "What makes death peaceful?" Peaceful means the absence of pain, first and essentially, on the physical level, because the presence of physical pain distorts both life and death and becomes a barrier to the peace we are hoping for at life's end.

Secondly, the emotional pain of strained or shattered relationships prevents peace from entering the patient's life at this time. This, to me, is the most excruciating of all, the pain of mental anguish caused by the lack of completion or closure in our human relationships.

Lastly, attaining peace on the spiritual level is exceedingly important as life comes to an end, since forgiveness and reconciliation with the divine, however experienced, appear to be necessary components in many people for peaceful death to become a reality.

Hope for a peaceful death possesses its own intrinsic power. Once your primary hope is for death, this hope actually empowers you to let go of life and become focused on death. This major shift from holding on, to releasing life, changes one's demeanor, attitude, and behaviors, allowing death to become more and more real. In fact, it becomes more real than life itself. The dying become preoccupied with the reality of death, as life and all that life symbolizes loses importance and no longer holds the dying's attention or life energy. At this point, death often comes quickly to the patient who is now open for it. Many appear to let go with resignation; others are resigned initially, then as their interior dynamic reality is tapped, they are filled with the serenity of acceptance, as their hope for peaceful death becomes reality.

There are, however, as we all realize, those who never come to peaceful death because they cling so tenaciously to life or loved ones that peach in death cannot find them. These are the people who die "kicking and screaming," who do not go "peacefully into that dark night," those who fight to the bitter end.

The Progression

By respecting a person's expressed hopes, we support the patient where he really lives and nourish the vitality intrinsic to the moment he is in. By allowing him to experience each stage of hope at his own pace, we maximize the potential of his own interior energy to organize and guide him at a speed he can handle in the way his hope system knows best. In the previous chapter we learned that though these stages exist on a continuum in theory, in people they commingle, and a patient can go from one to another stage of hope and back again in the flash of an eye. This is a good thing because it allows the inner dynamism of hope its full reach, but it can be a confusing thing for those of us on the outside looking in.

When I was the first person to be licensed by New York State as a clinical nurse specialist in oncology and thanatology in 1975, I was only just beginning to learn how elegantly these various stages of hope can coexist—and work for—a patient. They spiral back upon one another to gain power, giving the last stage its much-needed energy, almost like a pitcher's windup before the final throw.

Perhaps a real life clinical example will make four stages of The Hope System come alive for you.

Frank

Frank, the patient of mine we met in Chapter 2, had been readmitted to the head and neck surgery service and he requested that I come to see him. Frank had five prior admissions in two and one-half years, and, when last discharged, he had a permanent tracheotomy and feeding tube. That visit, for all intents and purposes, had been considered his final visit. At that time, we had sent him home to fulfill his hope, to enjoy spring in his garden. My predominant hope based on previous experience with Frank during his prior hospitalizations was hope for a peaceful death. Frank had been through so much and, in my mind, had suffered enough. Herein lies the danger of clinical thinking.

To my surprise, an elated, animated, though weakened man, greeted me. In a lively manner, communicating by using penciled notations on a pad of yellow paper, he began to describe a new surgery the doctor was going to try that perhaps would enable him to be rid of the feeding tube at last. He then left for the radiology department, giving me time to reflect and reexamine my own feelings. In order to be effective in this or any therapeutic trust relationship, it was necessary for me to be clear on my own hope system, which was affected by my knowledge, intuition, diagnosis, clinical experience and, of course, my personal feelings for the patient.

First, I had to be clear about what I had hoped for Frank. In all honesty, I was still hoping for a peaceful death for him. But, what was his predominant hope? Certainly, hope for treatment predominated, with underlying hope for cure, and, at the least, hope for prolongation of life. He wanted to have the surgery, be rid of the tube, and go home again.

Second, I had to avoid imposing my hope for a peaceful death on a person whose hope system had returned to hope for treatment. The support, information, and understanding that this patient required to support and strengthen his own hopes at this time differed greatly from the attention he would have needed had his predominant hope moved to the peaceful death phase.

Yet, I soon realized that Frank did not fit nicely into one stage anymore. His years of endurance under the gun had seasoned his hope system into something like the solar system. All the stages of hope he'd been through were now interconnected, revolving around each other, harmoniously, it seemed. He was hoping to have the surgery, be rid of the tube and go home again. For him, now, a new hope for cure was supported by hope for treatment with hope for a prolongation of life a steady hum underneath it all. How could I impose my hope for a peaceful death on a person whose hope system was revving for life?

Whether or not my hopes for him also shifted at this realization was immaterial. My behavior had to shift into line with the patient's hopes, not with my own and not necessarily with those of family members or loved ones. None of us had cancer of the head and neck except for him. So I had to release my thought that he had suffered enough and go where he and his wife needed me to be.

In addition to this, I was assigned several other roles to support his needs and hopes—again written on sheaves of yellow paper. These written hopes and needs were clearly his reality. First, he asked me to find out from the doctor exactly what the surgery entailed and then explain it to him and his wife. He also asked me to continue to be there for his wife.

How clearly he had written out his hope for prolongation of life with hope for treatment and ultimately hope for cure, using these words: "For me, life is to be able to go home without this feeding tube!"

How necessary it is for caregivers to hear the predominate hopes of our patients so that we may more realistically accompany them on their individual journeys.

I consciously adjusted to being the swing person, moving from my comfortable hope for a peaceful death to wherever he and his wife needed me to be to make his clearly-expressed hopes become reality.

I then set about coming in early to meet with his surgeon. This truly tested my own ability to support his primary hopes. I did not like his doctor and my clinical mind questioned how he could do this surgery. It included a special graft to the affected area, which I was not sure contained enough viable tissue due to the previous extensive surgeries and radiation. Would the graft take? After explaining the surgical procedure, I felt compelled to share my misgivings with Frank because I cared about him and took seriously the trust he and his wife placed in me. They both smiled knowingly as I spoke and were relieved by my honesty. Having shared my concerns about the surgery, I then was able to commit myself to being there for them and supporting them in their hopes, not my hopes. This I did with the totality of my personal and professional being.

Frank did have the surgery and, despite the odds, he came through the procedure beautifully. He also healed, even with all the damage from radiation therapy. The feeding tube was removed and he went home.

Without the embarrassment of the feeding tube, he was able to travel to Florida to see his aged mother in a nursing home and to say good-bye to her. His hope for cure enabled him to finish this important business. He lived almost another year with a high quality of life.

At his last admission to the hospital, he wrote on those same yellow pages, "Cathy, do you think the medicine can keep me comfortable until…," and, "Cathy, I hope you can continue to be there for my wife." This time I knew we were both at the same place and that the predominate hope was indeed for a death that was peaceful.

Again, both husband and wife requested my presence, but this time it was not for information but for palliation, comfort, and care. Frank did die peacefully in the arms of his loving wife. As a team of three, we enabled his hopes to come true. He accepted and understood the hope for peaceful death as the final stage of his life.

Using the metaphor of a patient's hope system being like a solar system, while you are within its reach (as you are in the role of caregiver), you are just another planet following universal laws. It is his world, it is his reality, that counts. If hope for cure pops up again after going home to die peacefully, so be it. Frank's hope for cure enabled him to have a final visit with his mother, which won him a feeling of satisfaction that, in turn, helped him live for almost another year in relative comfort.

The clinical application of The Hope System has proven effective by providing a language and guide to better understand and communicate with dying persons and their families. I feel it is crucial for all of us interacting with the dying because it enables us to get to the heart of the matter. That is, it helps us clarify what the patient is hoping for from his experience, his treatment, his surgery, his hospitalization. Thus, it helps us understand what both life and death mean to this individual in each step of his journey from initial diagnosis until life's end.

Chapter 4

How the Dying Speak to Us

The symbolic verbal and nonverbal languages of the dying are known as "separation behaviors" and are triggered primarily by the physiological changes that occur within the terminally ill person as the disease progresses. The behaviors that we see are the external manifestation of their inner world, that world within which is known only to them. It is part of the body wisdom, which alerts them to the changes that signal their demise. This mind-body interaction is given to them so that they may prepare for their own death and the resultant external, observable words, and behaviors are the language that they use to prepare those whom they love.

Thus, the interpretation of this special language is of prime importance for all those who would accompany the dying on their final journey. It has been my privilege to be taught this language by the best teachers, the dying themselves. It is now my privilege to share this with those of you who desire to learn it and wish to hear and understand the dying's final messages.

The Language of the Dying

I want to explain some of the words and behaviors I have observed so that when you see or hear one or two, or perhaps more, in a given situation with family or a patient, something will click. You will not only see and hear but understand what the dying are truly saying, and be able to interpret their language and symbols to help prepare yourself, no matter what role you have.

You, then, will be able to assist others who have a relationship with the dying person prepare themselves so the death is not as traumatic or devastating as it might have been without this knowledge and help.

I have never seen all of the following behaviors occur in one person. Yet, I have seen similar themes repeated time after time. These patterns emerged in the hundreds of dying persons I have accompanied on their final journeys. The behaviors and words are the language of the dying.

Between Depression and Acceptance

If one chooses to use the stages defined by psychiatrist Elisabeth Kübler-Ross in her book, *On Death and Dying*, to describe the dying process, a review of her work is helpful:

- The first stage is *Denial*: "No, not me."
- Then *Anger*: "Why me?"
- The third stage, *Bargaining*, is: "Yes, me, but…"
- The fourth stage is *Depression*: "Oh my God, I'm going to die."
- And the fifth is *Acceptance:* "I'm going to die, and somehow that's all right."

The time period I wish to discuss now occurs around the fourth stage as the person is moving toward the fifth stage. This period of resignation may be characterized as: "Yes me, and no more buts."

It is important that we clearly understand that the length of this time period is different for each person experiencing it and unique to their individual life-into-death transition. For example, over the years I have seen people in which several of the nonverbal behaviors occur in one day and then suddenly this person dies after having been on hospice care for several months. I have also observed nonverbal and verbal behaviors occur over months.

All of the symbolic verbal and nonverbal behaviors that follow are anecdotal evidence of the dynamic reality of hope within each of us. Our hope system comes to the surface, becoming real and observable when we face the crisis of our own death and all the things that mean life are being taken from us. When we are stripped to our core, we come in touch with our true-life force, wherein is our ability to hope.

We can observe all of this in others. As the disease progresses, it is like layers of an onion peeling away. The roles of work, family, and responsibilities that have constituted the person's life drop from importance. Now that the external life raiments have been stripped away, a deep inner dynamic—hope—is freed and comes to the foreground. It comes up to consciousness now because its power is needed so that the dying person may live each day the way he hopes to live it until he dies. This deep inner connection with self is what keeps one alive. It stems from the same deep reservoir within that all human beings share, and becomes activated when life is threatened.

Inner Sustenance

An aspect of The Hope System that has come to me over the years of observing the life-into-death process of so many people is that there seems be a shift in attention from "outer" to "inner" sustenance within each individual's unique way of letting go of life in order to grasp the reality of their death. The phases of The Hope System and the separation behaviors that follow capture and describe how this process takes place. Hope begins their journey, hope sees them through it, and hope brings them to its culmination in death.

For clarity, I have divided the symbolic language into two categories—nonverbal and verbal. I shall begin by describing the passive nonverbal behaviors, which form a significant part of the separation behaviors utilized by the dying to prepare themselves and their loved ones for their death. It is my hope that as you read on you will be able to see or hear more clearly, and now perhaps understand, the communications so lovingly delivered to you by those who have gone before you in death. You will also see that death is not a passive process, but a process that possesses within it a tremendous dynamism.

Passive Nonverbal 1

Behavior: They stop eating, drinking, and taking medicine.

Interpretation: They stop doing all the things that mean life and socialization and begin to disconnect from life and loved ones. They may also be taking charge of their life and death by choosing these actions.

Action: Don't force them to eat, drink, or take medication. Dehydration is a normal and natural part of the dying process. Their bodies are shutting down, and they don't require the nutrition and hydration they did in the past. It is important to adjust the method of pain and symptom control as the patients change to insure their comfort.

Passive Nonverbal 2

Behavior: Their eye contact changes. Initially, the dying look deeply into the eyes of loved ones, absorbing each feature. Over time their gaze shifts. They seem to be looking through us, beyond us, as if we were no longer there. They look to the left (heart side) or up to the ceiling as if looking at someone or something behind us.

Interpretation: Their change in gaze and focus indicates movement from those who are in their life toward their death. This often-subtle shift symbolizes the disconnection or letting go of physical life and loved ones. Often they begin seeing loved ones who have died or other spiritual beings at this time.

Action: Don't question this. Try to understand the subtle but powerful message contained in this behavior. They are now able to see beyond us, to see where they are going. Their life is no longer with us. They don't see themselves with us here any longer, but are now able to see the reality beyond this world. They now seem to be more "there" than they are "here."

Passive Nonverbal 3

Behavior: They pretend to sleep.

Interpretation: They are closing their eyes on the world and life and us. The things and people of this world are no longer important to them. The eyes are our windows on the world, and they are shutting theirs. They need to withdraw into self, to begin their inward journey.

Action: Allow them to rest. Do not try to wake them up or engage them in conversation. Explain this behavior to family as, "Sleep in preparation for death." It is not a rejection of loved ones.

Passive Nonverbal 4

Behavior: They request that we close the blinds or curtains on the window.

Interpretation: They are closing out the light of the outside world. They no longer wish to participate in life outside. They are retreating into their own world, which is necessary for their transition and signals the life-into-death process.

Action: Darken the room for them; don't argue with them. Respect their wishes. They need to close out the outside world and distractions. Focusing on the outer world is not as important now as inner-world focus is.

Passive Nonverbal 5

Behavior: They ask that the curtain between them and their roommate be pulled closed.

Interpretation: They are blocking out others, stopping communication and participation in life and community. They need time and quiet to focus within.

Action: Do as they ask. They need their energy directed inward. They need privacy to connect with their inner self, so they can finish their business. Inner communication is now more important than outer communication.

Passive Nonverbal 6

Behavior: They display changes in visage, from furrowed brow, facial grimacing, or a look of distress. Over time facial expressions change and relax. They appear calmer and more peaceful.

Interpretation: Physical relaxation response indicates the struggle of holding on is ending: "He's not with us anymore." "It feels like she's drifting away." Reality of death is present and with it comes resignation and relief.

Action: Observe and learn from this behavior. Do not hold onto them. Let them go. Give them your blessing and permission. This may be their final gift to you: "She looked so peaceful at the end. No more suffering."

Passive Nonverbal 7

Behavior: They become quiet and withdrawn, no longer talking.

Interpretation: By not communicating with loved ones, they are further withdrawing into self, not wanting to be part of the world or life. Interior communication is the most important task at this time.

Action: Respect and understand these important changes. This behavior is difficult for all caregivers, as we want to do something. In this behavior, the dying are trying to teach us the importance of being rather than doing, a crucial life-death lesson. In sharing the silence and just being present, we create a safe place for the dying to complete their journey. You might say, "I know you don't want to talk anymore. But, may I just come and be with you?"

Passive Nonverbal 8

Behavior: They turn their back on visitors.

Interpretation: They are turning their back on life, the world, and us. Their life energy is now more and more involved in their personal inner journey than the things and people in this world.

Action: Don't say, "Turn over; look at me," or interfere with this behavior. Allow and understand it, not as a blatant physical rejection, but rather with knowing that they are, with love, preparing us for a life without their presence. The deeper meaning to this is, as they turn away from us, they are turning toward their death. They are no longer part of us or our world. Silently, they ask us not to hold onto them, but let them go to their death. This is a powerful cross-cultural theme.

Passive Nonverbal 9

Behavior: They go into the fetal position.

Interpretation: They are turning physically inward. This movement signals that the dying are now, on all levels of their being, more and more involved in their inner journey. They are intensely preparing for their transition and delivery from life into death.

Action: This is an extremely powerful separation behavior. Analogy and symbology of this behavior is necessary for death as it is necessary for birth. Both can be seen as transition from one life into another. It is not only symbolic, but it is a necessary component of the life-into-death process. That's why it's so difficult for people who are tied down in ICUs or a nursing home to die, as they are not able to go into fetal position and complete their transition. We must allow the dying to die in their most natural way.

Active Nonverbal 1

Behavior: They physically push away those close to them, not allowing them to care for them anymore. They push caregivers' hands away if they try to feed or medicate them.

Interpretation: After having attempted the passive nonverbal behaviors and turning away without success, the dying now need to do something more active and direct to get their message across. They are symbolically pushing us away from them and death into a life without them. This communication is used by the dying as a last act of love.

Action: While you or the family may feel rejected, don't get upset or angry or feel the person doesn't love you anymore. The dying person feels frustrated. This is not done in anger but rather because they love us. They are trying to prepare us for, and spare us from, the moment of death. They are pushing us to understand and to let them go.

Active Nonverbal 2

Behavior: They move the arms back and forth from the center of the body to the sides. This movement usually occurs with fists clenched, as if breaking out of a shell. I have also seen pushing with open hands, as if moving through a web or cocoon, trying to get out.

Interpretation: They are breaking out of the physical shell which has encased them in life. The dying have a powerful need to free the spirit or life force. They are attempting to free themselves from their physical confines and pass into a new dimension of being. This behavior may intensify as death comes closer, but cease as the actual moment of death nears and their struggle is over.

Action: Do not attempt to stop or restrain them. However, it is important to protect them from harm. Understand and appreciate their silent words and hear the message this graphically signals, "It's my time to leave here and be freed from disease, pain, suffering, and life itself." It also demonstrates how difficult it is to leave, to let go of what was known as life. But this is crucial in order to die.

Symbolic Verbal 1

Behavior: They verbally push people away. The dying frequently use anger or language they never used in life. Family members are surprised and apologetic. "He doesn't mean it." "It must be the medication." "I never, ever heard him use words like that."

Interpretation: The dying often use anger or shocking words to get their loved one's attention. This is employed when all passive behaviors have failed to get the message across and their loved ones are still holding onto them.

Action: Don't react with anger or stop them. Rather, listen to their pleas, hidden within the anger or foul language: "Please listen. Hear my message. I'm dying. Release me. Let me go." The dying are vehemently requesting that their loved ones give them permission to die at this time.

Symbolic Verbal 2

Behavior: They ask loved ones and others working with them to leave. "Mommy, go home. Jimmy needs you more than I do now." "Nurse, I'll be okay. Go over there, that woman is crying; she needs you."

Interpretation: They are sending loved ones into a life without them. This is especially dramatic when seen with children who often send parents home and, no sooner than the parents leave, the child dies.

Action: By stating the needs of others before theirs, they are symbolically releasing loved ones to re-engage with others or their life without them. This gives family members the opening to say, "I hear you. I'll go on without you. Do what you need to do. I'm not alone; I have what I need."

Symbolic Verbal 3

Behavior: They use illogical travel metaphors or analogies. "Hurry, we must find Henry. He has the plane ready to take me." "I have to go. I don't want to miss my train." "I don't want the bus to leave without me. The tickets are in my purse."

Interpretation: Many use travel analogies to indicate movement toward death. These are symbolic assurances to the family that it's time to leave. They are used to calm loved ones. The dying are telling them they have a way of getting there; they are going home; that others know the way and will take them to their destination.

Action: Listen intently to their message. Don't hesitate to ask questions about people and mode of travel: "Where is the bus going?" "Was Henry a pilot?" The dying want loved ones to know that others know the way, have the means to take them, and that they are not going alone. It's important to tell them that you understand and that it's okay for them to leave.

Symbolic Verbal 4

Behavior: They speak to and see those who have gone before and/or religious figures that bring peace to them. "My mother came to me last night. She smiled at me." "God is there, waiting for me with open arms." "The angels came to get me one: big one and two small ones." "I saw my brother." "They're all there waiting for me, just across the river."

Interpretation: They are symbolically telling those close to them that "It is my time." They are ready, and they can, and must, go to see and be with spiritual beings and those who have gone before them. The dying "see," and now know for certain, that others are waiting for them and are able to help them come to them and find the peace and presence they have been longing for.

Action: Encourage them. Don't negate what they say. Ask them questions: "Tell me about them." "How many angels have come to you?" They are symbolically telling us where they are in the dying process. They are giving us assurances that others are there to help them cross over. "I will be with the others who have gone before and are at peace." "No more suffering." "You can let me go now." "I'll be just fine. I'm not alone and I'm going to a better place."

Reactive Depression

Many of these behaviors, such as the cessation of talking and eating, withdrawal and isolation, if seen in any other population would be called depression. In the dying population this pre-death phase is called "reactive depression." They are reacting to what is happening in their body and an increasing awareness of their impending death. This depression, like dehydration, is a normal part of the dying process and it is very important for the dying and for us. To help us understand this behavior I have divided it into two parts—anticipatory and preparatory.

Anticipatory

It is anticipatory for the dying person, who, on a deep and profound level, is anticipating his own death, thus the going inward. He may seem far away now, withdrawing into himself, completely absorbed with doing his interior work. "He's not really here with us anymore." "I can't reach her now; she seems so far away." "He's more there than he is here."

Preparatory

It is preparatory for the family and caregivers alike. The dying are trying to prepare us for their death by dismissing us from their life. "You don't need to come and see me anymore." "I'll be saying good-bye now." Frequently, I have heard them say to a spouse of many years, "Only come and see me once a day (or skip tomorrow). It's too long a bus ride." These statements have nothing to do with how long the bus ride is, but rather have everything to do with the deep awareness of the reality and proximity of their death and the need to prepare the other for it.

Since this reactive depression is part of a very important process, I recommend the individually-determined and judicious use of antidepressants for the dying. Antidepressants should be given only to take the edge off the depression and thus assist the dying in doing their work. They should *not* be given because this depression makes the doctor, family, or professional caregiver uncomfortable. Depression is an essential and normal part of the final journey and should not be interrupted. We must always remember it is not about us or our comfort; it is their dying, not ours. I've had patients say to me, "Cathy, please take that pill away; I can't do my work; it's hard for me to focus on what's important since they gave me that new medicine."

Final Words

The verbal and nonverbal cues contained in the symbolic language of the dying are an attempt to prepare those closest to them for their death and a life without them here on earth. They desperately want to ease the trauma for their loved ones in every way possible. These separation behaviors are triggered by the physical changes they are feeling as the disease progresses and they become aware from the inside out that they really are going to die, and they become aware of *when* they are going to die. Thus, they seek the right words to help their loved ones hear their final messages, prepare for living without them, and to be able to let them go.

Chapter 5

The Hope for a Peaceful Death

As we observed in previous chapters, the last stage of hope takes the most energy, though it may seem to require the least. As the patient's hope for a peaceful death takes priority, he may become passive and quiet, retreating into his interior world. Try not to take offense. Having accepted death, he is turning away from life and is preparing for the final transition. You can help by respecting that his strongest advocate and ally in this busy preparation is his own dynamic inner reality of hope.

The power of hope at this stage is in looking forward or anticipating and expecting the best outcome, not for life, but for a death that is peaceful on all levels. But before the dying person can fully access the positive energy available in this kind of hoping, the roadblocks have to be removed.

It is at this time, when death becomes more real, that a process called "life review" may occur. This is when the person who is dying takes stock of his life and its many roles—such as who he has been to himself and others; what he has done or accomplished; what is left undone. Has he done enough? Been enough? Is he still thinking, "If only…," as he looks back over his time on Earth. How will he be remembered, for good or ill? Or, more important, will he be remembered at all?

The understanding, acceptance, and resolution of one's life review has a direct bearing on the type and intensity of pain one might experience before arriving at a peaceful death. Since this review plays a pivotal role in both pre-death behavior and post-death fears which impact the life-into-death experience, I will discuss it here in relation to the levels of pain that emerge from this process.

Four Levels of Pain

Basically, a peaceful death, or "a good death," requires the absence of pain on four levels. This chapter should guide you in assisting the dying person on this final leg of the journey. You'll learn how to help the dying achieve relief on these levels:

- first, *physical pain,*
- second, *emotional pain,*
- third, and perhaps the most excruciating, the *pain of mental anguish,*
- and last, the *pain of spiritual alienation.*

What's required in letting go of life peacefully—what allows one to hope for the best in whatever lies beyond death—varies in its specifics for each individual. It is essential, in assisting the patient in managing his pain, that we help him find the root of the pain; from what level or levels does it originate? Once this is known, the most effective method to bringing relief can be employed.

As in the four stages of hope, the four levels of pain often overlap and spiral back and forth continuously before resolving themselves.

The important question at this stage of hope, hope for a peaceful death (and at each level of pain), is: What would make death a peaceful prospect *for this individual?*

Relief from the primary or most-felt pain of the moment is the prerequisite for achieving peace on every subsequent level, and so, first and foremost, caregivers need to help eliminate, or at least modify, the presence of pain on the physical level. Physical pain distorts the experience of both life and death. It becomes a barrier to not only the peacefulness hoped for at life's end, but also the unexpected growth that can happen. Of course, excessively strong doses of painkillers can distort a patient's perception as well—and sap the energy they need to make the final transition. So, finding the right balance of pain medication—and monitoring it so as to keep it in balance—is of primary importance at this stage. Keeping the patient as comfortable as possible, while allowing for some alertness, lays the foundation for him to do the rest of his work.

The second level of pain is emotional pain. This often develops due to:

- strained relationships, perhaps due to unresolved issues,
- sadness from having to say good-bye to loved ones,
- regrets for what has been missed or for what might have been,
- social roles which will be left unfulfilled, such as not being there to help guide and protect others,
- fear of the process, and
- fear of the unknown.

Any and all of these can block peace from entering the patient's life at this time.

In my experience, the third source of pain—mental anguish—can be the most excruciating of all. Mental anguish often has its roots in emotional pain but has a more heartbreaking quality often stemming from shattered relationships—separation and alienation from loved ones—and the realization that completion or closure will not be forthcoming. Knowledge that the way one has lived his life has hurt or damaged others may also cause mental anguish. A type of fear of the hereafter often appears here: the fear of meeting those who abused or rejected the dying person in life or the fear of meeting those who were illtreated by the person dying. Comments such as, "Will my father turn his back on me, as he did in life?" and, "I'm afraid to see my mother again. I caused her so much pain in my life," are common.

The fourth level of pain is that of spiritual alienation. Attaining peace on a spiritual level is very important as life comes to an end. It can go far in overcoming all the other levels of pain. And vice versa: I've seen forgiveness and reconciliation drive away the pain of spiritual alienation in an instant. By accomplishing the mending of fences, as they attend to their needs on the emotional and mental anguish levels, the dying are taking care of the last level, making spiritual peace.

Strategies for Helping

Assist the patient manage his pain of the moment by helping him find the root of the pain: From what level does it originate? Once this is known, the most effective approach to bringing relief can be employed.

Here are some things you can do to help the dying deal with their pain:

- Show that you care in any number of ways, including by asking, "How may I help you?"
- Alleviate the fear of the unknown by explaining or having a physician or other caregiver explain what is likely to happen from here on.
- Let them know that they still have a say in what will happen in terms of care and treatment.
- Express that you are trying to appreciate what they are going through.
- Help them mend fences if necessary. Make calls to estranged relatives or friends; act as an intermediary.
- Reinsure them that their loved ones will be okay without them. Use specifics.
- Let them know that they will be remembered and missed.
- Emphasize the positive experiences and accomplishments in the person's life. De-emphasize the "what ifs" and the "if onlys."
- Encourage others to visit or call, especially those close to the person. Visits or cards from children are especially helpful.
- Assure them that they are not going to be abandoned, that someone will be available 24/7.
- Help with the writing of letters to say unsaid things to loved ones.
- Share beliefs.
- Bring in a pastoral care professional, such as their own minister.

Pain is such a uniquely individual and mysterious human experience that it is important to listen and hear, not only from where the pain of the moment stems but what it means to each person. The stories of Carmen and Marguerite presented below show how the levels relate to one another and how meeting the need based on the pain of the moment enables the other levels to be addressed.

Carmen

Carmen was one of my special patients in this category. She was in her mid-thirties, had five children, and her Stage 4 breast cancer had been diagnosed eighteen months earlier when her daughter, Carmencita (Little Carmen) was born. Carmencita's name fit her; in fact, she was the image of her mother before the ravages of the disease and treatment changed her.

Carmen and her family lived in Spanish Harlem, a very bad area...As her hospice nurse, Jeanette, our escort, and I entered her building, we stepped over garbage, needles, and bodies of people sleeping off a crack high.

When you entered Carmen's apartment, it was another world; although sparsely furnished, it was immaculate. You could eat off the floor it was so clean. How this skinny woman kept it so clean amazed me. No sooner were we inside, when "Cita" came running to us, squealing with delight. She had lovely, dark curls that bounced as she ran, a beautiful face, and the biggest, most extraordinary, sparkling dark eyes. It was in her eyes that I really saw the resemblance to her mother, but the sparkle in Big Carmen's eyes had been diminished by pain and disease.

Carmen's pain was constant: severe head pain due to the metastasis (spread) of the primary cancer to her brain. She had been treated with a Fentanyl transdermal patch at high dosages, high doses of steroids to decrease the swelling of her brain, and two short courses of radiation therapy to shrink her brain tumors. One of her most severe and distressing symptoms, in addition to pain, was projectile vomiting caused by the brain swelling. This further weakened her. Getting enough calories into her was becomming a real problem.

Jeanette was at her wit's end. When I first came in to help Carmen, she had been healthier. Now, due to the progression of the disease, Carmen was but a shadow of her former self. I greeted her with a hug. Jeanette had been using a complementary healing technique with

Nine Tips

Over the years I found that the following nine strategies are helpful to those dying, because they help us be there for them when it counts. Yet, the major value in utilizing these tips is found in their benefit to friends and family of the dying. Doing these things enables them to live on with fewer regrets, knowing they assisted the dying person and did not abandon him.

1. Visit. Don't feel awkward about what to say or do. Being there is more important than saying or doing the "right" thing.

2. Ask if they need or want anything. "How may I help you?" goes a long way in showing you care. Do your best to meet their requests.

3. Call if you can't visit. Even a telephone call maintains contact. It is important for all of us to hear a voice we recognize. Encourage others to call.

4. Send mail. Cards, letters, and pictures let them know you are thinking of them and gives them something tangible to see and read. Again, encourage others to send cards. Cards and letters from children are especially helpful.

5. Allow for silence. Let them know that there is no pressure to talk. Silence allows volumes to be said and heard.

6. Leave an object—something that has meaning to the patient—when you have to go away for a while. This may be a religious item, a colorful plant, a wedding album, or even a stuffed animal. This helps, because symbolically you are still there with them.

7. Send gifts. Select ones that signify the relationship you have had with them over the years.

8. Reassure them that they are not forgotten. Let them know that you and others are thinking about them.

9. Keep your promises. If you say you are going to do something, such as return at a certain time or meet with a doctor, make this a priority for you, as it will be for them.

Carmen called "Therapeutic Touch," which had been helping with the pain until now.

Jeanette had been with Carmen and had experienced her changing, fluctuating hopes throughout the journey since her first surgery. Carmen asked for my help, due primarily to my question, "What are you hoping for?" "I hope for peace," Carmen told me. "Help me find peace for me and my kids and soon."

Hearing the hope for a peaceful death come up so strongly, Jeanette and I knew we had to move quickly in order to help Carmen. We sat on the cot that was Carmen's bed. I was on the left side, holding her hand and gently rubbing her back. Jeanette was on her right, with Carmen's head on her shoulder, her right hand clasping Carmen's hand. Then suddenly Carmen tightened up, squeezing our hands. She took a deep breath and let out a scream that I have never heard before and hope I never hear again. It came from deep within her soul and filled the room with pain and anguish. She spoke in a scream, "How can I leave them? I was an orphan myself!" Upon hearing this, we were all crying. Carmen's male companion came in to help and Cita was crying, too. She ran to pat her mommy and hug her.

We just kept sitting there in shock, rocking and crying, patting and rubbing. Then, after what seemed like an eternity, I heard Jeanette say, "I didn't know you were an orphan. How can we help you with the kids?"

Through tears and deep breathing, Carmen told us that two children had the same father, but the other three each had different fathers. She made it quite clear who should go with whom after her death. As we spoke, relief and clarity began to flood through us and through Carmen. Her pain, though, manifested on the physical plane, stemmed from her love-need bonds, her emotions and, primarily, her mental anguish: "How can I leave them?"

Once we knew the root cause of Carmen's pain, relief fell into place. From her cry for help we knew she needed to put into writing—legally—who she, as the custodial parent, wanted to raise each of her children. The biggest problem we faced, however, was getting a lawyer to come to her apartment. After six or so lawyers said no, the hospice program made arrangements for a lawyer to meet Carmen, her mother, Jeanette, myself, and our social worker at the hospital when Carmen next went for radiation therapy.

Very quickly, Carmen's hope for a peaceful death was being put into place and her physical pain decreased remarkably.

But we weren't finished. On our next visit, Carmen turned to Jeanette, the social worker who had come with us, and me. "You know real peace only comes when you and God are on good terms," she told us. "So, before I can leave, I need to have Little Carmen baptized. Then my work is done."

We had a wonderful pastoral care gentleman on the team who came to see Carmen. They clicked. Carmen was able to confess and release her past. The hospice team got excited. This man had performed many funerals and several marriages, but this would be his first baptism in a hospice program.

It was by far the most joyous, lively, love-filled baptism I have ever witnessed. In the Puerto Rican tradition, baptism is held in high regard, as the children are welcomed into both the natural and spiritual family in a special way. We were all given lovely favors with lace and "Carmencita" written on beautiful blue ribbon in gold. I still have that memento from one of my most special teachers.

Carmen's pain originated from several levels and she taught me that each person is like an onion. We need to help them trust us enough to encourage them to peel away all the layers of their pain so their hope for a peaceful death may become a reality.

Carmen wrote each of her children a letter to be opened when the child turned thirteen, and her pain decreased as she finished each letter. She died with minimal pain, surrounded by her children, mother, friends, and Jeanette—her faithful nurse—to the end. Carmen also had letters for both Jeanette and me. I still treasure mine.

Marguerite

I met Marguerite when she came to be evaluated for external and internal radiation for cancer of the uterus. She finished her external course of treatment with no complications and was encouraged by this news. She was thrilled when I told her I had set up a cesium hotline to work as a support network for women undergoing internal radiation with cesium implants in the uterine cavity (a form of radiation therapy). At that time, this procedure was given over several days and the patient was isolated in a special room with minimal visitors and interaction, due to the effects of the radiation. This was scary for those receiving the treatment, and to help patients cope, I encouraged them to stay connected with each other via calls, the lending of books, and the like. After her discharge from treatment, I had left that department and Marguerite took over coordinating the program.

Nearly two-and-a-half years later, Marguerite was again my patient in the Visiting Nurse Service Hospice Program. The cancer had spread and there was no more curative treatment for her. She had a huge belly, which needed to be drained frequently, and her legs were swollen to three times their original size. She often had difficulty breathing and had pain from the fluid pressure. I was called in to help with her pain management. We made arrangements for her son to come home from the service to "see her one more time before…" They had a lovely visit and we were able to keep her comfortable. After his visit the hospice team thought things might change for Marguerite since she had been able to say her good-byes and tell her son—the only family she had left—about her affairs.

Even with all the pain, fluid retention, difficulty breathing, etc. she never complained.

Her legs began to leak clear fluid, and one day, while I was changing her many dressings, I told her, "I'm so glad your son was able to get to see you. Is there anything else you are hoping for now?"

"I hope to have the strength to endure this to the end," she told me. "How can I help you?" I asked her. With that question, she grabbed my hands and whispered in my ear, "I'm not welcome in Heaven."

"You're not welcome in Heaven, Marguerite?" I asked.

Looking me straight in the eye and still whispering, she said "I'm not forgivable. That is why I got this cancer and I have to suffer." She sighed and held my hands even tighter and looked even more intently, deeply into my eyes. "Cathy, I had an abortion when I was a teenager. I just knew I couldn't raise a child. I was a child myself. I had no other choice."

Tears welled up in our eyes and we just clung to each other. She began sobbing and I held her until she stopped. When she looked up, she was a vision of peace and relief. I said to her, "Is it enough that you have shared this with me or do you need to speak to a priest, rabbi, pastor, or anyone else?" She answered, "No, Cathy, it's enough that I was finally able to say it out loud to someone else. Thank you for listening and not saying anything when I told you my secret." She had carried it for fifty years.

Being able to finally share her secret was essential to allow Marguerite to come to a peaceful death. I don't think I realized the true meaning of being an accepting, open, listening empty slate until that magical day when I saw freedom flowing in and filling Marguerite with profound joy. Her physical pain decreased greatly after that. She did die peacefully not long after. Her newly-discharged son and I were with her. I know she waited for me to return from vacation, as she had told me she would, for our final good-bye.

What Marguerite shared with me is what I call "sacred material," and it must be treated as such. Therefore, when we chart such an interaction or report it at a team meeting, we just need to say something like, "…shared something very important with me today and saying it brought great relief and peace." The details need not be told; the client's privacy and secrets remaining confidential.

Marguerite was a special teacher for patience and silence to me. I hope her story helps you listen and hear in a special way those in your care, be it family members, friends, or patients.

At this point, death often comes quickly to the patient who is now open to it. They are often filled with the serenity of acceptance. Many of the dying have told me that, from this serenity, "helpmates," emerge for them, bringing uplifting thoughts or images that promise to lend a hand in crossing over, bringing them great joy.

Coma as a Choice

I would now like to present and discuss a phenomenon that has become clearer and clearer to me over the years as I have accompanied the dying on their final journey. It is the reality of coma as a choice, rather than merely a response to physiological changes in the dying person. Early on in my career as a Nursing Sister of the Sick Poor, as I sat with and observed the dying in their own homes, I became fascinated with the differences in how the dying process took place. I found the going into a coma or not going into a coma was something that peaked my curiosity. Why did some patients go into this state at the end of their lives, while others did not? I made some cursory observations and notes about these patients and their families at that time, but drew no conclusions.

When, during the mid-1970s, I was the director of nursing at Calvary Hospital, a specialized hospital caring for the advanced cancer patient, I found that my interest in the phenomenon of coma was once again aroused. I began to do my own very informal study as I attended rounds on the patient wards. Two hundred patients were cared for at any given time at Calvary Hospital, many with the same cancer diagnosis, so I had many patients to choose from, as well as on-site laboratory facilities.

I was able to compare patients with the same diagnoses, similar ages and similar blood work over a six-month period. What I learned from that very rudimentary observation was that entering a comatose state did not appear to be determined by changes in the patients' blood, organ function, or disease process, but rather in the realization of the patient that their loved ones needed more time to prepare for the reality of death.

As I looked at the results of my inquiry, suddenly it all came together. With a smile, I silently thanked all the patients whom I had the privilege to care for at this special time in their lives and for the lessons they taught me. It became clear to me that coma is often used by the dying when all the symbolic verbal and nonverbal language has failed, and their family just can't let them go. Coma is a dress rehearsal for their death.

Coma is utilized by the dying to gently prepare families and give them the time they need to say "good-bye;" "I love you;" "I'm sorry;" "forgive me;" "I forgive you;" "thank you;" or whatever else is needed.

Initially, when the person first goes into a coma, we hear their loved ones say, "When will they wake up?" or "They look like they are sleeping." Time passes—the length differs for each patient, family situation, and need—then we hear family members say, "Gee, they look so peaceful now, they don't seem to be suffering anymore."

As more time passes, we begin to hear the family speaking about the person in the past tense as if they were no longer there with them. Shortly thereafter the person dies. How wise are our teachers, the dying, and how gently they lead us and help us to envision their death and thus be prepared for it. Coma looks just like the sleep of death. It is the absence of physical suffering and the appearance of being asleep that helps us be able to let them go into death.

I have observed the phenomenon of patients going into comas many times over the past forty years in a variety of situations. I have seen it frequently in people who have been ill with a chronic or terminal illness, in people following normally lifesaving surgery that went awry, as well as in people following a sudden traumatic accident. Let me now share with you several powerful, poignant, and preparatory messages spoken silently by those who have made the choice of coma, as their final gift to those they love.

My first example is that of a little girl hit by a car who, due to the extent of her injuries, should have been dead on arrival to the emergency room. Instead, to the amazement of the entire medical team, she survived and lapsed into a coma, thus, giving her family, especially her parents, time to adjust to the shock. This gave them time to say their good-byes and helped prepare them for her death. Over the time she was in the coma, her parents began to slowly accept the fact that she would not have wanted to live with the disabilities she suffered from the accident, and thereby they could accept her death a little easier.

Scott

After a diving accident that should have killed Scott, an active teenager, or at the least left him a quadriplegic, the coma he entered enabled all involved to say to him what they needed. In the end, his mother freed him by saying, "Go home, Scott. You always told Dad and me after Jim's accident, 'If I'm ever paralyzed like that, please let me go.' It's tearing me apart to see you like this; they tell me you're not suffering, so I can let you go. I know it's your choice."

Paul

One of the most powerful examples of coma as a choice came from one of the patients at Calvary Hospital. We made a point of celebrating life events and especially the birthdays of our patients. As was our way, we began to discuss how Paul, one of our favorite and longtime patients, wanted to celebrate his birthday, including his choice of an everything-chocolate cake. Suddenly, or so it seemed to us, Paul went into a coma for no apparent reason. His coma lasted for six weeks. It didn't seem possible for him to know day from night and the passage of time, yet he lived until his birthday. Not for a party and his everything-chocolate cake, but so that his wife would receive his social security and pension benefits. In addition, it gave her just enough time to be eligible for senior-citizen housing so she could sell their family home.

Paul took care of her and protected her in death as he had in life. They had been married for almost fifty years and as they both had said many times, they lived for each other. However, as the weeks went by, Helen, seeing him so peaceful and no longer suffering the severe pain that had racked his body for so long, was finally able to say, "Good-bye, thank you for being my husband; I love you and now go home to your maker; I'll always love you but now I know I can go on by myself." With these loving words, Paul's wife was able to give him her permission to let go and die. At one point, I remember her saying, "Paul, it's okay for you to celebrate your birthday in Heaven, with your God."

This example demonstrated to me and now, I hope, to you, the uncanny wisdom of the dying and their knowing exactly how much time their loved ones need in order to let them go.

Diana

My final example concerns Diana, the mother of a young teen-ager who attended a high school bereavement group that I facilitated. Diana had been diagnosed with a brain aneurysm and was being closely monitored by her doctor and surgeons. She and the family had been told she was an excellent candidate for this surgery, as she was in her forties and very healthy. Her brother had died suddenly two years before, followed by her mother, whom she was very close to, and an aunt who had died within the last six months. Her husband was not well and she was looking forward to the surgery, as she had been suffering with headaches from the aneurysm and had not been able to help him or be there for her daughter over the last several months.

The surgery was performed on schedule but she never woke up after the operation. The family was devastated and in shock, as were her doctors, who said, this should not have happened. Diana remained in a comatose state for several weeks. While still reeling from the terrible shock, her family came to see her and say their good-byes, as they had been unable to do with her brother, the teen's favorite uncle. Miraculously, there were no other organ problems or deterioration after her surgery, which was extremely unusual following this operation. Diana's husband and daughter were able to say what they needed to say during this time and were encouraged to do so by the nursing staff.

This was essential for her daughter, as they were having some of the usual mother-teenage daughter problems and she needed to tell her mother how much she loved and appreciated her, to express her remorse for her past behavior.

Diana remained in coma just long enough for tissue typing, which enabled her to donate a kidney to her sister who was on dialysis. Just when her family was being asked to consider her quality of life and they began to talk over her and about her as if she were not there, she gently and quietly died, with her daughter and her favorite sister singing to her. In dying when, how, and the way she did, she spared her family the agony of having to make difficult decisions as had been her pattern in life. For her daughter, having the time to finish her business, say her good-byes, and be with her mother, singing to her as she died, signified her mother's final gift of love to her. Having the time to do this made the daughter's grief and bereavement process much less difficult than if her mother had died suddenly on the operating table.

Coma as a Gift

The dying, who have chosen this powerful nonverbal language, have taught me how important it is for those of us who are health care providers to teach, support, and encourage families to not waste the gift of a coma. I explain that hearing is one of the first senses we experience when we enter this world and one of the last to go when we leave it. I encourage them to take advantage of this precious time, using it to finish their business with the person who is dying.

Time after time I have had loved ones say to me, "But Cathy, I don't know what to say to them." In order to help with this, I devised a special strategy. I believe it has helped many people.

First, I tell the family member to try to put himself into the mind and thoughts of the person dying and to look at himself through the dying person's eyes. Next, I ask him to try to think of what it is that the dying person *needs* to hear him say that will allow the dying person to let go. Then, and this is equally, if not more important for the family member than the first question, I suggest he ask himself what does *he* need to say to this person in order to finish his business so he can let this loved one go to his or her death in peace.

Being able to say these important things to the dying while they are alive often eases people's bereavement process. They are saved from having to symbolically say that which they need to by letter-writing or other rituals after the death. Saying what we need to say, post-death, can also prolong the grief process.

It is my hope that you understand and resonate with these examples and that you will share this knowledge of coma as a parting gift of love with all you know who are experiencing a death in their family.

Terminal Agitation

The final separation behavior I would like to present and discuss is called "terminal agitation." It occurs just prior to the actual death and is characterized by severe agitation and high anxiety with or without physical discomfort. This occurrence is very upsetting for the family and is extremely challenging for caregivers, professional and non-professional, alike. From my experience and observation, in terminal agitation, the struggle is within the dying themselves. It is the final struggle between the body and the spirit. It is the body saying, "I can't do it anymore," and the spirit saying, "I must stay; I can't leave now." It is a graphic description of the final essential ambivalence between holding on and letting go.

Although I have seen it in elderly patients who were leaving sick or dependent spouses they were caring for, I have seen it most often and more dramatically in younger patients—usually in their thirties and forties—who were leaving a spouse or young children. Often, these patients were long-term cancer survivors, having endured many surgeries, chemotherapy, and radiation. Youth had been on their side, but at the end, the spirit was still willing but the body was weak, weakened by all the treatments and pain they had endured.

To help this come alive for you, I would like to share two examples.

The first story tells of a young father with neurofibroma of many years duration. Since adolescence, he had suffered pain of varying intensities, multiple surgeries, radiation, and chemotherapy. He came into hospice with insufficient medications for his severe pain, but his pain was soon controlled by the hospice team. The patient became peaceful, pain-free, and alert. Although his wife had not been sure she could honor his wishes that he stay at home with his family until the end, with the help and support of the hospice team and her family, she decided she could keep him at home.

During this time she gave him permission to die by saying, "You know how much the girls and I love you, but I just can't see you staying and suffering anymore." Their three girls, who ranged from two to ten years old, with the help of a bereavement counselor, made cards for their daddy and told him they loved him.

Eventually he became increasingly restless and, as death became more and more real to him, terminal agitation began. At one point he said, "It's just so hard to say good-bye to the kids; I wanted to be here to see them grow up." Exhausted after several days of this restlessness, he suddenly became calmer and, surrounded by his girls, wife, mother, and sister he quietly slipped away. At last, his struggle had ended.

The second example is of a young wife in her mid-forties, who had been battling breast cancer for several years and had tried everything she could, including experimental therapies. It was the second marriage for her and her husband, and they had both found "the love of a lifetime."

"We live for each other," her husband frequently said. "I don't think I can go on without her."

She had been on hospice for almost six months, her pain control like a roller coaster ride, when terminal agitation set in. She requested to see the pastoral counselor and told him, "I've been everything to him; I'm afraid he won't be able to make it without me and our love." And he was unrelenting in his hope, stating, "She's a fighter; she'll pull through again."

As her agitation continued, he eventually questioned her quality of life. Finally, with the help of the hospice nurse and chaplain, he finally was able to tell her, "I'll miss you and always love you, but I'll be able to go on without you somehow. By enduring all the suffering you have all these years, you have given me the courage to go on without you." Upon hearing him say these words, her agitation ceased, she breathed a deep sigh, and died peacefully, cradled in her husband's loving embrace.

Chapter 6

Wisdom of the Dying and the Choice of the Moment

How important is it to be present at the moment of death? You may think that your spouse (or mother, father, daughter, son, grandmother) is counting on you to be there. Yet more often than not, the person closest to the dying, the most beloved one, is not in the room at the final moment of passage. Why is this so? And how can you bear it, when your commitment is not to abandon them? In a moment, I'm going to explain why you need not feel you've abandoned them—or that they've abandoned you—if you are not there at the bedside at the moment of death.

The point is you have no choice in the matter. However, the dying often do.

In this chapter, I share a phenomenon, taught to me by the dying themselves: how they choose the moment they leave the earth, and who they want to be with them at that moment.

In my workshops I ask, "How many of you were with the person you loved when they died, and how did you feel being with them at that moment?" I am struck by how universal the responses are: "It was an honor." "She died holding my hand." "I crawled into bed with him and held him till he died." "Wonderful." "Scared, sad, but glad." "My aunt and I sang her into death just as she sang me to sleep as a child."

And then, I ask those who were not there at that moment, "How did that make you feel?" Again, people give such similar responses:

"Terrible."

"I failed him."

"Guilty."

"She rallied, so we thought it was okay to leave her."

"He woke up and sent us to get something to eat."

"My son told me to go home, saying Jimmy needed me more than he did."

"If only I hadn't been so tired."

"If only I hadn't gone to have that cup of coffee."

The "if only" syndrome cuts to the quick of many of the survivors of this world. How well I know it. My father died suddenly when I was nineteen, and I wasn't there. My mother was ill for several years in a nursing home. All of her five children and eleven grandchildren visited her at Easter one year and, kissing us, she said, "I love you" to each of us and then she said, "Good-bye."

Now, we are not a good-bye family; we're a so-long-see-you-later kind of family. But I didn't hear the difference that day. Even having taught the symbolic language of the dying in dozens of workshops by that time, I didn't hear the finality in her message of love; I didn't interpret this as her way of preparing us for her death, as well as sparing us the pain of the actual moment.

I didn't hear it because I couldn't hear it. At that final farewell, I wasn't her nurse, a teacher on death and dying. I was just her daughter. I didn't want to hear her good-bye because that would mean she was really going to die and hearing that would be too painful. She died peacefully two days later. When I received word of her death, it didn't matter that I was the consummate professional on duty in my serene director of nursing office…and, in a totally unprofessional but completely human manner, I screamed.

I learned an important lesson at that moment, one that has helped me in my work with dying people and their families ever since. I learned that every death is a sudden death to the families of the dying. It didn't make any difference that my mother had been ill for several years and that I knew she might die at any time. I thought I was prepared, but when it actually happened I was shocked. I also learned that two people could be at the same stage of their hope systems in hoping for a peaceful death, but your vision of how that might transpire is probably not the same as your loved one's.

In some way, the dying may know what is better for them—and for us—than we do. Our vision of their peaceful passage may well include ourselves at the loved one's side. But in the final moment, we have no more control over the choice of the moment of life's end than we do over the outcome. How a person dies is as individual as how he's lived. And no matter how well you know him—or yourself—you can't predict when he'll go or how you're going to react at the last breath. On some level, every death is sudden, and no matter how you anticipate you'll react to it, you can't really know till it happens.

But the dying may know.

In my observation—and I'm not alone in noting this—the dying seem to understand and anticipate, better than we do, how we're going to feel and react to their death. I've seen it time and time again: The dying seem to choose their moment of death. And intuitively, they know the person or persons who are able to be with them at that moment, and those who can't handle it.

Statistically, most deaths occur in the middle of the night. I see this as yet another example of how the dying protect those closest to them. Operating from some depth of internal wisdom, they manage this final gift of love: to spare you the pain of the moment of the final separation.

I ask people at my workshops, "As you look back, since time has passed, do you think you could have coped with being there at that moment?" I've taught hundreds of workshops on both sides of the Atlantic, and the answer is the same: "I wanted to be there; I really did. But in all honesty, I'm not sure I could have stayed until he died."

You see, the dying are very wise. They are acutely aware that there is something very powerful in the moment of death, and they "send us out for coffee." There are several reasons the dying choose when and around whom they make their final passage. It may simply be that they are selecting those who need to be spared the physical or emotional pain of witnessing the actual moment. But the dying also recognize when we're not able to let them go, so they depart when we're not there to hold onto them. Oftentimes, they wisely choose someone else to take our place, someone not as personally attached to them.

In this way, they spare us not only the pain of bearing witness but also the burden of wondering whether they felt we had abandoned them at the end. This explains the expressions of relief that

I've heard so many times—remarks like, "Even though I wasn't there, I'm so glad he didn't die alone," or "I'm so happy his favorite nurse was holding his hand at the end."

The dying's choice of the moment of death can be as varied and as unique as their lives have been. Yet the manner in which they have treated others or the roles they have played in life often are borne out in both their timing and choice of companion at the very last moment. Frequently, for example, if a person has been the "protector" in life, then he waits for the arrival of another protector—someone he knows and trusts—to be there for his loved ones at the moment of his death and to be there to comfort them afterwards.

I have seen dying people hold out against all odds, choosing to wait for their favorite nurse, home-health aide, or chaplain, to be with them at the moment of their death. In this instance, their wisdom is twofold: first because the dying person had a special relationship with them, and second because this person would be there to help their families deal with their death. I have seen countless examples of parents waiting for the oldest or the most responsible child to arrive, to support their spouse before they die. Armed with an uncanny wisdom, many stay alive until the strongest person arrives before letting go.

They choose not to die on Thanksgiving, Christmas, or anyone's birthday. They hang on by a thread until the day after a special event. I have heard the bereaved say things like, "My dad chose my birthday to die because I was special and he knew I would never forget him." "I'm so glad he didn't die on our anniversary." "He didn't want to ruin my wedding, so he hung on until I was on my honeymoon."

The dying wait, far beyond medical expectations—"We don't know what is keeping her alive; she should have been dead by now." They wait for that special child, for the birth of a first grandchild, for people to return from the armed services, or traveling from far away. They hold on for a child to ask for forgiveness, to reconcile themselves with others or with God, or simply to say that special "Goodbye," or "I love you," whatever will bring peace to their survivors or to themselves. These examples show just how inextricably linked the last two stages of hope are.

The hope for prolongation of life will last as long as it takes for the dying and their loved ones both to achieve the peace they each desire. When this happens, it makes the grieving process of their survivors far easier, because they and the dying have both completed their final business.

The dying may also be waiting for their families to give them permission to leave. Therefore, it is most important that they hear loved ones say:

"I'll be all right; you don't have to worry about me."

"It's okay for you to go. I'll miss you but I know we'll meet again."

"I don't want to let you go but I know it's your time to leave me."

"I'm okay, I can balance the checkbook now!"

Sometimes, the silence of a coma speaks for the dying, as we discussed in the previous chapter. We learned how the dying who are in coma seem to know exactly how much time is needed for their loved ones to be able to release them. The coma has passively, yet powerfully, prepared them, and peaceful death comes at last. I have seen this frequently and dramatically with our hospice families. The patient awakens from a semicoma or coma, sends the spouse on an errand, for a meal or coffee or to bed, saying he is comfortable. As soon as the loved one has bustled away in relief—sometimes within minutes—the patient dies.

As a witness to events that cannot be medically explained, at the time of thousands of deaths, I've recognized that children are the clearest teachers of this innate knowledge. They are not as cluttered as adults, and the messages come right through them. I have seen children awaken from a semicomatose or comatose state, ask for their favorite food (usually ice cream), then signal their families to return home. Mission accomplished, they fall back asleep and into death in a very short time, sometimes as soon as the parent or family member is walking out the hospital door.

Often, as in the story that follows, the dying separate from those closest to them, in order to spare them the actual moment of their death. My working definition of "closest" is the presence of a bond based on love and need. Called the "love-need bond," it characterizes a relationship in which your need for the other person is equal to your love for them. The bond is very intense in the mother-child and the sibling relationships, as I'll explore in greater detail in the following chapter on the hope system of the family. But for now, I'd like to tell you about a tiny and very special teacher of mine named Danny.

Danny

Danny was only three years old and he had a fibrosarcoma of the lung that had spread to his brain. As this was an unusual cancer in one so young, Danny had undergone numerous treatments at the world-renowned Memorial-Sloan Kettering Cancer Center in New York City, even though his family lived two hours away on Long Island. I had two roles with this family: I was the night nurse, and I was also a counselor to help them face the crisis of terminal illness in one so young.

When I met Danny he had already endured surgery, radiation, and chemotherapy. Our meeting took place when he came home after his fifth admission to the hospital. Due to the progression of the disease into his brain, Danny was now blind and deaf; thus our major form of communication with him was by touch.

Touch and body language, as we learned in Chapter 4, often become the primary language of the dying as the unrelenting progression of the disease cuts off various avenues of the senses and other normal ways of expression. Therefore, we used many finger foods that the child could pick up and feed to himself. Although many years have passed, I think of Danny every time I see Cheerios—how much he enjoyed eating that cereal! In the midst of the overwhelming devastation of his illness, we all felt such joy to see him behave as a typical toddler, covered with Cheerios from head to toe.

Another lasting impression, again tactile in nature, is the image of Danny holding onto his "corner," the smooth satin corner of a blanket that his mother had lovingly replaced over and over again in his brief life. The way he reached out for his blanket—and clung to the corner with his little hand, or rubbed his cheek with it—expressed to us in nonverbal language that he had pain and how severe it was. It signaled to us as caregivers that, in addition to medication, he needed to be rocked for comfort or walked in his stroller, as this motion soothed him.

Upon his return from the hospital after each of his prior admissions, there had always been a very special and joyful homecoming welcome and celebration between Danny and Amanda, his sister, who was six years older. However, when he came home this time, he pushed Amanda away. Needless to say this was very hard for her and she required a great deal of time and help in understanding that he was not rejecting her and her love. Rather, he was pushing her away from his illness and back into life.

In my dual role as night nurse and counselor with this family, I was constantly with them. Thus, I began to notice the pattern and its deeper meaning emerge. Normally, we see children turn away when you go to wipe their mouth or kiss them when they don't want you to. But now Danny was pushing us away, not just with one hand, but with both his hands, every time. He was not just being fussy and he was not just being a toddler; it was clearly a dismissal. I recognized this subtle shift in his actions as a symbolic separation behavior, and I sensed it was time to help prepare his mother for his death.

One morning at the end of my shift, when I was bringing Danny's laundry down to be washed, an opportunity presented itself. In the most sensitive and gentle way that I could, I suggested that Danny might be trying to prepare Amanda, and the rest of us, in the only way he knew how. I remember the sparks that flew from her eyes and the anger in her voice, directing her words, like daggers, right at me: "Prepare Amanda, prepare us for what?" she shouted, and stormed off. Softly, I retreated into the laundry room. But the seed had been planted.

It was crucial that Danny's message be delivered, so that his mother would be able to let him go. However, because she was the one closest to him, this reality would be most difficult for her to hear and accept. As the life-bearer, she had brought him into this world and was his primary caretaker now. Parents must always protect the child, and when death prevents them from accomplishing this task, they feel that they are not being true to their primary role and responsibility. Thus, they frequently respond with anger toward the messenger as well as toward the bad tidings. Therefore, because the message is so important and the dying need message-takers, it is essential that caregivers not take this anger personally (For more on this, see Chapter 8).

More poignant lessons were to come from this tiniest of teachers. Shortly after pushing Amanda away, Danny pushed away his day nurse. Next, he pushed away his grandmother, then me, the night nurse and counselor. Slowly, over a three-week period, he became progressively weaker and increasingly ill. He then had a seizure and would have to return to the hospital. I had worked in Danny's home the night before, and in the morning, after I had gotten him ready to leave, his mom came in and took my hand. Looking deeply into my eyes, she said, "I am beginning to understand what you meant that day about Danny's preparing us." The daggers were gone, and I felt the sadness and sorrow in her words and in her heart.

Accompanied by his faithful three—grandfather, mother, and father—the child was again admitted to Sloan Kettering. Once stabilized in the hospital, Danny took up where he left off, in using the separation/preparation behaviors, by physically pushing his grandfather away, which signaled his final good-bye to his "Pop-Pop." Later on, his grandfather shared his interpretation of this behavior with me: "For the first time ever, when I went to kiss him he wouldn't take my hand. He pushed it away, in a gesture that said I'm finished with you, then opened his hand and waved me away from him. I knew in my heart it was his final good-bye to me."

After sending his Pop-Pop away, Danny had been going in and out of consciousness when suddenly he awakened, drank some water for his mother, then very powerfully and clearly pushed her away. His mother decided at that moment to go and get a cup of coffee. No sooner had she left than Danny turned to his father. Grasping his blanket's corner close to his face, he reached out for his father's hand. Danny held it tightly for a long moment, then released his grip and gently pushed it away, and slipped peacefully into his death.

His mother returned and became very upset that she had not spent her child's last moments with him. Her normal feelings of sorrow and grief were intensified because, as his mother, she had been so intimately involved with his first moments. She felt that she had somehow failed him by not being with him as he breathed his last.

This moving story graphically illustrates the reality and the depth of the innate wisdom of the dying, and how they choose the moment of their death. How else could such a young child know to push away those closest to him and be able to understand their ability to cope with his death?

There is no possible way that a three-year-old could have *learned* to do this. Since such a small child exhibits such knowledge, we can confidently propose that the same profound interior wisdom operates in adults as well, when they are face-to-face with death.

Danny knew that the only person strong enough to be there for him, and yet be able to let him go, was his father. His choice of the moment of his death was to be with the person who had always been there for him with quiet strength from the moment he came into life. As he most clearly pushed his mother away, he simultaneously accomplished two important tasks that helped him die a peaceful death. First, he was doing all he could to ensure that the person holding fastest to him would be out of the room at the moment of his release. Second, because of his closeness to and love for his mother, he chose— as a final gift of love to her—to spare her the final moment, which he *knew* would be too painful for her to experience.

Studies show that the death of a child is the most difficult loss of all to cope with. It seems against nature for a child to precede the parent into death. I saw Danny's mom for bereavement counseling after her son died, and as is so often the case, the passage of time made a crucial difference. The actual moment of death can be uplifting and profound, but it is also frightening and final. Eventually, loved ones can admit, as she did, that although they wanted to be on hand at that moment, it would have been overwhelming for them. Freed by this admission, they usually realize the depth of the dying person's intuition and love for them. At last they understand what the dying so clearly know, that the anguish of parting may be more difficult for us to endure than for them.

And our anguish can make it more difficult for them. Physician and author Bernie Siegel, M.D., theorizes that most people die in the middle of the night because that's when the caregivers have left and they can die without guilt. There is no question that the dying process requires a lot of energy, and when we don't accept their hope for a peaceful death, we deny them that energy.

We may rail against the dying in the night, as we need to, after the death. And, day-by-day, there is no need to hide our grief as they slip away. Their acceptance of death may outpace ours, but we do our loved ones and ourselves a lot of good when we honor and respect their acceptance, regardless of how we feel. People don't change each other. We can only change ourselves. And in the end, just like in the beginning of this process of life and death, what makes life worthwhile is exactly this, the ability to make our own choices until the last breath.

A Conscious Choice?

Many have asked whether the choice of the moment is made consciously or unconsciously. Science is actively working on this question, but as yet we do not have a definitive answer. So far, all we can point to are the well-documented separation behaviors described in Chapter 4 which, in The Hope System, signal the transition from hope for prolongation of life to hope for a peaceful death. The primary internal force that initiates this chain of events in the patient is the cluster of physiological changes that the person is experiencing. The dying seem to register an inner knowing that their life is coming to an end. And, at some point, this inner knowledge prompts them to say "Good-bye," instead of, "So long, see you later." The precise nature of this inner knowing is still a mystery. But we see clues to how it functions within ourselves and in how the dying speak to us with their actions and behaviors, when we learn how to listen and really hear.

The dying themselves are our greatest teachers. They alone experience this unique process, and only they can impart this special knowledge. I have *been there* with literally thousands of people at the special time of their passing into death. I know on a deep level that the knowledge that the dying have so generously shared with me has been given to me for a specific reason: so I can help other professional caregivers and families recognize the deeper meaning in the choice of the moment of death as the person's final gift of love.

As I have shared this understanding in my workshops and with thousands of dying patients and families over the years, it has become clear to me that when we understand the wisdom of the dying and the choice of the moment of death, we are relieved of the burdens of guilt and the if-only syndrome. This understanding helps immensely in the grieving process.

While I don't presume to speak for them—the dying speak for themselves—in this instance, allow me to take this message to you on their behalf: As you read this, if it strikes a familiar chord and even brings forth tears, I entreat you to let go of any feelings you might have that you abandoned a loved one. We do not abandon the dying. The choice of the moment is not ours to make. It belongs to the dying.

And, to take the logic one step further, they do not abandon us, either. In their final act, by the choices they make, they do what they feel is best for us, whether that is to be with them at their side, or not. If they are allowed to, they choose the timing of their death as an affirmation of their life and their love for us.

And then it becomes our turn to release whatever *we* need to release. We can take that affirmation and run with it: As the living, we can choose to put regret and guilt aside and live with intensity until we die, just like the dying teach us to do. That is our decision to make, our own choice. The rest is out of our hands. So if your thoughts and feelings of guilt have weighed heavily upon you, release yourself from them as your loved one has released you—and released their life as well.

Our role as caregivers is to inform, affirm, and support the choices the dying make, and to recognize that these choices come from an inner wisdom. The exact thing they are hoping for changes, as they move through and around the four stages of hope. But hope itself—as the driving force of their inner reality—never changes. The act of hoping—looking forward, expecting the best—is synonymous with living and it continues until the moment of death. No matter how much courage seems to falter, hope prevails even over fear into our last moments.

In pushing you away, the dying are directing you back toward life, and away from death—because they know that is where you belong.

At the same time, the dying are also clearing a space for themselves to turn in their own direction, as they travel deeper on their inner journey. In fact, although they may seem absolutely passive, the dying are actually very busy. They are looking within and, perhaps, ahead. We commonly describe their condition as without hope, yet they are full of hope.

It is hope's role, and not ours, to conquer this fear of the unknown that may affect the dying, and hope intensifies accordingly at the end to help make this death a peaceful one. At the end, hope is all that the dying have left—but it is more than enough.

Chapter 7

The Hope System and Loved Ones

In the previous chapters, I described The Hope System as it applies to the patient in detail. Now I would like to turn my focus to The Hope System as it applies to the significant others who have a relationship with the dying person.

It is a crucial element in our discussion here that the dying and their family and loved ones be considered as a single unit, much as mother and child are often addressed as one. The significance of our viewing them in this integrated way has a direct relationship to their hope systems. They should be seen in this way because, in a unique and special way, they are all dying.

The expression that most aptly describes this special relationship is "closeness." As I mentioned in the previous chapter, my working definition of closeness is the presence of a love-need bond. We often hear family members and others closest to the dying express this bond: "Not only is she my mother, she is my best friend." We may hear a woman speak lovingly of her husband: "He is not only my husband, but my strength. He has always been my protector."

Often caregivers enter the patient's room and find the dying person sleeping soundly while the spouse of twenty, thirty, or even fifty years sits beside him or her in tears. In effect, the person who is dying with the greatest intensity at that moment is the spouse, not the patient who is sleeping peacefully.

It is important that we who are caregivers, either as part of our personal or professional role, understand this fact clearly if we are to be effective helpers. Understanding that, in a special way, each is dying enables us to shift our focus to all parties. Sometimes we have difficulty with this because we were taught that the dying patient is our primary focus and responsibility. While this is true, since all are dying, all need understanding, help, and support to deal with the dying process and its ultimate outcome.

Bearing this shared need for support in mind, also realize that family members tend to be somewhat more consistent with the first three hopes than the patient; that is, they maintain a more constant hope for cure, hope for treatment, and hope for prolongation of life. They do not seem to fluctuate as much as patients do. This is because they are not continually bombarded by doctors and other health professionals presenting new treatments, discussions, or other possibilities. Families seem to respond more to the bond of their relationship with the patient than to the process or changes in the treatment regimen.

At different ages and developmental periods in our lives, our love and need bonds change, as they do in times of stress and crisis. The crisis of impending death causes the intensity of these bonds to increase dramatically.

This significant love-need relationship responds to the special and unique sustenance needs of the patient throughout his illness. Hope is nourished by communion with others. Friends and family can spark hope that those who love and need him are waiting for him to return home.

On the other hand, the dying person's hopes for cure or treatment stokes his loved ones' desire to accompany him through the most rigorous of therapies even when they know he will not return to his previous physical level.

Hope for prolongation of life offers the possibility that they can have a new, enriched life together despite severe physical changes or disease progression.

It is definitely these hopes transmitted by the family, coupled with the person's own hope system, that enables the dying to undergo difficult and devastating treatments and live through them. People's ability to withstand so many debilitating surgeries and therapies demonstrate that hope and love do more than simply coexist.

Support for the Family

Since the loved one's role is so important to the life potential and development of the patient, support for the family members is essential and can take several forms. These include education, especially in the all-important interpreting and translation of a patient's hopes. Changes experienced by a dying patient cover the range of physical, emotional, psychological, and spiritual planes. At this time the patient is especially vulnerable and often deeply connected to the love-need bonds of those who are closest to him.

The always-necessary listening presence includes counseling the patient as needed, which has a direct and beneficial effect on him as well as those close to him. If the family feels informed and confident of outcomes—both negative and positive—these feelings are readily conveyed to the patient. They can sustain him throughout the death process, no matter how difficult it may be at each moment.

The caregiver's sharing of knowledge and observations with the family on a continual basis, which I call the "communication loop," teaches the family to tune in and hear the subtle nuances that indicate changes in the patient's hopes for himself *and* their hopes for him. They learn to be open to hear the movement from hope for cure or treatment, to hope for prolongation of life, and finally to hope for a peaceful death both within the patient and within themselves.

Protective Coping Denial

The closer and more bonded people are, the greater the difficulty everyone has in letting go. Intense love-need bonding makes the thought of separating all the more painful for both parties.

Those closest to the dying have the greatest difficulty in accepting or coming to terms with the death. They often experience intense denial while trying to accept the diagnosis, the dying process, and ultimately the death itself.

If we understand the love-need bond, then we can understand the need for and mechanism of the family's denial. It is just too painful for them to think or let into their consciousness that their loved one could possibly die and leave them. Those closest to the patient often maintain the initial shock, disbelief, and denial stage for a long time.

I have named this initial or lead-in denial *protective coping denial.* Denial—our universal coping mechanism—comes into play from the moment of diagnosis. While acknowledging the presence of a change in the body, such as the presence of lumps, abnormal discharge, bleeding, or other symptoms, both the patient and family are protected from the too-painful fact that this presence may signify or herald the reality of death. The closer the bonds, the more intense and prolonged the denial.

Usually, after a while, both the patient and those near and dear to him are able to let down the protective shields of their denial to allow treatment to begin. The initiation of active treatment and therapy becomes a beacon signaling that help and a possible cure are on the way.

I liken this fascinating defensive mechanism—protective coping denial—to the Lucite shield found in many of our modern banks that separates tellers from their customers. It is clear, yet quite strong, and it allows the tellers to see us as we see them. However, tellers are protected by the shield should there be any threat of danger, harm, or death. Protective coping denial acts in a similar manner, protecting patient and family from the threat of danger or death. It enables them to see the problem, seek help, and activate their own hopes for cure and treatment.

Protected by their denial, they begin to cope with the diagnosis and plunge with strength and commitment into therapeutic regimens, either as the participant or as the observer.

As time and treatments continue, the same denial reaction may become evident again as both patients and their loved ones move into what we often call the "conspiracy of silence." They move into different corrals when *he* knows and *she* knows but they don't talk about it. This behavior is seen by each as a type of protection of the other and once again stems from the love-need bond: "Because I love you, I must and will protect you from this horrible truth, this death over which I have no control."

Denial is one of the most powerful coping and protective mechanisms and we have it because we need it. Because it is so vital to our survival, it must be recognized and treated with respect. It must *never* be attacked, negated, or taken away. Removal of this important protection leaves the patient and families open and vulnerable.

Balancing Denial with Reality

On the other hand, we know how important it is for the dying and their loved ones to finish their business and say their good-byes prior to death. This communication frees the patient to die peacefully and helps the family live on more peacefully after the death has occurred. So, how can we help them to get together in one corral before it's too late?

Come with me now as Jenny and her husband, Chris, show us how they were able to accomplish this crucial task—just in time.

Jenny and Chris

Jenny was my patient for several years and was in the latter stages of rapidly advancing melanoma. She had survived many disfiguring surgeries and treatments all over the United States and Europe, empowered by her intense hope for cure and hope for treatment and supported in these hopes by her husband and their three loving children.

But the disease was taking a heavy toll on Jenny. She an her husband, Chris, both knew it, but they were protected by their denial.

I went to see Jenny and found Chris crying in the hallway. "She's not good today," he said. "I think she's losing the battle. I don't know what to do to keep her spirits up." I asked him the question he had heard many times as we shared Jenny's journey, "What are your hopes for Jenny, now?" He answered, "I hope she doesn't suffer at the end. I know I have to say good-bye to her soon."

This told me that Chris had shifted from hope for prolongation of life to hope for peaceful death for Jenny. Now I had to hear where Jenny was. Later that day she answered my query with, "I hope it's peaceful." Then, tearfully, "It's so hard to say good-bye to Chris and the kids. I have so much I need to say to them."

All of us knew that time was running out. My role as mediator/messenger could not have been clearer. Their conspiracy of silence was no longer protecting them; it was now preventing them from saying what they needed to say so that a peaceful death was possible.

To help them accomplish this task, I enlisted an approach that I have used with many families to help them align their hopes into a unified hope for a peaceful death and communicate openly.

I sought Chris out and said to him, "Chris, it's clear to me how much you love Jenny, how you have protected her and have been her cheerleader from the beginning. Things are changing and the way you are acting and speaking is making her feel left out."

There is something powerful in the expression of this thought that immediately helps the patient and/or the family to see reality clearly because we *never* want our loved ones to feel left out and we will do anything, to get them back in sync with us. Also remember we are fulfilling the first basic need of dying. They need to know they will not be abandoned.

Chris realized right away, "Oh no. I thought I was helping her and protecting her. Cathy, help me say and do what is best for her to get us back together."

"Let's start by sharing with Jenny what you shared with me this morning. I spoke to her later and she's hoping for the same things you are; it's important for you to really talk to each other now."

Relief flooded Chris' face as he thanked me and ran off to Jenny's room. My understanding of The Hope System and how it applied at this step of Jenny's journey enabled me to be the swing person and to help them accomplish this important task.

With the denial removed, Chris, Jenny, and their children were able to use the precious time they still had to complete the important tasks that would free them to be with each other, say their good-byes, and to say, "I love you."

This enabled Chris to lovingly give Jenny permission to make her transition in peace. Inspired by the openness and the example of their parents, the kids, in their own teenage ways, expressed what they needed and wanted to tell their mom. As they shared in her death, they were also helped to share feelings and support each other through their bereavement process. This was made easier because there were few, if any, regrets: "We said what we needed to and she knew we loved her to the very end."

I hope I have helped you see that the best way to deal with denial is not with a sledgehammer, but gently, using love and need, helping the patient and family to hear how their hopes have changed so that they can be there for each other and to respectively die in peace and to live on in peace.

Double-Bondedness

An intense love-need bond may be a contributing factor in the sometimes almost immediate death, for no apparent reason, of a surviving spouse after the death of his or her mate. You may have heard this situation described as someone having died from a broken heart, but it might be more accurately defined as the severing of the sustenance of the love-need bond. This double-bondedness is seen most dramatically and powerfully in the parent-child relationship, and of course, goes back to the concept of the patient and loved one both dying.

Hazel and Bobby

Perhaps the story of Hazel and Bobby will demonstrate the potential intensity of both the love-need bond and concurrent denial.

I had worked with Hazel, a young mother whose son, Bobby, was dying of leukemia, from the day of diagnosis through aggressive therapies and I was with her at the end.

Bobby did not die easily, and at the point our story begins, he had pain in his joints and throughout his body and was bleeding through several openings. The mother's loving and tender care was beautiful to behold, and as I sat with her, it was becoming clearer and clearer to me that the child was ready, and in fact, wanted to die.

I had been trying to share and interpret his nonverbal language, wishing to indicate this to her in a very gentle way. As we sat together, I used an analogy that has helped me describe denial with many patients and their loved ones.

We talked about death being like the sun, and that sometimes, in order to look at it, we have to put on sunglasses. At other times, when it appears nearer and brighter, we go indoors to escape it. At other times, when it becomes especially bright, we might not only go inside, but also pull down the shades to protect ourselves from its blinding rays. If it were then to find a way inside, we might jump into bed and pull the covers over our heads for more protection.

At that moment, tears welled up in her eyes. Slowly she picked up Bobby and cradled him in her arms saying, "All during the treatments I even threw the sunglasses away. For a while, I was all right in the shade of the treatments and the partial remission. Later the house provided enough safety until I had to pull down the shades after the bone marrow transplant failed and the leukemia was out of control.

"Eventually I thought that if I stayed inside under the covers, I could protect him forever. Even though he's bleeding and he has pain, I thought, I still have him and I can still hold him, and I will take care of him forever."

Thus we sat together, she rocking him in her arms, and I sitting next to them with one hand on her shoulder for strength and the other gently touching his head, the blonde fuzz growing back in after the chemotherapy and radiation treatments. Slowly his breathing changed as she sang to him. She called upon his guardian angel to help him on his journey and to enable her to let him go. After his breathing ceased and he gently drifted away, she kissed him and placed him on the bed. With loving hands, she covered him with a light blanket, turned to the windows and opened the blinds to let in the sun. The tears were our means of communication until she broke the silence and said, "Who will take care of him now? Am I still his mother?"

In that instant, I understood in a most powerful way the complexity of the feelings of the person closest to the dying and their need for protective coping denial throughout the dying process up to and including the very moment of death. I think that I also appreciated in a very deep way that much help is needed by the family to be able to let them go on in peace.

Feelings of Guilt

Sometimes a person's hope for a peaceful death for another is equated with wishing that this person die. One thing we as helpers must not allow is for people to think that, in the act of letting go, they have *wished* their loved one dead. How the survivors think of this time and the death itself has a direct bearing on their bereavement process and healing. If they think they wished their loved one dead, they may have the added burden of guilt, which impedes their healing.

When Roles Vary

It is important to note that the individual closest to the dying person may or may not be in a normal socially designated role, such as parent or spouse. They may not even be in a socially accepted role. This person may be anyone from the oldest, youngest, or most needy child in a family to a dear friend, illicit lover, or surrogate parent.

It is necessary for those of us acting as helpers—whether we are professional caregivers, volunteers, or family members or loved ones—to be sensitive to the closeness of relationships and to be there with compassion for all involved— and always without judgment.

Chapter 8

Especially for the Professional

I would like to turn now to the role of the professional caregiver as educator, mediator, and translator. Health-care professionals need to let their patients know that they are respected and valued as unique persons, not just as patients. With this in mind, the goal of this chapter is to show health care workers why they should support a patient's hope system, and how they can do so without compromising their professionalism.

In order to accomplish this, the caregiver must be an empty slate, allowing the dying patient to write his own story. The caregiver, as an empty slate, possesses an attitude of openness, respect, and sensitivity to patient and family. This enables the caregiver to recognize and interpret the hope systems of his patients and their families, as well as recognize his own hopes for his patients.

Caregivers have the power to be inspiriting to their patients. Sidney Jourard, a leading force in humanistic psychology, and a pioneer in the fields of self-disclosure and body-awareness, describes *inspiriting* as delivering "an invitation to continue living, to develop each individual's exquisite potential." In the case of terminal illness, the attainment of this potential culminates in a peaceful death.

Professionals can clarify and support hope in various ways, but primarily they do so by helping the patients understand and draw on the resources found in their individual hope systems. The health-care provider must determine which phase of The Hope System—hope for cure, hope for treatment, hope for prolongation of life, or hope for a peaceful death—predominates for the patient at any given moment. Once this is ascertained, it is the responsibility of the caregiver and care team to provide the patient with the supportive care needed during that phase. For example: Encouragement, information—including an explanation of the diagnosis—and treatment are essential during hope for cure and hope for treatment, as opposed to the comfort, care, palliation, and presence needed during the hope for a peaceful death phase.

It must be clear to the caregiver that the patient's hope may not be the same hope that the caregiver has for him at that time. Support of the patient's hope system is always a priority. In the terminally ill, hope becomes the patient's real world, an inner reality that takes precedence over all other realities. Hearing others deny this reality, saying it is unrealistic or unimportant, doesn't change this; it simply sends the patient's thoughts and feelings underground and frustrates the satisfaction of two basic needs: the need to not feel abandoned and the need to express one's self.

In acknowledging the validity of the patient's inner reality of hope, caregivers go a long way in supporting this process and can better accompany the patient on the final leg of his journey to a peaceful death.

Working with the Family

The fostering of sustaining relationships is also a key responsibility of the caregiver. The patient's loved ones, not the caregiver, have the most powerful influence on sustaining the patient's hopes. The caregiver should work directly with those closest to the patient initially by explaining the concept of The Hope System to them and the interrelationship between their hopes and those of the patient.

It is essential that the health-care professional attain and maintain open communication with both the family and the patient—the group interaction that I call the "circle of care." From this focal position, the caregiver can assist loved ones and help other team members clarify their hope system for the patient, thus providing additional support.

The caregiver should guide the family in personalizing their understanding of the hope system by asking, "What are you hoping for your loved one at this time?" This important query helps them grasp the reality of The Hope System from the inside out, just as it does with their loved one. This knowledge demonstrates to them how powerful they are in nurturing the individual hope system of the patient.

Mutual Trust

It is also extremely important for the health-care professional to realize how crucial her interaction with the patient is. This is especially true in the area of trust. A special bond of nonjudgmental trust between the dying patient and caregiver facilitates the open communication of the deep and essential hopes from within the patient. Because of this mutual trust, the patient knows that whatever he shares is heard and not judged. The caregiver thus becomes the empty slate, helping the dying to write his own story, dot his own *i*'s, place his own commas, and finish his life with a period, an exclamation point, or a question mark.

Watching for the Changes in Hope

Being able to perceive when the patient's hopes change is primarily the responsibility of the caregiver who can be more objective than family members since he is not as affected by love-need bonds as is the family. He takes on the roles of educator, mediator, translator, and supporter, helping both the patient and family read and understand the words written on the empty slate.

These multiple roles are essential so that the dying person's hopes for himself, as well as those of his loved ones, can each be realized. Assisting the dying person to unearth his own hope system is crucial and begins early on by explaining that both the presence and the power of hope is always active within him and that hope has been and is now making an impact on every facet of his life. His grasp of the power of hope deepens each time he is asked, "What are you hoping for?" By answering this question time after time, his awareness of the reality and power of hope within him emerges more clearly.

Doing this enables the professional caregiver to help the patient live his hope each day of his life and to bring about his final hope for a death that is peaceful on his own terms.

Being to Becoming

Hope is the activator for an individual's process of becoming, and it allows the movement from *being* to *becoming*, which is possible at every moment of human existence. Hope is like an entrance door through which we gain access to the reservoir of both our own and our patient's hope systems.

Hope not only helps to maintain our existence, but encourages us to develop our deepest potential throughout all our lives. Hope becomes stronger and all-pervasive as we proceed on our path toward death.

91

Thus, death is seen as the final "becoming" and the last stage of human growth.

Synchrony

The professional caregiver who is in synch with the dying person and his family creates a climate in which all hopes can be realized. This is a climate that is imbued with hope and helps the caregiver to clarify his own as well as the patient's and the family's hope systems. As we have discussed, the family is a patient's main source of sustenance throughout the dying process.

Often with just a word or suggestion, the professional can help ease the dying process profoundly. For example, as I mentioned in Chapter 3, my response to Frank's final question to me—"Yes, Frank, the medication will keep you comfortable until..."—reassured him that the peaceful death he envisioned would come to pass.

Diane, a single mom who was concerned about her teenage daughter, was greatly relieved when I told her we had a social worker who has a gift with teenagers. "I'll ask her to come to see you. I know she can help you with your daughter."

Tim was a fighter all the way and I was happy to help honor his final request: "Cathy, I don't want to be snowed with medication at the end." I told him, "Tim, we have a pharmacist who will work with you and your physician to enable you to die pain-free and alert."

When we realize hope is a dynamic process among patient, family, and caregiver, we begin to understand the necessity of the caregiver to be in synchrony with each person.

The professional is in a good position to serve as an interpreter of behavior that signals a shift in the patient's hope system, a change that the family often doesn't clue into right away. The professional can be especially important in helping the family understand the movement of hope for a peaceful death into the foreground for the patient. As we've seen, enabling patient and loved ones to communicate prior to death facilitates the grief process and healing after death.

The sensitivity to and understanding of the subtle and the more overt changes in both the patient's and the loved ones' hope systems enables the professional to resonate with each in a different and unique manner. This special resonance is called the *trust relationship*, wherein both patient and family are freed to share their personal hopes aloud to the caregiver and to each other without being judged.

This is a real-life application of the caregiver's role of messenger and translator: helping each party to hear and understand the hopes of the other. Frequently, both the patient and the loved ones find it easier to share their personal hopes with an open and unbiased caregiver. Then after listening and hearing the hopes of both, and with their permission to share them, she takes the message from one to the other or brings them together to hear each other's hopes, whichever is the most helpful to each situation. This helps them hear how their hopes may differ or agree and how they may be brought into alignment with one another. This often happens with the insight and support of the caregiver guiding them.

Try as we may, some patients and families are not able to come together in mutual hope for a peaceful death for a variety of reasons. It is important to remember that people choose the way they die and the way they live, and they will have different requirements both during the dying process and after. However, if a trust relationship can be established, all are assured they will be accepted as they are regardless of the outcome.

Through all this, we need to remember that, although we create the climate by being the best nurse, social worker, doctor, home-health aide, chaplain, or volunteer we can be, it is always the patient who chooses the person or persons they trust to be there as his path twists and turns till journey's end.

Caregiver as an Authority Figure

Because of his uniform and medical expertise, the professional appears as an authority figure. What he says carries great impact. He needs to tell the truth in the form of pertinent information, of course, but he does best when he bears in mind that medical prognoses are largely based upon statistical likelihoods and that there is a deeper truth within each individual, a truth called hope.

The Hope System is an extremely dynamic process. As we've discussed, the caregiver's hope system for a patient will change as he perceives changes in the patient's clinical, psychological, and emotional state. Yet, the caregiver must simply be there for the dying. He should not tell his patient what to do or how to act or how to be. And the caregiver should never impose his own hopes on the patient just to make it easier on himself.

What Are You Hoping for?

From the moment of the diagnosis, people are asking the patient important questions:

"How are you feeling today?"

"Did you sleep last night?"

"Do you have pain?"

"How is your appetite?"

And, of course, the ever popular, "Did you have a bowel movement today?"

The answers to these questions indicate where the patient is regarding his physical condition and how his disease is progressing. And although important, they do not touch on his interior world where he lives to a greater and greater degree as his physical world deteriorates.

It is the role of the caregiver to ask, "What are you hoping for?" When we ask what the person is hoping for today, what he or she is hoping for from one treatment or another, or another similar question about his or her hopes, we cut through the person-as-patient role and connect with the deeper part of the person who is experiencing this process. Then, and equally important, when we ask the family members this same crucial question, we can learn the hopes of the loved ones supporting him.

It is important to respectfully acknowledge the patient's and their loved ones' hopes as they are expressed. When we do this, we are maintaining both the circle of care and the primary communication loop between patient, family, and caregiver.

The simple fact that both the patient and loved ones are being asked what it is they are hoping for imparts to each four important points.

- First, that the caregiver sees each individual as a unique person.
- Second, that the caregiver acknowledges and affirms that he knows this person has hope.

- Third, that the caregiver is willing and anxious to listen to each person's hopes.
- Fourth, that the caregiver accepts the patient as he is and accepts where he is at in this moment of time.

This approach frees the patient from responding in the traditional compliant-patient role and establishes a more human interaction—the trust relationship mentioned earlier—where hope can be easily shared and articulated. The usual response of the patient to this approach is to experience a sense of relief. Often it seems he has been waiting for someone to relate to him in this way: "At last someone is trying to understand me and what is important to me."

The empty slate and the trust relationship are two very effective approaches for accompanying the dying on his own path toward death in a way that frees both patient and caregiver to be true to themselves.

Ed and Tina

I was working in the radiation therapy department of a local hospital when I met Ed and Tina. It was immediately apparent how close they were. Ed was being prepped for radiation therapy to shrink a lung tumor that was pressing on his trachea, causing him pain and making it difficult to breathe. Following radiation, he would have surgery, then chemotherapy, and all would be well again. At least this is what they had "heard" their oncologist say to them.

As I sat with them, I listened to their hopes for cure and treatment. Ed said, "My brother had radiation too and he's okay. I know I'm gonna' beat this thing, just like him." Tina spoke to me while he was being tattooed so the radiation would be directed only where his tumor was and spare the surrounding tissue. "I know he'll be okay; he's such a fighter."

Unfortunately, Ed had a rough time with the radiation. His skin was sensitive so we had to interrupt his treatments to allow him time to heal. Ed said, "I'm not happy about the setback, but I know the radiation will do the trick." Tina encouraged him by saying, "I know you'll be okay Ed; you're a fighter."

Even though we had blocked his organs, Ed developed a severe tracheitis with continuous coughing. Eventually, we stopped his radiation altogether.

His response to my question, "What are you hoping for now?" was, "I'm sure the radiation worked well enough for them to do surgery." Tina's response to the same question was, "I know he'll get through this; he's a fighter."

Surgery was successfully performed and Ed started chemotherapy. Ed, at the hope for treatment stage, said "I've made it this far; I'm gonna' beat this thing." Tina supported this hope, "See, you're a fighter Ed; you'll get through this, too."

Halfway through his chemotherapy protocol, Ed came in to visit me. He was limping; his routine bone scan showed metastasis to the thoracic and lumbar areas of his spine. His response to the hope question was, "I hope the radiation can do its magic again; our daughter is getting married in June." Tina's response was, "I want him to be well enough to walk Susan down the aisle."

For this couple, hope for prolongation of life had entered the spotlight. As his disease progressed, radiation therapy offered temporary relief, and, when questioned, Ed answered, "I only hope the pain medication keeps working." Tina added, "I hope they can keep him comfortable. June is just around the corner."

Empowered by his own and Tina's constant hope for life, and with the help of more radiation and stronger medication, Ed did walk his daughter down the aisle to the joy of all concerned.

After this momentous event, Ed began a slow but steady decline. Eventually he was hospitalized for a morphine drip. At this point, hope for a peaceful death was expressed by both husband and wife. From Ed: "I hope it's over soon. I'm so tired." And from Tina: "I hope, for his sake this is all over soon. He fought the good fight."

Asking "What are you hoping for?" helped me stay connected with Ed and Tina from diagnosis until death.

Swing Person

A key attribute of a caregiver is the ability to listen and to be present to both family and patient. By identifying his own personal hope system and using it as a point of internal reference, the professional caregiver can clearly understand what he is hoping for at each interaction. This knowledge has the power to stabilize and ground him. He knows what he is feeling in relation to the patient and the patient's family, and what he is hoping for the patient at any particular time. This awareness helps to enable him to let go of his own hope system stages and thus be available to respond to the changing hopes of others as needed. He becomes the *swing person*.

It is crucial that the swing person has the ability to emotionally travel with the patient and family as hopes shift and to give the support necessary as each stage of The Hope System appears. From the secure position as the professional helper, the caregiver is able to hear beneath words and behaviors to the deeper, more consistent themes and hopes. As these messages emerge from the patient's private interior world into the light, the caregiver is able to interpret them for the dying, those closest to him, and members of the care team, as needed. This strengthens the trust relationship, allowing for increased understanding, energy exchange, and support throughout the entire process.

How May I Help You?

This approach of open inquiry has assisted me to ask another very important question, one that has helped me to enter the world of the dying person. It is simply, "How may I help you?"

This question is essential for deeper communication because, in fact, we don't truly know what individuals in our care are experiencing in their personal journeys from life into death. Asking this question, listening to the answer, not assuming or imposing, and utilizing The Hope System, has helped me work in a different, more real way with the dying. This is demonstrated in the story of young Krystal below.

We Aren't All Knowing

Being present for the dying does not mean that we know or indeed should know all the answers to the mysteries of dying and death.

My life as a helper to the dying changed dramatically when I was able to let go of the burden of the erroneous belief that I should know all of the answers, after all, "I am the professional."

What the dying *do* need, is for us to listen, hear, and respond to their pain and concerns, to really *hear* their story and, on occasion, to act as messengers, communicating their wishes and hopes to their loved ones.

Other Helpmates

There may be others, ones much more effective than you and I, in easing the profound passage from what we know as life into what we don't know. As death comes closer, the dying—whose focus now moves within—turn away from us, perhaps to another listening presence that they have recently become aware of. As this happens, they appear to be more "there" than "here with us."

Krystal

By telling the story of this young girl, I want to show one way a child reported the presence of such helpmates. Real or imagined, these hopeful visions comfort the dying through the transitional moment. The story that follows also illustrates how caregivers and loved ones can avoid becoming a distraction and can respond to this phenomenon in a way that maximizes the inner power of the dying person's hope.

Krystal was a beautiful, blue-eyed, blond-haired girl of three when I first met her in the pediatric unit of Long Island Jewish Medical Center. I remember thinking she looked like a porcelain doll because her features were so perfect. When she smiled, she lit up the room.

In my role as clinical nurse specialist in oncology and thanatology, I spent a great deal of time working with the staff of "Four South" and their little ones who were caught at a very tenuous juncture between a young life and young death.

Since caregivers should never separate the parent from the child, I became involved with the parents and other loved ones of these special patients in strollers and tiny wheel chairs. Over time, the staff and I formed a special circle of care embracing each of these tiny tots.

Such was the case with Krystal, whose blue-white sparkle was dulled by the unremitting progression of the cancer that was slowly and surely draining her life away. I had been working with mother and child for almost a year. Krystal had been in a special chemotherapy protocol for her type of leukemia. The protocol was not working and little Krystal was becoming paler and paler with each passing day.

One day, I received a call from the unit saying Krystal's mother needed me. The unspoken plea that I heard beneath the staff member's words was, "We need you, too, Cathy. We don't know what to do." At my arrival on the fourth floor, I was greeted by a staff with anguished faces and beseeching eyes. They quickly told me that Krystal had just told her mother that she had to leave soon and that her mom had to go with her.

Both Krystal's comment and her request were not only understandable, but developmentally correct for her age and her needs. For the young child, separation is viewed as death. Thus, it was perfectly natural and normal for Krystal to want and need her mom to go with her. Of course, in the magical thinking of the child, Krystal had assumed that her mother could leave with her on her final journey. Since her mother had been the most consistent parent figure for her, the two, in effect, had never been separated during Krystal's short life.

Nevertheless, the staff, her mother, and I didn't know what to say to Krystal in response to her request. I knew there was nothing else I could do but be a listening presence. With the help of the wonderful question that had taken me many miles on my walks with the dying and those close to them, I queried both mother and daughter, "How may I help you?" The response was instantaneous. "Just walk with us, Cathy."

What a relief for me, as I didn't know what to do or say. As we walked along, I placed one hand over the hand Krystal's mother was using to push the high stroller and the other lightly on Krystal's shoulder.

The pediatric unit was shaped in a large oval with a core area in the center. The children's rooms formed a ring around the core. At one point, I spoke to Krystal and said that I knew she had to leave, but I wondered where she was going. This family did not have a tradition that included a sense of God, Heaven or the Hereafter.

Little Krystal answered that she was going far away and that it was dark there, but she quickly added, "Mommy has to go with me." After this exchange, her mother and I just held tightly to each other's hand and occasionally traded glances as we continued along, pushing Krystal and her ever-present IV pole around the circle.

Suddenly Krystal turned to us with an animated smile on her face and a sparkle in her eyes. She said, "It's all right, Mommy. You don't have to go with me." Both her mother and I were dumbfounded, relieved, and in shock—all at the same moment.

"Mommy doesn't have to go with you, Krystal?" I finally was able to say. "No, Cathy, Mommy doesn't have to go with me because where I'm going I'll be with Jimmy and Todd and Jennifer and Melissa," Krystal told us, while pointing to rooms as we circled the unit.

Krystal was naming children she knew who had been patients in the rooms we had passed. It was as if she were reading the small nameplates that were on the doors of the rooms these children had been in when they died. What was even more uncanny was that each child she named as she pointed to the rooms had in fact died of her type of leukemia. If only in her mind, these children had returned as Krystal's helpmates.

Lessons Reinforced

During this tiny patient's pain, confusion, and searching as her life came to an end, Krystal and her mother reinforced for me the importance of being a listening presence, mediator, translator, and educator. As you can imagine, I had traversed the ever-fluctuating hope system of both parent and child over the time they were in my care. I had accompanied them from intense hope for cure and hope for treatment, both supported through the rigors of experimental protocols, continuous tests, and a bone marrow transplant, to hope for prolongation of life, hoping for long-term remission until a cure for her type of leukemia was developed.

Because I was so clear on Krystal's hope system and my own for her, I was armed with clarity and strength. This enabled me to be present with her mother's pain, confusion, and feelings of utter helplessness—feelings which we both shared on each admission—to a degree that I had never before experienced in my work with the dying and their families. Thus, I was able to walk with them and hear Krystal say, "Mommy, you don't have to go with me."

My involvement in their hope journey continued with my helping Krystal prepare her mother by interpreting significant verbal, nonverbal, and behavioral changes. The interpretation of the verbal and nonverbal language of the dying is an important role for the professional caregiver when working with the dying, but is enhanced with dying children and their parents. It is only from the children themselves that the parent can hear and begin to accept that their child is really dying and leaving them.

Krystal's hope for a peaceful death was signaled very powerfully for me when I was dismissed by the dying child, who said, "That little girl over there who's crying needs you now, Cathy." In addition, Krystal had maturely told her elder sister that she was to "take care of Teddy [Krystal's stuffed animal] now and tuck him in at night. Don't let him get lonesome." In both of these powerful symbolic messages, Krystal clearly demonstrated her understanding and acceptance of her own hope for a peaceful death, indicating "I have to leave now."

The Take-Away for You

In this clinical example we see clearly demonstrated the trust relationship between Krystal, her family, and myself. I became the empty slate upon which Krystal wrote the final words of her life story in a way we were all able to understand and, thus, having understood, we were able to let her go.

Because I had taken the inward journey of my own personal hope system many times and was clear about what I hoped for Krystal at every step of her own process, I was able to be present to mother and child in the ways in which they needed me. I did not waver in my ability to be present because I was continually and consistently clear within myself. Consequently, I was free to be with them in their time of need.

For me and, I hope for you, this demonstrates very powerfully that we, as professional caregivers, do not have to have all the answers since the questions of life and death are often unanswerable. However, we must be willing to listen and to respond with the ever-changing hope systems of our patients and their loved ones so that we may walk with them as a true friend would, making contact eye to eye, then ear to ear, walking shoulder to shoulder with them, because it is not easy to let go and die, and finally connecting heart to heart, resonating with their hopes for life and death. By doing so, we will in fact be accompanying them on their final journey as they hope it will be.

****

What I have attempted to describe in this chapter is the evolution of hope within the patient, family, and professional caregiver, and the intricate ever-changing pattern and interaction that it creates. Hope is the dynamic life force that exists first within and then outside each person in relationship to self, environment, and their loved ones. Each of us possesses unique embodiments of hope, hope for ourselves, our families, our profession, and our world.

Acknowledging Your Own Hope System

Each of us as professionals has his or her own unique clinical knowledge, expertise, and competence. I invite you to take this uniqueness to a deeper level. Come to know and respect the individual resources of your own hope system. Take hold of this dynamic reality within you. Once it is yours, you will have the ability to respond and resonate with the needs and hopes of your patients and their families in a more real manner. This will enable you to establish and maintain therapeutic relationships at the highest level of your capabilities.

Take Care of Yourself

In order to take care of others we must take care of ourselves on all levels. To live a full and happy life when one deals daily with death and loss is truly a balancing act.

I have been able to work so long with the dying only because I work as hard at keeping my life in balance as I do on my work with the dying. I want to end this chapter by sharing with you some of the things which enable me to live a full and happy life:

- Sharing the burden—peer and staff support, process groups
- Meditation—quieting the mind
- Exercise—running, biking, walking, Tai Chi
- The beach or lake—healing water
- Retreats—silent, spiritual
- Dancing—freeing the spirit, fun
- Music—soothes the savage beast
- Nature—forest, mountains, hiking
- Being with children—playing
- Massage—manicure, body work

I hope that you find these suggestions helpful. The dying need energy and they will get it however they can. We need to remind ourselves everyday, "It is not my death. It is their death."

We each must die our own death. Yes, we are there to help them face their dying and death in a special and hopeful way. But we can't do it for them. What has enabled me to continue to be present for so many patients over the years is something I learned early on: I do my best, then, I let it go, for the outcome is not in my hands. Internalizing this phrase has helped me to be free to live my life fully.

Chapter 9

The Hand-Heart
Connection

Since the "letting go" of someone or the "giving permission" for that person to die is so difficult for loved ones to do, I would like to share with you something that I have learned which has helped both the dying and those near and dear to them.

Because the letting go and the subsequent separation appear to happen at the heart level, an approach I call "The Hand-Heart Connection" serves as a facilitator of the dying process, enabling both the dying and those close to them to "let go" in mutual release.

There is a direct relationship between the hand and the heart (in Eastern teachings, the heart is the fourth chakra or energy center). Thus, when we hold someone's hand, in a very special way, we are in fact holding his heart. In this we see an even deeper and more powerful reason and symbol for the commonly-seen practice of holding hands.

As the dying person comes nearer and nearer to death, we see the physical changes that indicate a marked decrease in his total life energy. These changes are manifested by increased weakness, lethargy, and even emaciation in some instances. He, in fact, seems to be fading away right in front of us. This—plus the other symbolic verbal and nonverbal behavior of the dying such as the cessation of speaking, eating, or even looking at those close to them—is very difficult for the family to endure, as fulfilling social and physical needs have been the family's primary ways of relating to and caring for this person.

What this often creates in those closest to the dying is an overwhelming feeling of helplessness, since they feel that they no longer have anything to offer the person, and they are losing contact with him even before his death occurs. This entire set of circumstances can bring on feelings of guilt, rejection, and abandonment before the person actually dies. These feelings are very powerful, and, on occasion, lead to behavior directly opposite to fulfilling the first basic need of the dying, which is that they will not be abandoned.

I have devised The Hand-Heart Connection to help families and other direct caregivers maintain necessary contact and to help decrease the feelings of helplessness and pain. This technique appears profoundly simple, but in reality it is simply profound. Just as touch was the primary mode of communication when we came into this world at birth, so too it remains the basic and most powerful medium of communication as we leave this world.

I will describe this approach in detail, as it has been one of the most effective and teachable tools to help those closest to the dying person to hold on, while they are in fact letting go, and to do this with less pain and more love. First, move to the left or heart side of the patient and place the patient's left hand gently in your own left hand, palm to palm. As the patient's hand sits in your upturned hand, begin to consciously think of and direct peace and love to the ill person, imaging tranquility and love filling and overflowing the dying person's heart.

Holding the hand is the connection and is all the contact that is necessary. Since this is an already-known and well-practiced action in many relationships, it is often something that anyone close to the dying feels comfortable doing. However, if you feel that you would like to increase this connection, here are some additional steps you may take.

After placing the person's left hand in your left hand (if it is inconvenient or awkward to hold his left hand, you may hold his right.), cover it with your right hand. This increases the sense of contact and security that the dying feels from you. I had a woman patient respond in a very special way to this touch. She awoke from an almost semicomatose state as I covered her hand with mine. Looking at me with bright eyes she said, "Oh, you're holding my heart!" and at that very moment, I had the sensation of a tiny heart beating in my hands as well.

If you are comfortable with it, gently move your right hand up the person's arm and place it on his left shoulder with your hand pointing to his heart. Again consciously send or direct peace and love to the heart of the dying person. The patient (who, we must remember, is not a passive participant in this interaction) may move your hand down nearer his heart, or perhaps place your hand in the center of his chest above the heart. I have seen many people do this as death comes closer and closer and they, although peaceful and accepting, become afraid of the unknown and of taking the final leap.

Fear Centers

This area in the center of the chest near the collarbone seems to be the place where fear lives in the dying. I compare it to the scared or panicky feeling we experience when we feel as though an elephant is sitting on our chest and we cannot breathe. Another area of fear or anxiety may be the area just below the stomach in the region of the solar plexus, which is often called the seat of emotion. It is in this area that we, throughout our lives, might have felt "butterflies" when confronted by a situation in which we felt afraid or experienced stress.

If either you or the patient are not comfortable with this hand placement, this can all be done from the back. Simply leave your hand on the left shoulder or place your hand in the center of the back at the chest and heart level and continue to send peace and love to him.

Breaking the Connection

When you feel that this connection is lessening, the loved one has loosened his grip on your hand, or you feel it's time to release the contact—perhaps the patient is sleeping soundly or you need to leave for awhile—it is important to remember that the disconnection is as important as the connection. If you have done the whole technique, simply retrace your steps, moving from the heart or chest area back to the left shoulder, and gently move your hand down his arm and place your right hand over his left hand, again cradling his hand (and heart) in your hands. Pause there and say or think your good-byes, tell him you love him, wish him peace, or say whatever comes to you. Then gently place the patient's hand back on the bed or on his lap.

As stated earlier, the simple act of holding the dying person's hand is sufficient to set this exquisite love connection into action. However, I have found it almost instinctual for the patient's loved ones to cover or cup their hands and gently touch or massage the upper back, neck, or shoulders as a way of maintaining contact or staying connected by touch with those whom they love.

This essential connection tends to decrease the tremendous feelings of helplessness felt by those closest to the dying.

Required Energy

An equally important reason for my devising this particular approach was to provide the dying person with the love and energy needed to complete this final life task. We utilize the heart in this approach for a very special reason, because it is here that separation and letting go must occur. The task of dying is separating from or letting go of all loved and known things and this, as we well know, is not an easy task, but one which requires energy. The dying person in fact loses life energy on all levels and therefore requires a tremendous influx of energy to complete the task of dying.

The Hand-Heart Connection helps provide the patient with the energy needed to release loved ones, especially those bonded by love and need. It can facilitate the saying of things previously left unsaid.

The Hand-Heart Connection also serves a very important third purpose. Because of the outgiving nature of the interaction, consciously directing peace to the dying, those staying behind are helped to let go via the flow of love and peace they are sending. This outflow of love energy helps them to loosen their grasp and relieves the feeling that they are abandoning the dying. They have, in fact, stayed in contact by maintaining a loving touch with them until the final separation we call death occurs.

The influx of love and life energy via The Hand-Heart Connection certainly can ease the dying process. It enables the dying to let go, while still having the feeling of being connected to and held onto by their loved ones. This connectedness insures the dying person that the basic need of not being abandoned is respected and honored until the end; it actually enables them to let go and die peacefully.

A Final Word

I believe that certain people come into our lives for a reason and that we are given opportunities through them to grow in ways that we would not have if their paths had not crossed ours. I have shared with you my own patients' voices and stories. Their wisdom was given to me and it has been my goal to pass it on to you. Please spread their wisdom to others who, at the difficult juncture when the Known meets the Unknown, may help make each dying person's transition more peaceful.

Resources

Resources for Family and Friends: Hospice, Palliative Care, and End-of-Life Care

Academy of Hospice and Palliative Medicine
      aahpm.org
Aging Parents and Elder Care
      aging-parents-and-elder-care.com
American Hospice Foundation
      americanhospice.org
Approaching Death: Improving Care at the End of Life
      nap.edu/readingroom/books/approaching
Barbara Ziegler Palliative Care Education Program
      Memorial Sloan-Kettering Cancer Center
      mskcc.org/zpep
Before I Die
      wnet.org/bid/index.html
Caring Connections
      caringinfo.org
Center to Advance Palliative Care
      capc.org
Disparities at the End of Life
      rwjf.org
Elder Rage
      elderrage.com

End-of-Life Nursing Education Consortium (ELNEC)
> aacn.nche.edu/ELNEC/about.htm

End of Life Physician Education Resources (EPERC)
> eperc.mcw.edu

EndLink: Resources for End of Life Care Education
> endlink.lurie.northwestern.edu

Griefworks BC
> griefworksbc.com

Growth House, Inc.
> growthhouse.org

Hospice Foundation of America
> hospicefoundation.org

Legacies
> legacies.ca

Life's End Institute: Missoula Demonstration Project
> lifes-end.org

NPR, The End of Life: Exploring Death in America
> npr.org

National Hospice and Palliative Care Organization
> nhpco.org

National Prison Hospice Association
> npha.org

On Our Own Terms: Moyers on Dying Thirteen/WNET New York
> pbs.org/onourownterms

Promoting Excellence in End-of-Life Care
> promotingexcellence.org

Robert Wood Johnson Foundation
> rwjf.org

Share the Care
> sharethecare.org

Spiritual Care Program
> spcare.org

The National Center for Advanced Illness Coordinated Care
> coordinatedcare.net

Toolkit of Instruments to Measure End of Life Care
> chcr.brown.edu/pcoc/toolkit.htm

Support Services and Support Groups for Patients and Loved Ones Facing Chronic/Terminal Illness

American Cancer Society
cancer.org/docroot/home/index.asp

American Heart Association
americanheart.org

American Lung Association
lungusa.org

Cancer Care
cancercare.org

Resources for Professional Caregivers: Hospice, Palliative Care, and End-of-Life Care

Naropa University School of Extended Studies
Contemplative End-of-Life Care: A Certificate Program for Healthcare Professionals
naropa.edu/contemplativecare

National Hospice and Palliative Care Organization
nhpco.org

Medical and Nursing Organizations Providing Education and Research for the Science and Art of End-of-Life Care

Academy of Hospice and Palliative Medicine
aahpm.org

American Holistic Medical Association
holisticmedicine.org

American Holistic Nuring Association
ahna.org

Hospice and Palliative Nurses Association
hpna.org

Oncology Nursing Society
ons.org

Suggested Reading

Adding Value to Long-Term Care: An Administrator's Guide to Improving Staff Performance, Patient Experience, and Financial Health
Lazer, Dianne and Schwartz-Cassell, Tobi

Affirming the Darkness: An Extended Conversation About Living with Prostate Cancer
Wheeler, Chuck and Martha

All Kinds of Love: Experiencing Hospice
Jaffe, Carolyn and Ehrlich, Carol H.

An Ocean of Time: Alzheimer's Tales of Hope and Forgetting
Mathiasen, Patrick, M.D.

Another Morning: Voices of Truth and Hope from Mothers with Cancer
Blachman, Linda

By No Means: The Choice to Forgo Life-Sustaining Food and Water
Lynn, Joanne (editor)

Caring in Remembered Ways: The Fruit of Seeing Deeply
Davis, Maggie Steincrohn

Choices at the End of Life: Finding Out What Your Parents Want Before It's Too Late
Norlander, Linda, R.N., MS, and McSteen, Kerstin, R.N., MS

Companion to Grief: Finding Consolation When Someone You Love Has Died
Kelley, Patricia

The Courage to Laugh: Humor, Hope, and Healing in the Face of Death and Dying
Klein, Allen

Dancing With Mister D: Notes on Life and Death
Keizer, Bert

The Death of a Christian: The Order of Christian Funerals
    Rutherford, R. and Barr, T.

Death: The Trip of a Lifetime
    Palmer, Greg

The Denial of Death
    Becker, Ernest

A Different Kind of Health
    Justice, Blair, Ph.D.

The Diving Bell and the Butterfly
    Bauby, Jean-Dominique

Dying: A Book of Comfort
    McNees, P. (editor)

Dying At Home: A Family Guide for Caregiving
    Sankar, Andrea

Dying Well: The Prospect for Growth at the End of Life
    Byock, Ira, M.D.

Dying with Dignity: A Plea for Personal Responsibility
    Kung, Hans and Jens, Walter

Elder Rage—or—Take My Father... Please!
    Marcell, Jacqueline

Facing Death and Finding Hope: A Guide for the Emotional and Spiritual Care of the Dying
    Longaker, Christine

Facing Death: Images, Insights, and Interventions: A Handbook for Educators, Healthcare Professionals, and Counselors
    Bertman, Sandra L.

Fading Away: The Experience of Transition in Families With Terminal Illness
    Davies, Betty, et al.

A Few Months to Live
    Staton, Jana; Shuy, Roger; and Byock, Ira, M.D.

Final Gifts: Understanding the Special Awareness, Needs, and Communications of the Dying
    Callanan, Maggie and Kelley, Patricia

Forced Exit: The Slippery Slope from Assisted Suicide to Legalized Murder
    Smith, Wesley J.

The Four Things That Matter Most
    Byock, Ira, M.D.

The Gift of Peace: Personal Reflections
    Bernardin, Joseph Louis

The Gifts of the Body
    Brown, Rebecca

The Good Death: The New American Search to Reshape the End of Life
    Webb, Marilyn

Grace and Grit: Spirituality and Healing in the Life and Death of Treya Killam Wilber
    Wilber, Ken

Graceful Passages: A Companion for Living and Dying
    Malkin, Gary Remal and Stillwater, Michael

Grief and the Healing Arts
    Bertman, Sandra L. (editor)

A Grief Observed
    Lewis, C. S.

Grieving: A Love Story
    Coughlin, Ruth

Handbook for Mortals: Guidance for People Facing Serious Illness
    Lynn, Joanne, M.D., and Harrold, Joan, M.D.

Hard Choices for Loving People: CPR, Artificial Feeding, Comfort Measures Only and the Elderly Patient
    Dunn, Hank

The Healing Art of Storytelling
    Stone, Richard

The Healing Power of Creative Mourning
    Yager, Jan

The Helper's Journey: Working with People Facing Grief, Loss, and Life-Threatening Illness
    Larson, Dale G., Ph.D.

Helping Grieving People: When Tears Are Not Enough: A Handbook for Care Providers
    Jeffreys, Shep J., Ed.D.

Hospice Care for Children
    Armstrong-Dailey, Ann and Zarbock, Sarah, (editors)

The Hospice Choice: In Pursuit of a Peaceful Death
    Lattanzi-Licht, Marcia; Mahoney, John J.; and Miller, Galen W.

The Hospice Handbook: A Complete Guide
    Berresford, Larry

How We Die: Reflections on Life's Final Chapter
    Nuland, Sherwin B.

I'm Here to Help: A Guide for Caregivers, Hospice Workers, and Volunteers
    Ray, Catherine

Illness as Metaphor and AIDS and Its Metaphors
    Sontag, Susan

Improving Care for the End of Life: A Sourcebook
    Lynn, Joanne; Lynch Schuster, Janice; and Kabcenell, Andrea

In the Shadow of Illness: Parents and Siblings of the Chronically Ill Child
    Bluebond-Langner, Myra, Ph.D.

Intimate Death: How the Dying Teach Us How to Live
    De Hennezel, Marie

Kitchen Table Wisdom: Stories that Heal
    Remen, Rachel N., Ph.D.

Last Rights: Rescuing the End of Life from the Medical System
    Kiernan, Stephen

Lean on Me: Cancer through a Carer's Eyes
    Kember, Lorraine

The Least of These My Brethren: A Doctor's Story of Hope and Miracles on an Inner City AIDS Ward
    Baxter, Daniel J., M.D.

Liberating Losses: When Death Brings Relief
    Elison, Jennifer, Ed.D., and McGonigle, Chris, Ph.D.

Life Worth Living: How Someone You Love Can Still Enjoy Life in a Nursing Home: The Eden Alternative in Action
    Thomas, William H., M.D.

It's All Good: Emails from a Dying Best Friend
    Widran, Jonathan

Living Our Dying: A Way to the Sacred in Everyday Life
    Sharp, Joseph

Living Posthumously: Confronting the Loss of Vital Powers
    Schmookler, Andrew B.

Living With Grief When Illness is Prolonged
    Doka, Kenneth, Ph.D., and Davidson, J., (editors)

Living with Life-Threatening Illness: A Guide for Patients, Their Families, and Caregivers
    Doka, Kenneth, Ph.D.

Long Goodbye: The Deaths of Nancy Cruzan
    Colby, William F.

Love is Stronger than Death
    Kreeft, Peter

Managing Death in the Intensive Care Unit: The Transition from Cure to Comfort
    Curtis, Randall J. and Rubenfeld, Gordon D. (editors)

Man's Search for Meaning
    Frankl, Victor E.

Medical Care of the Soul: A Practical and Healing Guide to End-Of-Life Issues for Families, Patients, and Health Care Providers
    Bartlow, Bruce G., M.D.

A Midwife Through the Dying Process: Stories of Healing and Hard Choice at the End of Life
    Quill, Timothy E., M.D.

More Than a Parting Prayer: Lessons in Care Giving for the Dying
    Griffith, William H.

Mortal Acts: Eighteen Empowering Rituals for Confronting Death
    Feinstein, David

Mortally Wounded: Stories of Soul Pain, Death, and Healing
    Kearney, Michael, M.D.

Mourning & Mitzvah: A Guided Journal for Walking the Mourner's Path Through Grief to Healing
    Brener, Anne, L.C.S.W

Mourning Has Broken: A Collection of Creative Writings about Grief and Healing
    Mara, Koven and Pearl, Liz

My Grandfathers Blessings: Stories of Strength, Refuge, and Belonging
    Remen, Rachel N. , M.D.

My Own Country: A Doctor's Story
    Verghese, Abraham , M.D.

The Nature of Suffering and the Goals of Medicine
    Cassell, Eric J.

Nothing Left Unsaid: Creating a Healing Legacy with Final Words and Letters
    Polce-Lynch, Mary, Ph.D.

On Death and Dying
    Kübler-Ross, Elisabeth , M.D.

The Open Road: Walt Whitman on Death & Dying
    Vest, Joe, (editor)

The Oxford Book of Death
    Enright, D.J. (editor)

Oxford Textbook of Palliative Medicine
    Doyle, Derek; Hanks, Geoffrey W.C.; and MacDonald, Neil (editors)

Palliative and End-of-Life Pearls
    Byock, Ira, M.D., and Heffner, John E.

Part of Me Died, Too: Stories of Creative Survival Among Bereaved Children and Teenagers
    Fry, Virginia Lynn

Patience, Compassion, Hope, and the Christian Art of Dying Well
    Vogt, Christopher P.

Physician-Assisted Suicide
    Weir, Robert F. (editor)

The Presence of the Dead on the Spiritual Path
    Steiner, Rudolf

Raising Lazarus: A Memoir
    Pensack, Robert Jon, M.D., and Williams, Dwight Arnan

Readings in Thanatology (Death, Value and Meaning)
    Morgan, John D., (editor)

Refuge: An Unnatural History of Family and Place
    Williams, Terry Tempest

R.I.P.: The Complete Book of Death and Dying
    Jones, Constance

The Rights of the Dying: A Companion for Life's Final Moments
    Kessler, David

Rituals for Living and Dying: From Life's Wounds to Spiritual Awakening
    Feinstein, David and Mayo, Peg Elliot

Saying Goodbye to Daniel: When Death is the Best Choice
    Rothman, Juliet Cassuto

Seduced by Death: Doctors, Patients, and the Dutch Cure
    Hendin, Herbert, M.D.

Share the Care: How To Organize a Group to Care for Someone Who Is Seriously Ill
    Capossela, Cappy; Warnock, Sheila; and Miller, Sukie

117

Signs of Life: A Memoir of Dying and Discovery
    Brookes, Tim

The Singing Bird Will Come: An AIDS Journal
    Noonan, John Richard

Six Months To Live: Different Paths to Life's End
    Byock, Ira, M.D.; Staton, Jana; and Shuy, Roger

*Stay Close and Do Nothing: A Spiritual and Practical Guide to Caring for the
    Dying at Home*
    Collett, Merrill

Surviving the Fall: The Personal Story of an AIDS Doctor
    Selwyn, Peter A. , M.D.

The Tibetan Book of Living and Dying
    Rinpoche, Sogyal

A Time to Grieve: Meditations for Healing After the Death of a Loved One
    Staudacher, Carol

To Live Until We Say Goodbye
    Kübler-Ross, Elisabeth , M.D.

Tuesdays with Morrie
    Albom, Mitch

The Troubled Dream of Life: In Search of a Peaceful Death
    Callahan, Daniel

The Undertaking: Life Studies from the Dismal Trade
    Lynch, Thomas

What the Dying Teach Us: Lessons on Living
    Oliver, Samuel

When Bad Things Happen to Good People
    Kushner, Harold S.

When Life Becomes Precious: A Guide for Loved Ones and Friends of Cancer Patients
    Babcock, Elise NeeDell

Who Dies? An Investigation of Conscious Living and Conscious Dying
    Levine, Stephen

Words to Live By: A Journal of Wisdom for Someone You Love
    Marshall, Emily and Kate

The Wounded Storyteller: Body, Illness, and Ethics
    Frank, Arthur W.

You Can Help Someone Who's Grieving
    Frigo, Victoria; Fisher, Diane; and Cook, Mary Lou

About the Author

Cathleen Fanslow-Brunjes is an internationally acclaimed expert in the fields of death, dying, grief, nursing, and hospice care.

Over the years, Cathy has worked with more than 40,000 dying persons, their families, their caregivers, and the professional staffs involved with them. She has worked extensively with dying children and adolescents, as well as with adults.

Cathy has been an acclaimed pioneer in the field of hospice: She created the Hospice Program for New York's Visiting Nurse Service; she worked at the first certified hospice in Long Island; and she created the first free-standing hospice in Switzerland. She was director of nursing at Calvary Hospital in New York, the specialized hospital for advanced cancer patients, considered by many to be the first hospice in the U.S.

One of Cathy's most impressive professional accomplishments has been the development of the "Standards of Care for the Dying Patient." This protocol is used throughout the U.S. Veterans' Administration Hospital System, one of the largest health-care systems in the world, with thirty-five medical centers throughout the U.S.

Cathy has received many awards over the years, including the National Hospice Organization's President's Award, the Award for Excellence from the National Hospice Association, and the Healer of the Year award for outstanding achievement in the field of healing from the Nurse Healers Professional Associates. She also received an award from the New York State Hospice Organization in recognition of extraordinary service to the New York Hospice movement.

Senator Clayton Templeton and
Mrs. Neva Templeton
request the honor of your presence
at the wedding of their daughter
Carling Templeton

to

Kane McClellan

on Saturday, June 20

at

the Triple M Ranch

2 p.m.

Reception
to Follow

Please address questions and book requests to: Silhouette Reader Service
U.S.: 3010 Walden Ave., P.O. Box 1325, Buffalo, NY 14269
Canadian: P.O. Box 609, Fort Erie, Ont. L2A 5X3

Western Weddings

BARBARA BOSWELL
THE BRIDAL PRICE

Published by Silhouette Books
America's Publisher of Contemporary Romance

SILHOUETTE BOOKS
300 East 42nd St.,
New York, N.Y. 10017

ISBN 0-373-30107-3

THE BRIDAL PRICE

Copyright © 1990 by Barbara Boswell

Celebrity Wedding Certificates published by permission of
Donald Ray Pounders from *Celebrity Wedding Ceremonies*.

A Letter from the Author

Dear Reader,

I was delighted to learn that my book *The Bridal Price* had been chosen to be reissued in the HERE COME THE GROOMS series. *The Bridal Price* is to be included in the Western Weddings category, and this is a particular thrill for me because it was the first "Western" book I'd written. I've always been a major Diana Palmer fan and have read every ranch romance she's ever written. I'd been wanting to write my own ranch romance for a while, so I reread some of my Diana Palmer collection for inspiration.

I began to picture Kane McClellan's ranch in Texas, maybe around the area where Diana's characters live. It was fun to pretend they were all part of the same circle. Since I'm also fond of the "Taming of the Shrew" theme, I decided to make the heroine, Carling Templeton, a citified shrew in major need of some taming. But in all fairness, Kane needed his macho streak mellowed a bit and Carling seemed just the woman to do it. Both Kane and Carling are strong, stubborn characters accustomed to having their own way, and it wasn't hard to keep the conflict going between them, even though they're locked away together down on the Triple M ranch.

Since *The Bridal Price* was first released, I've had a number of letters from readers asking about the secondary characters in it, especially Kane's sister Holly and her "rat" boyfriend, Webb Asher. He appears again as a secondary character in my second ranch book, *The Wilde Bunch,* an August 1995 Silhouette Desire, where he meets an unexpected fate. Holly is still waiting for Mr. Right, but hopefully she's having fun!

I hope you enjoy reading *The Bridal Price* as much as I enjoyed writing it.

Barbara Boswell

One

___

"Carling, you have a visitor," Senator Clayton Templeton announced as he knocked lightly on his daughter's bedroom door. "It's Kane McClellan and he's waiting downstairs in the living room for you."

Carling was sitting in the window seat and staring blindly at the neat rows of tulips that filled the wide flower beds in front of the Templetons' Bethesda, Maryland, house. She tensed, but made no reply.

Through the closed door she heard her father clear his throat and murmur, "Don't keep him waiting, my dear."

Don't keep him waiting? Carling's mouth twisted into a scowl. It wasn't enough that she'd been forced into the position of slave on the auction block; she was also supposed to spare the bidder the inconvenience of waiting!

The force of her anger carried her out of her room and down the stairs, but a few steps short of the living room a sudden tidal wave of tension and anxiety brought her to an abrupt halt. Waiting inside was the man she was supposed to agree to marry. *A man she hadn't even dated.* She'd only met Kane McClellan a few times and very briefly at that, but she'd known in those short, infrequent moments that she didn't like him and never would.

Her stomach began to churn and her mouth went dry as the nervous tension escalated to panic. *Marry him?* The notion was positively medieval. She couldn't go through with it; there had to be a way out. Not only was being forced into an alleged "marriage of convenience" ridiculously archaic, not to mention horrifying, but Kane McClellan just wasn't her type in any way.

Physically, he was too big, too tall and too dark for her tastes. From what she knew of his life-style, it was too reclusive for an extrovert like herself. Even worse, he was aggressive and unyielding with a domineering streak a mile wide. She'd immediately picked up on that from the few words they'd exchanged during their mercifully quick meetings.

She had been told by her father that Kane McClellan owned a large cattle ranch several hundred miles from Dallas, and that he also possessed an unerring acumen for real estate and business investments, which had made him a very wealthy man. She'd heard McClellan described as a loyal, longtime Templeton supporter by members of her father's inner circle. Translated, that meant he was a generous financial contributor to Senator Clayton Templeton's campaign coffers.

Carling had managed to find out a little more about the man on her own and what she'd heard further convinced her that she had been absolutely right to turn down his invitation to dance at that Houston fund-raiser last summer, that her refusal to have dinner with him following a campaign rally on another evening in Dallas had been right on the mark.

Her father might admire Kane McClellan's wealth and financial prowess, but she'd seen no reason to further her own acquaintance with him. She'd learned that McClellan rarely left his ranch, preferring a reclusive life-style far from the glittering social world which she inhabited in Washington, D.C., where her father served as the senior senator from Texas. Kane was equally a stranger to the Texas social scene, while she was firmly established in both Dallas and Houston circles.

Carling peeked into the living room and saw Kane standing in front of Great-Grandmother Templeton's mahogany tea cart, on which an antique china tea set was placed. His presence seemed to dominate the elegant room and Carling inhaled sharply as the sight of him impacted on her senses.

His hair was straight and dark, almost coal-black in color, and was cut short in a style that would never require the upkeep of regular salon trims, hair dryers and sprays. If he needed a haircut he no doubt went into a barber shop, probably one with spittoons for the chewing tobacco habits of its patrons. The first time she'd met him, Carling had imagined him washing his hair with a bar of soap in the shower, toweling it dry, running a comb through it and then forgetting about it. A decidedly different attitude from many of the trendy, style-conscious men she knew.

His features were hard and sharp and as frankly masculine as the rest of him—the firmly set jaw, the sharp blade of a nose, the wide, sensual mouth and thick, dark eyebrows.

He was six foot four with a powerful masculine frame, broad-shouldered and muscular with a physique that radiated virility. He looked strong and powerful and she knew the image was in no way an illusion. He *was* strong and powerful. The one time he had touched her—that night in Houston when he'd taken her hand and asked her to dance—she'd felt the strength and power in his long, well-shaped fingers. She had refused him and for just a moment, before he'd let her go with a shrug and a smile, he had tightened his hold on her, making her irrevocably aware that had he chosen, he could have kept her with him for as long as he wanted.

A man of his size and strength could make her do anything he wanted her to do and for one unguarded moment, she had found that sheer, feminine helplessness intriguing. Shocked with herself, she'd quickly allowed outrage to prevail instead. The disconcerting episode had redoubled her determination to have nothing to do with the man. She was too independent, too used to having things her own way, to cede to the demands of any man.

She watched him pick up a small antique silver frame, which contained an old-fashioned baby picture of her grandmother. The delicate frame seemed dwarfed in his big hand. Carling shivered. Big. He was certainly that. The sheer size of him had an unnerving effect upon her, and she didn't understand why. She only knew that he made her feel wary and hostile, that he made her want to run in the opposite direction.

Her eyes flicked over him once more. He was as solid as a chunk of granite, she thought with a disparaging frown. And he was wearing jeans—*again!* He'd worn jeans every time she'd met him. Didn't he have anything else to wear? His jeans weren't the trendy, designer type that were the only kind worn in Carling's crowd. Kane McClellan's jeans were practical and well-worn. Carling's blue eyes widened. And he wore them well. They fit snugly in the front and back, molding his long, muscular thighs and tight buttocks in what she considered a thoroughly unnerving sex-defining way.

Deliberately, she dragged her eyes away from that mesmerizing sight, but her gaze remained riveted upon the rest of him. She took in his crisp blue chambray shirt and his pale sheepskin jacket. She was certain that the fine leather Western boots he wore were part of his everyday garb, and were not strictly worn to parties with a Western theme. Her well-trained shopper's eye recognized the enduring quality of his clothes—expensive but functional. He was the epitome of the authentic, moneyed working rancher.

She gulped. What was the matter with her? Anyone who might happen to come by and see her staring into the living room at him, would think she was ogling him. Which she most definitely was not! Carling Templeton did not ogle men in general, and in particular not an overbearing, barbarous cowboy, who was determined to ruin her life. Or her father's career...

"How long are you going to stand cowering in the hall?"

Carling started violently at the sound of the deep, slow drawl. Kane McClellan turned slowly to face her. She went hot and cold all over. He had given no indication that he'd been aware of her presence, but as his slate-gray eyes locked with hers, she knew at once that he'd known she had been there all along.

She felt a hot blush sweep over her from head to toe and silently cursed her fair coloring and her penchant for flushing when in the throes of strong emotion. "I wasn't cowering," she snapped. Carling Christine Templeton did not cower or ogle! "I was bracing myself for the horror of having to deal with you."

Kane carefully placed the picture back on the tea cart. "The horror of dealing with me?" he repeated. Unfortunately from Carling's point of view, he didn't seem at all offended by the jibe. Instead he smiled, as if he was amused.

He began to walk toward her, very slowly. She stood rooted to the spot, transfixed by his confident, lazy stride.

"You've assiduously avoided dealing with me in the past," he remarked in that gravelly, husky voice of his. "Does this mean that you've decided to accept my offer of marriage, Miss Templeton?"

She could tell by the gleam in his eyes that he was definitely mocking her. Carling seethed. "As if I had any choice at all, you—you snake!"

He was standing in front of her now and he was much too close. Excruciatingly aware of his virile size and strength, she found herself in the grip of an overwhelming need to turn and run. He was so close she could feel the heat emanating from his body. The scent of him, a combination of soap and a woodsy aftershave, filled her nostrils when she dared to inhale.

"You do have a choice," he said calmly. "You can marry me or not. The choice is yours to make, Carly."

"My name is Carling," she said coldly, stressing the pronunciation. "Since you're trying to force me into marrying you, the least you can do is to get my name right."

"I know your name," he replied with maddening affability. "I just prefer my own shortened version of it. A pet name, if you will." He took a lock of her champagne-blond hair between his fingers.

Carling froze. She felt unable to breathe, unable to move. His nearness, his touch seemed to immobilize every part of her body. Helplessly, she raised her eyes to his. Their gazes held as his fingers slowly rubbed the strand of hair in a patently suggestive way.

She abruptly jerked away from him, as if she'd been scalded. "I don't want or need a pet name from you! I'm not your *pet* and I resent your chauvinistic, demeaning, overbearing—"

"I get the picture," Kane interrupted dryly. "Let me amend my explanation. I prefer Carly because I'm too lazy to tack on those extra letters. And because Carling sounds like the name of a brewery to me."

Carling fumed. "It happens to be my mother's maiden name."

"My mother's maiden name was Lacey," he said, shrugging. "I'm forever grateful to her for not having bestowed it on me. Can you imagine the schoolyard brawls that were avoided by naming me Kane instead?"

"Except she spelled it wrong. It should be C-a-i-n, like that murderous fiend in the Bible."

He had the unmitigated gall to laugh. His refusal to argue with her was wildly frustrating. She wanted to see him furious and insulted, to make him storm from the house in a rage and never look back.

"Do you want an engagement ring?" he asked instead, in an infuriatingly amiable tone.

"No!"

"Then there's no need to waste time picking one out. We can be married immediately." He reached into the pocket of his sheepskin jacket and pulled out a small box, flipping the lid open to reveal a thick gold band. "Here's your wedding ring. Let's go."

"Go?" Carling paled. "Now? Oh no, we can't. It's—we—" She broke off as she realized she had lapsed into incoherence.

"We certainly can. Your father was kind enough to inform me about a place in Fairfax, Virginia, which condenses the usual three-day waiting period for a blood test and license into a few hours. He tells me that we can have a civil ceremony performed there."

"You must be pleased to have such an accommodating future father-in-law." Carling felt bitterness gnawing her like acid. Disillusionment shadowed her deep blue eyes. It was difficult to grasp and almost impossible to accept—that her father who for years had doted upon her, his only child, should now be so eager to literally *sell* her to this man.

"I like your father, both personally and politically," Kane said blandly. "I always have. He's been an excellent senator for our state and done more for the interests of the oil and gas industry than anyone in Congress. That's why I've always supported him."

"And you're such a fan that you're buying his daughter?"

Kane smiled. "Is that how you see it? That I'm buying myself a bride?" He didn't seem unduly perturbed by the notion.

"Yes! What's even worse is that you're blackmailing my father and me into going along with you!"

A wave of rage swept through her, so fierce that she began to tremble from the force of it. He was towering above her, so vibrantly male that he evoked some wild and primitive feminine response from deep within her. But she refused to acknowledge it. She hated the man.

Kane shrugged. "I'm not blackmailing you, sweetheart. If you don't want to marry me, all you have to do is to tell me no and I'll leave."

"As if it's that easy!" Her voice rose. For the first time in her life she truly understood the phenomenon of "seeing red," as a rosy haze of fury swam before her eyes.

"My father owes you hundreds of thousands of dollars. He'd have to declare bankruptcy and even then he couldn't repay you. And—and it's illegal for a senator to accept such large sums of money in the first place. You have my father and me backed against the wall and you know it!" She felt her eyes fill with tears as depression abruptly replaced her anger.

Last night's scene with her father replayed vividly in her mind. They'd had another argument and she had gone to her room dispirited. For the past two years she and her father seemed to do nothing but argue, and she was confused and heartbroken by the change in their previously loving and mutually admiring relationship. Worse, the argument always centered on the same topic: Carling's unwillingness to marry a wealthy young man and give her parents the grandchildren they craved.

Or that they claimed to crave. Last night the senator, looking older than his usual debonair sixty years, had confessed the truth. As much as the Templetons wanted grandchildren, they wanted—they *needed!*— a wealthy son-in-law.

Carling had listened in stunned silence as her father confessed that the life she'd been living had all been a lovely fantasy fostered by the illusion that the Templetons were as rich as everyone else in their tri-city social circles. For the first time Carling learned that they were not at all rich; they merely lived well, relying on the senator's honorariums and the largess of his constituents and friends to supplement his congressional salary, while stretching credit to the limits and beyond.

Carling's mother, Neva, had never worked, but she loved to shop. Her exquisite taste was evident in her wardrobe and the family's two large homes, in Bethesda and in Dallas, as well as in the family apartment in Houston. Carling, at twenty-eight, had never worked for pay, either. There had never been any reason to. Occasionally helping out in her father's office, making public appearances during his various reelection campaigns, and her charity fund-raising work had always been her full-time occupation—along with socializing.

The senator hadn't confided his financial worries to his "girls," as he fondly referred to his wife and daughter. Instead, he'd opted to try his luck in the stock market and bought a lot of stocks on margin. Two days ago, his broker had called with devastating news: the stocks were dropping and a huge margin call payment needed to be made at once. Clayton Templeton didn't possess the necessary cash resources to cover the payment, which was so large that he would lose everything he owned.

Desperately, he'd called upon the man who had easy access to such substantial sums, the man who had been expressing a keen interest in Carling for well over a year: Kane McClellan.

Kane had readily agreed to cover the sum for the stocks, the senator told Carling, and she had blanched at her father's words. She'd been savvy in the way of politics since her teens; she knew that the Federal Election Act limited the amount of money that politicians were allowed to accept in campaign donations or personal loans. The amount Kane McClellan had paid for those stocks far, far exceeded that limit, making her father liable for an ethics investigation by the Senate and possible prosecution for accepting illegal loans.

And this was an election year! Carling thought of the other party's candidate for the senate seat, a young man who had managed to garner a surprising amount of statewide support. As things stood, Clayton Templeton's reelection was probably assured, but an ethics investigation and financial scandal could easily swing voters to the opposition.

His position as a senator from Texas was her father's life, his entire identity! Carling couldn't fathom how he would handle losing his career, along with his social status and prestige. And her mother! They would have to sell their houses and all the beautiful furnishings, the priceless antiques and objets d'art Neva Templeton so enjoyed collecting. Carling shuddered at the thought of her mother trying to cope with both the loss and the scandal.

Feeling as if her heart had turned to stone, Carling had listened to her father propose the only way out, a plan which required her cooperation. At least, that's how her father had described it. Offering herself as a human sacrifice was closer to the mark, Carling thought.

If Carling were to marry Kane McClellan, any threat of Senator Clayton Templeton standing in violation of the Federal Election Act would be eliminated. There was no law limiting the amount of personal gifts or loans an elected official could accept from a member of his family, her father explained with pathetic eagerness. And wonder of wonders, McClellan was willing to forget the loan entirely and personally absorb the financial loss himself—*if Carling were to marry him.*

Now Kane McClellan was here to collect his prize—the bride he had purchased. Carling felt tears of fear and anger burning behind her eyelids and tried to blink them away. She would not cry in front of this—this atavistic savage!

"Why are you doing this?" she whispered, staring disconsolately at the floor. The brilliant patterns in the Oriental carpet blurred in her teary gaze. "Why in the world would you want to marry me?"

"I turned thirty-five last month," he said simply, dispassionately. "It's time I settled down and started a family of my own. I've devoted the past twelve years to building up the ranch as well as various other business interests. Now I want to share my life and fortune with a wife and children."

"But what does that have to do with me?" Her voice cracked with desperation, but she pressed on, now determined to reason with him. "Surely you can find a woman who *wants* to marry you. Texas is a huge state and you're—" she paused and gulped "—you're not an unattractive man. And, of course, you're very rich. That's certainly a lure to some."

"Yes, isn't it?" he interjected dryly. "An irresistible lure, in some cases."

She thought of her father who had been pushing the idea of her first meeting, then dating, now *marrying* Kane McClellan strictly on the basis of his financial status. Her flush deepened as shame rippled through her. But that was her father's doing, not hers! she reminded herself. She couldn't let Kane embarrass or intimidate her into giving up her fight!

"There must be some nice young woman out there who would be glad to be your wife and—uh—raise a family for you." She bit her lip, afraid that she'd sounded insultingly patronizing. She hadn't meant to, she merely wanted him to realize his options.

Kane shrugged nonchalantly, but there was nothing simple or dispassionate or nonchalant in the fires burning in his gray eyes. His gaze was hot enough to melt steel. "But I want *you*, Carly. For my wife, for the mother of my children."

The uncompromising finality in his tone made her gnash her teeth in frustration. "That's ridiculous! We don't even know each other."

"We'll have plenty of time to get to know each other after we're married. It's going to work out very well between us, Carly," he added, his voice firm with that promise.

An involuntary whimper escaped from her throat.

"I'd seen pictures of you before we met," he continued. "You're a knockout. Great big blue eyes, high cheekbones, a beautifully shaped, sexy mouth, plus all that blond hair. The only reason I attended those fund-raisers for your father was to meet you. I thought to myself 'here is a woman who has it all—beauty, brains, class.'" He smiled a heart-stoppingly sexy smile. "Not to mention a great body. Do you want me to rhapsodize about your breasts and your legs and that sweet little butt—"

"No!" she interrupted, her face scarlet. "You're unspeakably rude, Mr. McClellan. Rude and crude and sexist and—"

"Assaulted by adjectives," Kane interrupted dryly. "I'm none of the above, Carly, but I am honest and outspoken. You'll always know where you stand with me."

"You'll always know where you stand with me, too! At the top of the list of people I detest."

"Right now, you probably do think you hate me," he conceded. "But you'll get over it."

"I will not!" Carling suppressed the urge to scream, regretting that she'd been raised to view such unbridled exhibitions as unladylike. She was getting nowhere in her attempts to fight with Kane McClellan, she admitted ruefully. Her barbs didn't come close to penetrating his thick hide or daunting his incredible ego. He'd obviously decided that he was not going to allow her to drive him away. She must find another way to make him want to be rid of her as much as she wanted to be rid of him.

"So I'm supposed to believe that you fell in love with me from my photographs?" she demanded scornfully. She was infuriated that her heart was thundering faster and louder than a speeding train. "Only a naive, moronic fool looks at a picture of a woman and decides to marry her. An apt description of yourself, Mr. McClellan? Or maybe you're so socially inept and so totally devoid of personality that the only way you could ever get a woman to marry you is to buy her?"

"I'm sure you'll understand if I don't agree with either of those theories," he replied smoothly. "Try looking at it this way, Carly. What red-blooded male wouldn't want a woman with your face and body? If you like, you could choose to view the situation as wildly romantic—your besotted suitor going to extraordinary lengths to win the woman of his dreams. Because once I'd met you, I decided that you were the woman I wanted for my wife."

His amused confidence set her teeth on edge. He hardly sounded like a besotted, romantic suitor. Unfortunately, he didn't exactly fit into the fool or social clod categories, either. He looked and sounded shrewd and hard and calculating, a man used to getting what he wanted. And he wanted her.

"Are you crazy?" Carling's voice rose. If things went on as they were, she might end up screaming after all, etiquette be damned. "The few times we met, I was horribly rude to you. I played the role of the snotty society bitch to the hilt!"

"I know." His gray eyes glittered. "You were very, very wary of me, weren't you, Carly? You still are. I might not be one of those fancy playboy types you like to party with but I certainly recognize sexual tension, and it's been vibrating between you and me from the moment we met. Right from the start you've been very aware of me and very eager to antagonize me, to fight with me."

"That's because I don't like you," she shot back furiously. "Oh, why bother to sugarcoat it? The truth is I hate you! And not only are you a blackmailing barbarian, you're self-deluded to the point of no return. The so-called *sexual tension* you've imagined in me is—is—really suppressed nausea."

"I see." He had the nerve to laugh at her and to cup her shoulders with his big, warm hands.

Carling stiffened. "Don't touch me," she warned in a voice that was not as commanding as she would have liked.

He didn't release her. "You're very skittish," he observed, arching his dark black eyebrows. "That's another thing I've noticed about you. You're too nervous for a woman who is accustomed to being touched by a man. That leads me to assume that you've kept your relationships with all those men you've been linked on a strictly platonic level."

She was aghast that he'd hit on the truth. She did not like sex. The one time she had tried it, at the age of eighteen after a college fraternity party, had been quite enough for her. She and her date—whom she'd never spoken to again—had both had a bit too much to drink and the volatile combination of adolescent hormones, alcohol and curiosity had led to the mutual loss of their virginity. The memory was a distant one, but still repugnant to her.

Never had she experienced anything so painful and messy, so clumsy and humiliating. She had decided then and there never to do it again, and she hadn't. Nor had she ever had any trouble sticking to her vow. She'd earned a reputation for coolness—her detractors, frustrated with her icy unresponsiveness, had amended cool to frigid—but that didn't bother Carling. She didn't like being touched and she didn't care who knew it.

Until now. She did not like Kane McClellan knowing. It made her feel vulnerable, which alarmed her. Whoever said that knowledge was power had a point; having Kane know about her aversion to sex gave him a power over her and she hated it. Oh, how she hated him!

"You have one hell of a lot of nerve assuming anything about me, Kane McClellan!" she snarled. She was well aware that a lady never cursed in the presence of a gentleman, let alone cursed the gentleman himself, but doing so was inordinately satisfying. And Kane McClellan was not a gentleman, anyway. "Now take your hands off me this instant."

He merely laughed, unperturbed by either her cursing or her command. "It's time for you to get used to having my hands on you, honey. Because after we're married I'm not going to keep them off you. You'll soon become very accustomed to a man's touch. My touch." He pulled her closer with such strength that she was unable to pull away. "And you'll be much calmer and more content when you've worked off all that high-strung, nervous energy in bed with me."

"No!" she cried, nearly choking at the panic roiling inside her. "You can't do this. I won't let you! I won't marry you. I'll pay you back every penny you lent my father! Please don't make—" Her own fierce pride abruptly silenced her. She had been on the verge of pleading with him! Never would she sink to that!

"You're working yourself into a world-class bout of hysteria," Kane pointed out and his air of calm was in dramatic contrast to her frantic loss of composure.

Her resentment heightened. "I have a right to be upset, dammit! I'm living every woman's worst nightmare! You want to force yourself on me and—and hurt me and—"

"I'm not going to hurt you or force you in bed, Carly," he said quietly.

She was breathing heavily and her blue eyes were huge as she stared up at him. "You—you mean that if I marry you, you won't expect me to—to have sex with you?" For the first time since last night, she felt a flicker of hope. If there was no way out of marrying him, at least she might be spared the mortification of sleeping with him.

"My uptight little darling, you're incredibly naive if you think I'd ever consider a celibate marriage, particularly with you." His smile was predatory, provocative and fairly brimming with sexy male confidence. "But maybe it's time to show you that you have nothing to be afraid of concerning the physical side of our marriage. There'll be no forcing or no hurting. You'll give yourself to me and I'll satisfy you completely."

The way he was looking at her...those lazy gray eyes of his...the soft, seductive words... Carling felt frissons of heat rippling through her, which paradoxically made her shiver.

"The only way you'll ever be able to satisfy me is to disappear from the face of the earth," she cried fiercely, hating the peculiar, unfamiliar shakiness in her limbs, the tight knots which were coiling deep in her abdomen, the wild racing of her heart. Nobody else had ever evoked these strange, primitive sensations and she hated them, hated that they were beyond her control, hated that Kane McClellan could do this to her.

"Oh, I don't think so. I think you're about to realize that you are as hungry for me as I am for you."

Two

His hands slid possessively over her. With one hand at the small of her back and the other between her shoulder blades, he molded her against him with effortless expertise. Carling gasped at the contact of his hard, muscled body and instinctively began to struggle.

Kane merely tightened his grip, rendering her efforts to free herself useless. "I've heard you're called the Ice Princess," he said softly, his mouth just an inch above her own, his warm breath mingling with hers.

She felt helpless and dizzy, fighting the almost overpowering urge to close her eyes and relax against him. Instead, she held herself tautly and glared at him with furious, disparaging blue eyes.

But Kane was undaunted. "All that anger is masking the passion that you've managed to freeze inside you," he taunted, brushing his lips lightly against her own. "It's going to be as explosive as a nuclear meltdown when you finally let yourself unleash it."

The touch of his mouth, brief and light as it had been, electrified her. Alarm bells seemed to go off in her head, and in a renewed attempt for freedom, she managed to lever her hands against his chest and push at him with her palms.

"Nuclear meltdown? Spare me the ridiculous hyperbole." She was irked that she couldn't seem to raise her voice above a whisper, but pleased that she was still able to insult him. She would *not* succumb to his barbarian physicality like some addle-brained twit straight out of those daytime television programs she occasionally—and accidentally, of course—tuned into watch.

"You're a brute and a bully and I promise, I *swear* that I'll never, never ever—" She paused, searching for the words, her face crimson with outrage.

"Give into me?" Kane suggested. "Respond to me? Enjoy making love with me? Is that what you're having such trouble trying to say?"

"Yes!" Carling gasped hoarsely. "That's what I'm trying to say. I'll never willingly give into you. You'll have to resort to rape because I won't respond to you. I'll never willingly have s-sex with you."

Their gazes clashed and for one tense, silent moment they stared deeply into each other's eyes. Carling saw the gray flames burning there, saw his pupils dilated with desire. She felt the powerful strength of his thighs hard against her, was excruciatingly aware of her breasts crushed against his chest.

"Is that what you think, my little fire-and-ice princess?" His voice was deep and husky.

A sudden tremulousness made her feel weak and soft inside. She fought against it. Clenching her hands and abandoning any attempts at propriety, she began to hit him.

Kane's hold was inexorable. He didn't let her go, he held her closer and buried his lips against the slender, graceful curve of her neck. She felt him nibbling the sensitive skin with his teeth, then soothing it with his lips. She whimpered. She wasn't used to being touched or caressed, and the surge of intense sensation rioting through her was both terrifying and darkly thrilling.

"Stop!" she demanded thickly. "Let me go!" Somehow her fists had become uncurled and her hands inched slowly to his shoulders. To push him away, Carling assured herself. His muscles rippled beneath her palms and her fingers gripped him.

Kane lifted his head and laughed softly. "No, baby, I won't let you go. I have you right where I want you at last. You're finally where you belong and soon enough you'll know it and admit it, to me and to yourself."

Outraged, she began to struggle again, but his superior size and strength easily kept her his captive. He wouldn't even let her hurt herself fighting him; he simply held her tightly until she exhausted herself and lay limply against him, gasping for breath.

And then slowly, his gray eyes glittering, Kane lowered his mouth to hers. Carling watched with a passivity she found appalling but couldn't seem to shake. He curled his hand into her hair and he held her head still as his mouth opened over hers and took possession of her lips.

His mouth was hard, hungry, demanding. He thrust his tongue into her mouth in an excruciating sexual simulation of what he intended to do with her body. Carling began to shake. Her mouth was open under his and she sampled the hot heady taste of him as she helplessly accepted the slow penetrating thrusts of his tongue.

He was so big, so strong; the masculine sound and smell and shape of him surrounded her. She felt her breasts swell and their sensitive peaks tighten as arrows of fire burned from her belly to the moist, secret place between her legs. Carling quivered.

She tried to tear her mouth from his, but his hold on her was inexorable. She had no choice. She couldn't get away. She had to stay in his arms with his tongue buried deeply in her mouth as his big hands moved over her possessively, gliding over the rounded curves of her bottom and positioning her intimately against the cradle of his iron-hard thighs, rubbing her, touching her.

Suddenly, she couldn't seem to stand. Her knees were too rubbery to hold her and she literally had to cling to Kane for support.

She wanted to scream, she wanted to faint. But she did neither. She was trembling and her body throbbed in response to the erotic rhythm of his movements. Neon lights were flashing in her head and she felt all coherent thought begin to slip away.

When his hand covered her breast in a gesture of pure male possession, she uttered a wild little cry from deep in her throat. His thumb traced the tight nipple beneath her teal-blue silk blouse, and seemingly of its own volition, her body arched against him.

And then, one disorienting moment later, it was over. He lifted his mouth from hers and his hands moved from their intimate positions on her breast and bottom. He stopped caressing her and held her tightly, but quite chastely, against him. "Someone's coming," he murmured against her ear. "Calm down, darling. Relax. We'll continue this tonight."

His words exploded in her head like a bullet to the brain. "No!" she cried, and she struggled against him.

To her surprise and infinite relief, he let her go. "No, you won't calm down or no, you won't relax?" Somehow he managed to look and sound both seductive and satisfied at the same time.

Carling longed to smack that smile of amused male confidence from his face. "I mean, no, we won't continue this tonight."

She wanted to melt into a puddle of pure embarrassment when he laughed softly and murmured, "Oh, yes, sweet. We're definitely going to pick up where we left off and you're going to be with me all the way."

Given her shocking performance in his arms, he probably felt quite justified in making his smug prediction. Carling suppressed the urge to wail in horror. Why hadn't she fought him tooth and nail? It must have been because he had caught her completely off guard; since she hated this man, there could be no other reason. He was everything she'd never wanted in a date, let alone a husband, yet something perverse and unpredictable inside her had nearly succumbed to his primitive sexuality.

Nearly? A nasty little voice in her head mocked her. She often heard and then firmly suppressed that voice because it inevitably made observations she didn't care to acknowledge. *Honey, you melted like wax in the sun and he hadn't even begun to turn up the heat. Wait until tonight, when he does . . .*

"Well, well, look who's here!" The clear oratorical tones of Senator Clayton Templeton sounded from the staircase, filling the foyer.

Carling whirled to face her smiling parents, who were descending the stairs together. While the senator was pulling off a credible impression of being surprised to see Kane McClellan in his home, his wife was genuinely so.

Carling knew that her mother was unaware of the senator's disastrous financial plight and Carling's impending fate. When Clayton Templeton had made his desperate confession and plea the night before, he'd begged his daughter not to mention a word of it to her mother. Carling, heartsick, panic-stricken and filled with dread, had agreed. After all, she'd reasoned glumly, why should her mother have to feel this way, too?

"Neva, you remember Kane McClellan, of course," Clayton boomed heartily, as they joined the younger couple. "He's a tried-and-true Templeton supporter from the Triple M Ranch southwest of Dallas. You've met him at some of the rallies . . ."

His voice trailed off. All three Templetons were fully aware that Neva mainly knew Kane McClellan as the man that the senator was forever trying to interest Carling in—the man whom Carling vociferously refused to have anything to do with. Yet here the pair stood in the hall. Carling's usually impeccably coiffed blond hair was sexily mussed and her lips slightly red and swollen, most definitely from being kissed. Carling saw her mother's eyes widen in confused amazement.

"We're very pleased to welcome you to our home, Mr. McClellan," Neva said, recovering quickly, her ingrained hospitality and never-failing political instincts carrying her through whatever private thoughts she might be harboring. "Carling dear, have you offered our guest some refreshments?"

"Oh yes," Kane said politely. The gleam in his gray eyes was positively wicked. "Thanks to Carling, I'm definitely refreshed."

Carling glowered at him. The charade was becoming unendurable—her father pretending that he hadn't arranged for Kane McClellan to be here, that he hadn't set the wheels in motion for Carling's ignominious plunge into slavery! And just when she thought she couldn't stand it for another moment, it got worse.

"Senator, Mrs. Templeton, I'd like to ask for the hand of your daughter in marriage," Kane interjected smoothly. "I've discussed it with Carling and she has agreed to do me the honor of becoming my wife. Having your blessing would mean the world to both of us."

Carling balled her hands into fists. Was she the only one to recognize his gallant-sounding words were spoken strictly tongue in cheek? She glared at him fiercely, and he countered by reaching over to grab her hand and holding it firmly in his. His eyes challenged her to contradict him, dared her to pull away and order him out of her house, out of her life.

Of course she didn't. And unless she wanted to bankrupt her family and kill her father's career, she was in Kane's power and they both knew it.

Her mother gaped at Kane, obviously dumbfounded by the news. After all, the last Neva Templeton had heard from Carling was that Kane McClellan was uncivilized and antisocial, an appalling throwback to some Neanderthal ancestors, and that she'd rather date a gorilla. "Carling, this is so—so—*so unexpected,*" Neva managed to say at last.

Kane grinned. "I believe Carling has said that nothing in the world could induce her to date me," he said cheerfully. "But it seems like marrying me is an entirely different matter."

"Indeed it is!" Senator Templeton exclaimed, reaching for Kane's other hand and shaking it heartily. He turned jovially toward his wife. "Neva, my dear, I hope you'll forgive this little deception of ours. You see, Carling and Kane let me in on their secret romance weeks ago and I convinced them to wait and surprise you. If you'll look at the Style section of this morning's *Post,* you'll see their engagement announcement, which I took the liberty of sending in."

"What?" Carling and Neva chorused.

"I've ordered several thousand copies to be delivered to the house later today," Clayton continued. "I want my staff to send clippings of the announcement to all our closest, dearest friends."

"Your closest, dearest friends number in the thousands?" Kane asked dryly.

The senator nodded, oblivious to the irony in Kane's tone. His sarcasm, however, hadn't eluded Carling. Her lips tightened as she glared at her newfound fiancé. She was equally upset with her father. Obviously he had been certain enough of her capitulation to mail an engagement announcement to *The Washington Post!*

She thought of the sad little scene last night, of her father's seemingly hopeless and pitiful despair. Since the announcement that would save his skin had already been prepared for publication, had his tears simply been a masterful piece of acting?

"Welcome to the family, Kane, my boy," the senator exclaimed expansively. "Nothing could make me happier than to see my little girl married to you!"

Truer words had never been spoken, Carling thought grimly. She swallowed back the protest of fury and indignation, which had welled up inside her, and turned her sapphire-blue eyes on her mother, silently willing the older woman to recognize her misery, to acknowledge that something very strange was going on and to demand an explanation.

Carling knew that there was only one person in the world from whom Senator Templeton would take orders and that was his wife, on the infrequent occasion she chose to issue them. If her mother were to learn of the mess they were in, if she were to forbid Carling to marry Kane McClellan just to bail them out of it...

Carling's heart leaped with hope. Oh Mama, please, say something! she mentally pleaded.

"This is such a surprise, I'm practically speechless, Kane," Neva exclaimed. She averted her eyes from the intensity of her daughter's gaze and turned her full attention to Kane. "And anybody who knows me knows that I'm seldom at a loss for words. Usually I have too many of them," she added with the charming frankness that had endeared her to countless voters, year after year.

"Well, I was surprised too, at first," the senator added quickly. "We kept singing your praises, Kane, but we didn't think our little girl was listening. Carling is so headstrong and independent that once she makes up her mind about something or someone it's usually impossible to make her change it."

He turned to beam at Carling, his voice utterly convincing in its sincerity. "You didn't want to tell your mama and me that you were secretly seeing Kane because you didn't want us to tease you or have to listen to us say I-told-you-so, isn't that right, my angel?"

Kane arched his eyebrows and made no comment, but Carling suspected he was secretly doubling over with laughter. In her opinion, her father was laying it on a tad too thick. What made it even worse was that three out of the four people standing here knew the truth!

"Carling certainly had us fooled," Neva said in a rather dazed voice. "She actually had us believing that she didn't want anything to do with you, Kane."

"The little minx," Kane said, his lips twitching with unconcealed mirth.

Carling wanted to smack him. She settled for shooting him a scathing look. "Mama, I believe my exact words were 'I'd rather date the gorilla in the National Zoo than Kane McClellan.'"

"Why, yes." Neva chuckled. "And now look, you're marrying him!"

"Maybe the gorilla was already spoken for," suggested Kane.

The senator and his wife laughed appreciatively.

"And he has a sense of humor, too!" Neva exclaimed, her eyes bright with delight. "Your young man is quite a catch, Carling. I'm thrilled to pieces for you. And for him, too, of course. And you're certainly going to make him a wonderful wife. Why, I'm thrilled for all of us!"

"So am I!" the senator added fervently.

Carling guessed that as the bride-to-be, she was supposed to make some sort of giggly, deliriously happy remark. She did not. She might be selling her body, but she would not sell her soul.

Her parents were too caught up in their own rapture to notice the lack of her own. "When can Carling and I begin planning the wedding?" Neva asked enthusiastically. "Oh, there is so much to do! But first things first—the engagement party! I'll call the Congressional Country Club right this minute and reserve the—"

"No need to do that, Neva," Kane cut in. His tone, ever polite, was also unmistakably firm. "Carling and I are skipping all the engagement hoopla. We're getting married immediately. Today, in fact. We're leaving for Fairfax, Virginia, right now."

Neva's giddiness was deflated as quickly as a balloon that had been pricked with a pin. "Oh." It was more of a gasp. "I—I see." She looked at Carling, and for the first time since the news of the marriage had been announced, she seemed to actually see her.

And Carling made no attempts to disguise her unhappiness, her anxiety and her nervousness.

"That place in Fairfax," Neva said, frowning. "That marriage mill where people who *have* to get married go immediately. Oh, Carling, at your age! And after all those years we attended the Planned Parenthood fund-raising balls! Now I truly am speechless."

Carling was appalled her mother thought she was pregnant out of wedlock at the age of twenty-eight! Her gaze flew to Kane and she blushed furiously. As if she'd let this reclusive brute from a cattle ranch take her to bed and make her pregnant!

"Mother, how could you believe such a thing even for a moment!" she cried indignantly.

"Don't be upset with your mama, sweetheart," Kane interjected soothingly. He casually swung one arm out and caught her around the waist, pulling her back against him, effortlessly, like someone reaching out to pick up a doll. But his arm was a steel band around her, holding her to him, an inexorable bond from which she couldn't break free or wriggle out of— though she tried to do both.

"I can see where your mother might misunderstand our haste," he continued, lowering his head to brush Carling's temple with his lips. "But let me assure you, Neva and Clayton, that my intentions toward your daughter are honorable and always have been, and I would never—" he paused and cleared his throat—choking back a laugh, Carling was sure "—sully her spotless reputation by anticipating our wedding night. Carling is definitely not pregnant now, but I hope she will be by this time next month."

Carling's heart plummeted and her stomach jumped, causing a dreadful upheaval in her middle. If she'd been made of weaker stuff, she would have burst into tears on the spot.

Instead, she tried to pry his arm from around her waist as she bared her teeth in a poor imitation of a smile. "Since we've cleared up that misunderstanding, let's rethink the entire Fairfax idea. If Mama has her heart set on giving us an engagement party and a big, fancy wedding, I certainly don't mind—"

"But I do mind, honey," Kane interjected. "I don't want to wait months while the wedding plans are in the works. Seems like a colossal waste of time to me. I want to take you home as soon as possible. It's settled, we're getting married today."

Though Carling burned to refute him, to refuse him, she stayed silent. She had no choice, and they both knew it. Kane McClellan was the one in charge and what he said, went. They both knew that, too. Like a master puppeteer, he controlled the strings and the Templetons, like marionettes, danced to his command—or else.

Carling and her father and Kane himself all knew what the unspoken but inevitable "or else" would be: the financial and political ruin of Senator Clayton Templeton and the public disgrace of the Templeton family. Carling looked at her mother, whose face was a study of confusion and concern, and tried to imagine the toll that such a scandal would have upon her.

The gossip, the gleeful speculation, the hounding by the media would forever change the pleasant, privileged existence which Neva Carling Templeton had enjoyed for all of her fifty-five years. As for Carling's father...well, she'd already spent hours agonizing over his fate if she were not to come to his rescue. She might be furious with him for putting her in this position, disillusioned with him for using her in this way, but he was her father. She loved him and would do whatever she could to help him. There was no use thinking about it anymore, no use looking for a way out.

She had to accept it. She was going to marry Kane McClellan today—in a quickie, impersonal marriage mill because his wish was literally her command.

Carling swallowed hard. "I guess we're on our way to Fairfax then," she said bleakly. Her acting talent didn't extend to pretending that she was happy. She turned her head slightly to look up at Kane, although she assiduously avoided meeting his eyes. "If you'll let me go, I'll get my jacket and purse and we can leave."

"Of course, sweetheart." Kane smiled. But before he released her, he dropped a quick hard kiss on her mouth in an unmistakable brand of possession. She shivered.

"Hurry back to me," he said. He deceptively made it sound like a request. Carling knew it was an order.

Her face flushed and blue eyes glittering, Carling raced up the stairs at a most unladylike breakneck speed.

Kane's eyes followed her until she reached the top and disappeared from view. He flicked his gaze to Senator and Mrs. Templeton, who were watching him uneasily. He read regret and wariness in the senator's eyes, curiosity and corresponding wariness in Neva's. He treated them to his most confidence-inducing smile. "There's nothing to worry about," he said reassuringly. "Everything is going to be all right, I promise you."

The senator nodded nervously. "Of course, we know that. It's just that—that—Carling is our little girl." His voice broke and he took a deep breath in an attempt to regain his composure. "We—Neva and I—have always wanted the best for her."

"I understand. I'm going to take good care of her," Kane assured him. "Perhaps she isn't too happy with the idea of this quick wedding, but she will be content and secure married to me."

"We've always dreamed we would give her a grand wedding with all the flourishes," Neva said mournfully. "Carling in a stunning white gown and bridal veil, Clayton walking her down the aisle of the National Cathedral, a wonderful reception at the club with all our friends . . .'' Her voice trailed off.

There was a long moment of silence. Kane guessed that he was now supposed to allow the Templetons to produce the kind of wedding extravaganza that they'd always dreamed of throwing for their little girl, who was not a little girl at all, he thought with a smile. Carling was most definitely a woman, and in a short while she would be his wife just as he'd wanted.

It didn't surprise him that he was about to realize his goal. He always managed to succeed in whatever he set out to achieve or acquire.

He remembered the first time he'd become aware of Carling Templeton. His younger sister Holly had shown him a pictorial coverage of a society party in one of the Texas monthly magazines. While Holly admired the glamorous designer dresses worn by the ever-fashionable belles, Kane found his attention riveted by one beautiful young woman in particular.

The caption under the photograph identified her as Carling Templeton, the senator's daughter.

Over the next few months, he found himself scanning sections of local magazines and newspapers he'd never bothered with before. Carling's photographic appearances were frequent, but it took him a while to admit that for some inexplicable, unfathomable reason, the senator's daughter—who was probably an airheaded party girl—intrigued him.

He'd been a longtime contributor to Clayton Templeton's campaign war chest and regularly received invitations to various political fund-raisers and constituency meetings. He finally decided to attend one featuring an appearance by the senator's wife and daughter. It was time to find out if Carling was a shallow little idiot or the woman he wanted her to be. . . .

The question was resoundingly answered on their first meeting. From that moment, Kane wanted Carling. His blood heated at the mere thought of her. She stirred his imagination as no other woman ever had. So he'd bided his time, waiting and watching, dropping hints, both broad and subtle, to her father.

Finally, it had all come together. As an astute businessman with faultless instincts, he had hardly believed the poor judgment and impulsive greed that had sent a desperate, disconsolate Senator Templeton to him. He'd seen his chance and taken it. Kane knew all about opportunity knocking and when and how to respond.

He also knew his own worth, but was under no illusions about his charm—or the lack of it. He was hardworking, outspoken and set in his ways; he preferred to lead a quiet life with few intrusions and little socializing. He knew he lacked the flair of a party-loving extrovert, and could have never wooed and won Carling Templeton in traditional, social fashion.

Then he'd noticed that no other man in her exalted circles seemed capable of wooing and winning her, either. She dated the most eligible young bachelors that Washington, Houston and Dallas had to offer and invariably the relationships went nowhere.

The first time he had observed her, he understood why. She was friendly but reserved, classy and cool, intelligent and charming, the ideal date for those exclusive parties, benefit balls and other elite social functions she was forever attending. But missing were any of those nuances that a sexually eligible and interested woman sends to a potential lover. She was strictly look-but-don't-touch, all polite, charming talk but absolutely no physical action.

"Carling Templeton is an icicle," he'd overheard one disgruntled charm-boy tell another. "Ask anyone and they'll tell you. She's so cold she could freeze liquid nitrogen."

Had anyone asked him, Kane would have disagreed. Carling played it cool—okay, icy, he conceded—but the chemistry arcing between them on their first meeting was as explosive as magnesium to a flame. And that was very explosive indeed, as he remembered from a botched experiment in chem lab. Adding to that was the way she had responded to him today when he'd taken her into his arms. The heat they'd generated was the embodiment of every fantasy he'd ever had about her.

Oh yes, Kane told himself with characteristic infallible conviction; this marriage was going to work out very well indeed.

"Kane?" Neva's voice intruded upon his reverie, jarring him out of it. "Could we possibly prevail upon you to set a wedding date several months from today? Though Carling might not have told you, I know how very much she would love to have the big wedding of her dreams. She used to absolutely adore playing wedding with her paper dolls when she was small. I bought her hundreds of those bride-and-groom sets and she would carefully cut out every single—"

"Mama, I'm sure Kane isn't interested in hearing about my paper doll games." Carling rejoined them in the hall, wearing a tailored beige jacket and matching pencil-slim skirt. She'd switched to a pair of teal blue leather shoes, the shade perfectly matching her blouse, the three-inch heels high and slender, bolstering her height to an impressive five foot nine. Still, she felt dwarfed by Kane's towering frame.

She had also recombed her hair, pulling it into a sleek, smooth chignon without a single strand out of place. She'd fixed her makeup, too, obliterating all traces of that deep, hot kiss they'd shared...

No, she quickly amended—that he'd *forced* upon her.

"Carling, dear, I was just explaining to Kane how we would adore having a wonderful old-fashioned wedding," Neva said eagerly. "Perhaps you two could talk it over and—"

"The thought of a great big society wedding makes my blood run cold," Kane said bluntly. "I can't think of anything I'd hate more."

There was a long moment of silence which wasn't broken until Senator Templeton cleared his throat to speak. "Neva, if Kane and Carling have made up their minds to have a quiet, private wedding, we have to respect their decision."

"Thanks for your support, Senator. I appreciate it," said Kane dryly.

A million nasty, caustic rejoinders leaped to mind, but Carling refrained from uttering any one of them. What was the point? Even if Kane had suggested getting married in a new-age ceremony deep in the bowels of some damp creepy bat cave, her father would have supported him.

"You two are welcome to come along and be our witnesses," suggested Kane. "Afterward, we'll have a celebration dinner at Washington's best restaurant, my treat. Just name the place and I'll phone for reservations right now."

"No, no, you two run along," Neva interjected quickly. "Clayton is right. If you want a private wedding, you should have it. And instead of going to a restaurant, why don't you come back to the house afterward? I'll have the cook prepare a special wedding dinner for us here—so much more celebratory and festive than merely dining out."

Neva shepherded them toward the door as she talked, while the senator stood in the background, staring silently at the floor. Within moments, Carling and Kane were standing outside on the small brick stoop, the front door closed firmly behind them.

"I can see that we come from two different worlds," Kane remarked dryly. "In my family, dining out is considered celebratory and festive—eating dinner at home is the everyday routine."

"That is only one of the minor differences between us. There are several million *major* differences as well," snapped Carling. "Which is why the idea of us getting married is not only absurd but sure to be calamitous."

"We're more alike than you realize. The fact that you agreed to marry me proves it."

"I didn't agree, I had no choice, so it proves nothing at all!" She shrugged off his hand when he placed it on her elbow to lead her to his rental car parked in front of the house.

"Doesn't it bother you to know that you're being married strictly for your money?" she demanded. The urge to provoke him, to goad him, was irresistible. "I thought rich men wanted to be married for themselves, not for their fortunes. But not you! What kind of—of weird misfit are you, anyway?"

"The kind of weird misfit who's about to become your husband," he replied complacently.

"That's it! I've had all I can take!" Carling shrieked, her eyes darkening with rage. Abandoning all attempts to stay cool, giving into the ferocious anger pulsing through her, she drew back her hand and slapped him hard across the cheek.

Three

The sound seemed to reverberate around them. Kane laid his fingers to his stinging cheek. "That hurt, Carly," he said coolly. "But you meant it to, of course. Now are you ready to pay the price?"

His other hand snaked out to seize her wrist. Slowly, deliberately, he started to pull her toward him.

She held herself rigid, trying to hold back, but once again his greater strength overcame her resistance. Against her will, she found herself inching toward him.

"You were asking for it! You deserved it and worse!" She sounded fierce, but her anger had been momentarily displaced by pure shock—with herself. "I've never slapped anyone before in my entire life. I happen to be a firm believer in nonviolence, but you forced me into it!"

"Let me get this straight—it's my own fault I got hit? I *made* you do it?"

"Yes!" She tried to jerk her wrist from his steely grip.

"You subscribe to the blame-the-victim school of thought, I see." One final tug brought her up against him. "Let's settle this issue once and for all, Carly. I don't believe in domestic violence and I sure as hell don't believe in letting my future wife haul off and belt me. I want an apology."

"I'm not sorry!" Oh, but she was. Not only for having hit him, but also for the consequences her rash action had provoked. The way he towered over her made her instinctively want to retreat. She frantically tried to take a step back, to put some much-needed distance between them, but it was too late. He had already wrapped his hard, muscular arms around her, firmly anchoring her against him.

"Go on and fight me, baby," he taunted huskily. "You know you want to."

"I do not! I'm hardly the fighting, spitting, scratching she-cat type, Mr. McClellan. If that's what you're looking for in a wife, I suggest you continue your search."

She drew her head back a little and looked up at him. He was so tall and so powerful, simply being near him made her feel vulnerable, and the sensation was intensified when she was in his arms. An alarming weakness began to spread through her, making her feel small and soft and....

"My search for a wife has ended, Carly," he drawled. "When you go to bed tonight, you'll be Mrs. Kane McClellan."

Her mouth went dry. A vivid image of herself lying nervous and naked, waiting for Kane McClellan to come to her, flashed across her mind. "I believe I should warn you that I'm as cold in bed as out of it." She tried for her most forbidding tone of voice, one that had never failed to discourage even the most audacious suitor. "Hardly an enticing bridal prospect for a—a hotheaded savage like yourself."

Kane was not discouraged. Far from it. "You've honed that prim icicle act of yours to such perfection that even you're beginning to believe it. But I don't buy it, Carly."

He settled her intimately against his big frame. For one heart-stopping moment, the soft mound of her femininity pressed against his erection. Carling gasped at the sharp, dizzying sensation piercing her.

"Under that glacial veneer is a little wildcat," Kane murmured softly, seductively. But he didn't release her; she remained a captive in his arms, the soft, warm curves of her body fitted against and into the sturdy masculine planes of his.

"Let go of me!" she cried, fighting the syrupy warmth stealing through her. That was the only struggle she could hope to win. She'd already learned that it was useless to pit her physical strength against his. She remembered only too well how she'd fought him in the hall earlier, how he'd effortlessly held her and kissed her. Those same hot ripples of pleasure she'd experienced then were building within her again.

He was holding her against her will, but he wasn't hurting her, and it horrified her that some dark primitive part of her was actually responding to his caveman tactics.

"If you don't let me go this minute, one of the neighbors will undoubtedly call the police!" she threatened. The need to lash out at him warred against the urge to melt into him—and won.

"They will?" He sounded genuinely curious. "Why?"

"Because you're molesting me in full public view!"

Kane laughed so hard that he let her go. "Molesting you?" Then he howled all over again.

"It's not funny!" Scowling, Carling quickly moved away from him. "I'm sure that in the isolated wastelands of your ranch your barbaric uncouth behavior goes unnoticed, but may I remind you that we happen to be in a civilized neighborhood where—"

"A man on his way to his wedding is not allowed to touch his fiancée?" Kane suggested helpfully. "Somehow I think that's permissible, even in the most proper neighborhoods."

"Dammit, what do I have to do, what do I have to say to make you take me seriously?" she practically shouted, her cheeks flushed with fury and frustration—and arousal.

"I do take you seriously, sweetheart. What could be more serious than marriage?" He opened the front door of the car, on the passenger side. "Get into the car, Carly. We're leaving."

"I didn't apologize for hitting you," she reminded him quickly. She was stalling for time, grasping at straws. The marriage mill awaited; once she'd gotten into the car with him, she would be doomed.

"You will, eventually." He glanced at his watch. "Carly, if you don't get into the car, I'm afraid I'll have to put you in myself, right in full view of your scandal-mongering neighbors."

It took her less than a second to decide. Tilting her chin regally, she climbed into the car, pausing only to shoot him a smoldering look of dislike. He couldn't have realized how effective his threat about the neighbors actually would be. The proliferation of newspaper and television tabloids had created a wide-open market for those wanting to cash in on scenes and scandals. Someone would be only too happy to report—or film with their home video camera?—Senator Templeton's socialite daughter brawling with a Neanderthal cowboy in front of the Templeton home.

It galled her that she had to obey him but she did, deriving some small satisfaction by sitting as far away from him as the front seat would allow. They drove in silence, Kane weaving in and out of the dense, early-afternoon traffic with an expertise that not even Carling could fault.

"Your father gave me directions to this place when he called me last night," he said. As a conversational sally, it fell flat. Carling stared in icy silence, her lips compressed tightly.

He fiddled with the radio, looking for a station and then asked her to suggest her favorite. She snapped that she didn't listen to the radio in the car. While driving, she preferred to play her foreign language tapes. Thanks to them, she was fluent in Spanish, did passably well with French and was currently learning conversational Japanese.

He shrugged and found a country-western station.

"Your favorite type of music, I presume?" she remarked caustically after a forlorn ballad about loneliness, fast nights and faithless women ended with a guitar-strumming finale.

"You presume correctly," he said. His smile was clearly a peace offering.

One she did not accept. "That figures. It's the only type of music that I absolutely can't abide."

Kane turned the volume higher and the sound of banjos filled the car. "I gave you first choice, honey. Now you're stuck with my choice. A little lesson for the future, maybe?"

"I don't take lessons from you!"

"How about some advice then? I'm more than willing to meet you halfway, but if you're determined to challenge me at every turn, I won't back down or back away. And, baby, you'll end up losing every time."

"That's what you think, you insufferable, arrogant macho clod! If you insist on marrying me, *you'll* be the one in need of lessons and advice. Because *I* do not lose and I'm not about to start now."

"You never lose?" He pretended to ponder that. "I guess it would be insufferable, arrogant and macho of me to point out that you once swore never to have anything to do with me, yet now you're on your way to our wedding."

He paused and reached for her hand, tucking it to rest beneath his hand on his thigh. Because she was sitting so far away from him, her arm was completely outstretched. It was uncomfortable and looked foolish, she knew, but she refused to move closer.

"I'm glad you consider our wedding your own personal victory, sweetheart," Kane continued silkily. "I feel the same. You see how alike we are? A perfect match."

His smooth tone didn't fool her for a minute. He was deliberately baiting her! Carling felt the rough denim of his jeans against her palm, felt the rock-hard muscle of his thigh beneath the cloth. His big hand was covering hers, engulfing it, his fingers lightly stroking hers.

A bolt of electricity rocked her. How could he manage to antagonize and arouse her at the same time? Confusion and rage ripped through her, short-circuiting her emotions. She felt like laughing and crying. Never had she met anyone who could rattle her this way. Everything he did, everything he said, got under her skin and provoked a wild reaction. In fact, he didn't even have to do or say a thing, she acknowledged grimly. His mere presence unsettled and unnerved her.

Glaring balefully at him, she jerked her hand away, rubbing the aching muscles of her arm with her other hand.

Kane appeared to be unaware of her turmoil. "I'm a bit surprised that your parents didn't come with us," he remarked as they passed the road signs welcoming them to the state of Virginia. "It's all or nothing with them, hmm? If their only daughter's wedding isn't a newsworthy super-spectacular, they can't be bothered to attend the ceremony."

"Don't you dare criticize my parents!"

"I wasn't criticizing—well, yes, maybe I was. Still, I admire your loyalty to them, no matter what."

"My parents deserve my love and loyalty and they'll always have it."

"Very admirable," Kane said, nodding his approval. "I understand and appreciate your support for your parents. You have a strong sense of family, Carly. It's a value I share, and shared values are a prerequisite to a successful marriage. That's one of the reasons why I know we're well matched."

"*You* have a family? Reptiles don't, as a rule, you know. I assumed you were hatched before you crawled out from under your rock, like the rest of your species."

He said nothing, irritating her further. She glanced at him covertly. He appeared to be concentrating completely on the roadway. Two of his fingers were lightly tapping the steering wheel, keeping time with the beat of the song blasting from the radio.

For some unfathomable reason, which Carling didn't even try to comprehend, she couldn't stand being ignored by him. Fighting with him was far more preferable. If being likened to a reptile didn't bother him, then perhaps an attack on his family would draw some blood?

"You have the nerve to condemn *my* parents for not coming to this—this farce of a wedding ceremony of ours," she began, her blue eyes alight with a combative glitter. "Well, where are *your* parents? I certainly don't see any evidence of this great family love and loyalty you're boasting about."

"My parents are dead," Kane said flatly.

Carling closed her eyes and suppressed a groan. Her social blunders were few and far between and rarely of this magnitude. "I didn't know," she mumbled. She was so mortified that her hostility was temporarily replaced by her horrified embarrassment.

"I'm terribly sorry." The words came easily, almost automatically. Because over the years she had accompanied her father to countless viewings and funerals of his assorted constituents and colleagues, it was natural for her to slip into that mode.

"Are you?" Kane challenged. "Since you didn't know my folks and you profess to hate me, why should you be sorry?"

She'd never had her perfunctory proclamation of sympathy questioned before. Carling was flustered. "Well, because—I—of course, I didn't know them but I'm sorry—that is, I'm certainly not glad to hear that they—uh—passed away."

Her face flamed. A practiced, smooth public speaker, she'd never made such a mangled mess of a remark in her life. She was determined to make amends and regain her composure. "How— When did you lose your parents, Kane?"

"They're not lost, they're dead," he said bluntly. "I know you probably mean well, but I detest euphemisms."

She swallowed. "I grew up speaking in euphemisms. It's practically the official language of politics."

"How true. Just this morning I heard two congressmen on the radio, debating the pros and cons of 'negative tax reduction' and 'revenue enhancement.'"

"Two of the more creative terms used in order to avoid that dreaded, guaranteed election-loser known as raising taxes," she admitted sheepishly.

The quick, droll smile he gave her made her feel a warm thrust deep in her abdomen. Carling forgot to exhale. When her body demanded that she begin breathing again, she had to gulp for air. She was in deep, deep trouble and she knew it. When his smile affected her so profoundly...when his touch made her burn with a restlessness she had never previously experienced . . .

Carling tensed. She couldn't be softening toward him! The thought was too appalling to imagine. She shook her head, as if to shake off the idea. She would not, could not, be seduced by this arrogant, infuriating man.

He was *buying* her, Carling reminded herself bitterly. He'd written a check to obtain her, as if he were paying for a bag of groceries at a supermarket. A helpless rage streaked through her. Being his bought-and-paid-for-bride would certainly mean the loss of her freedom and independence. A domineering man like Kane McClellan would settle for nothing less than total subservience to him.

He was forcing her to give up everything that was important to her, her home and friends and social activities, to lead a life of reclusive desolation on his wretched ranch deep in the middle of no-man's-land. But he couldn't force her to like him or care for him or want him, she reassured herself. He was her enemy and she wasn't about to forget it. And oh, would she make him sorry that he had purchased her so cold-bloodedly!

"You asked how and when my folks died," Kane said, breaking into her vengeful fantasies and successfully disconcerting her once again. "They were killed in a car accident twelve years ago, a week after my twenty-third birthday. One of my younger brothers was with them and was critically injured. He died ten days later."

She wasn't so cold-hearted that she could be indifferent to such a monumental tragedy, even if he was her avowed enemy. Carling temporarily shelved her diabolical fantasies of how to make his life unendurable. "It must have been terrible," she said quietly. "I can't imagine losing my parents. And to lose your brother, too..."

Her voice trailed off. It was too awful to contemplate, let alone put into words. Her all-purpose "I'm sorry" just didn't cover the enormity of it.

"It was tough."

She saw him tighten his grip on the steering wheel and somehow understood the volume of emotion behind those three simple words. "What happened?"

"They were driving my brother John back to college when they were hit head-on by a drunk driver going the wrong way on the interstate. John was twenty-one and a senior at Rice University. My old alma mater," he added with a slight smile.

"You graduated from Rice?" That was a surprise. She thought he'd never ventured from the old homestead.

Kane nodded. "I went on to the Wharton School of Business after graduation. I'd planned to become an investment banker—you know, live in New York, make a pile of money. I was just finishing up my MBA at the time of the accident."

Her eyes slid over him. From the moment she'd first seen him, she had thought he looked the part of the quintessential cowboy. This new information caused her preconceptions to shift as she tried to picture him in a custom-tailored suit, sitting behind a desk in a Wall Street office.

She simply couldn't. He looked like a man who worked outdoors, one who could chop a cord of wood in his spare time and not even get winded. A citified, desk-bound Kane McClellan was beyond her ken. "You—obviously didn't go to New York," she ventured a guess.

"No. I went home immediately. In addition to the ranch, there were the other kids—my two little brothers and my baby sister. There was a big age gap between the three of them and John and me. Our mother had had several miscarriages during those years and had given up hope of having any more kids. Then Scott finally arrived when I was eleven. Holly was born two years later and then Tim just a year after that."

"So they were very young when your parents were killed." Carling did some quick mental arithmetic. "Twelve, ten and nine. How sad for those poor children!"

"I was named their legal guardian and returned to the ranch to raise them. They're all grown up now. And doing well, too." He flashed a proud, fraternal smile. "Tim is a brilliant student at Rice. He's a senior this year and has already been accepted into medical school. Last year Holly graduated from a women's college in Atlanta and is currently living at the ranch, learning the ropes. I think she has her heart set on becoming a rancher's wife, and nothing could please me more," he added with satisfaction.

"She's very young. Does she want to get married?" Carling asked coolly. "Or are you arranging a marriage for her in your inimitable feudal fashion?"

He ignored the jibe. "The Waynes, our nearest neighbors, have a son, Joseph, who's Holly's age, and the two of them have been seeing a lot of each other since Holly returned home. They don't need me to arrange things for them. As for Scott, he majored in partying at the University in Austin, but after six years finally managed to graduate and, thankfully, seems to have settled down. He's now a bank management trainee in Dallas.''

''It sounds as if you did a good job raising them,'' Carling said with grudging admiration. It couldn't have been easy for a young man in his early twenties to take sole responsibility for three children, along with having to cope with the terrible grief of losing the other half of his family.

But somehow it didn't surprise her that Kane McClellan had successfully done so. She was already learning that he was the kind of person who achieved what he set out to do. And then she was struck by a ghastly insight: since Kane had been forced by fate to give up his plans and change his life, he probably had no compunction about expecting her to do the same!

He would never understand the magnitude of her loss of freedom. Hadn't he accepted and adjusted in a similar situation? No wonder he fully expected her to settle down to domestic life on that godforsaken ranch without regret or a backward glance—he had done the same thing.

''There were some rough times, though, particularly when the kids were teenagers,'' Kane admitted. ''Tim was always easygoing and dependable, a pleasure to have around, but Scott and Holly each went through a rebellious period. Fortunately, that's all behind us.''

''What do they think about your crazy idea of marrying a woman you hardly know and they don't know at all?'' she demanded. The brief frown that crossed his face was all the answer she needed. ''They don't know!'' she accused. ''You didn't tell them you were getting married. You're planning to spring me on them—''

"I don't have to clear my actions with the kids. They—"

"But I bet *they* have to clear their actions with *you*," Carling interrupted snidely. "You wouldn't have it any other way. Growing up with you in charge must've been like living in a totalitarian regime."

"The kids and I get along very well," Kane insisted. "In fact, seeing how well the three of them turned out has given me the confidence and inspiration to raise children of my own."

Carling froze. This was where she came into the picture. "I don't know very much about children," she said swiftly. "I'm an only child with no cousins near my age and I never had baby-sitting jobs when I was a teenager."

"You'll be a fine mother," Kane said soothingly. "Maternal instinct goes a long way and there are plenty of books and videos on child care to fill in the gaps. Besides, I'll be right there to help you. I intend to be a very involved father, not an absent one."

"I'm not worried about what kind of mother I'll be," Carling gritted out through clenched teeth. "But when I have children, I want it to be my choice and with the man of my choice."

"He's sitting right beside you, sweetheart. You just haven't realized it yet. But you will. As for when to have kids, for us it's the sooner the better. Our biological clocks are ticking away."

"I have quite a few years before the alarm goes off!" she protested indignantly.

"You may not have had much experience with children, but you like them," he continued, his voice smooth and sure. "You enjoy your friends' and neighbors' children. You want a baby of your own—

in fact, several of them. You don't want to raise an only child because you were often lonely growing up."

He was repeating comments she'd made in public over the years, and they were all true. But hearing him use her own words to bolster *his* position was like being shot down with her own ammunition. "Don't quote me to myself!" she snapped.

He merely smiled. "You'll be a conscientious full-time mother, who can devote herself completely to her family without the demands and hassles of an outside career interfering with your primary responsibilities."

Uh-oh! Carling gulped. She recognized that statement. She'd said it often enough to the various conservative groups, which were the foundation of her father's political strength. She tried to come up with an effective rebuttal, but nothing came to mind. When she opened her mouth to speak, there were no words to be said.

"No comment?" Kane asked mildly.

Carling clenched her fists. He had her there, and he knew it! Though his expression was calm and implacable, she was absolutely certain that he was silently, triumphantly laughing at her.

"I should've guessed that a sexist pig like you wouldn't approve of—of career women!" She had to admit to herself it was a rather weak salvo coming from her, the senator's daughter, who regularly took potshots at career women because they were easy targets in the domestic arena of the political battlefield. If Kane were any kind of a gentleman, he would let it pass and not call her on it.

Naturally, that didn't happen and call her on it he did. "Lame, Carly." This time he didn't bother to conceal his laughter. "You and your daddy and his crowd are the ones who lambaste women who choose careers instead of total domesticity, not me. I happen to respect them. That's why I would never ask a woman who has invested years of her life in studying for a profession, who has built a successful career, to leave it all to become a full-time wife and mother on my ranch. It wouldn't be fair to her."

"You mean if I were a doctor or lawyer or teacher or something, you wouldn't—wouldn't—"

"Be interested in marrying you? That's correct, I wouldn't. Because I'd know you would be unhappy, far from the city and your profession, and I don't want an unhappy wife. I told you I'd researched this very seriously, Carly. You were raised to be a wife and mother. You believe a woman is happiest devoting herself to raising a family. And that's exactly what you're going to spend the rest of your life doing. With me."

She couldn't speak, she couldn't breathe. For one wild moment, she wondered if he were an agent for one of those opposition groups her father and his allies were always at war with, an enemy whose assignment it was to make her live the words she so glibly espoused.

She was trapped, and the hopelessness of her situation struck her with renewed force. "Oh, what's the use in trying to reason with you? Talking to you is like talking to a brick wall." How she wished she could come up with something more original, but she was too overwrought to be clever. He had already bested her at every turn.

"So I've been told," Kane agreed with maddening good humor. "Relax, Carly, everything is going to work out fine. Do you really think I would marry you if I thought there was a chance that it wouldn't?''

''I have no faith in your judgment. I think you're insane! Who else but a crazy man would insist on marrying a—a woman who hates him, who is determined to make his life a misery beyond anyone's wildest imagination!''

''Is that what you're planning, Carly? To make my life miserable?'' He sounded amused.

''Oh yes,'' she vowed with heartfelt vehemence. ''I guarantee that you'll find living with me so intolerable, you'll soon be begging me to go.''

''And I guarantee that won't happen,'' he replied with equal intensity. ''Loyalty is an intrinsic part of your character, Carly. This marriage of ours proves how loyal a daughter you really are. It goes without saying that you will be loyal and loving to your husband, and to your children as well. Anyway, if you were to be honest with yourself, you'd admit that it's time for a change in your life. You weren't happy with things the way they were. The party-social circuit was beginning to pall for you,'' he added with a certainty that took her breath away.

''You've said a lot of outrageously arrogant things today, but you—you've outdone yourself with that one,'' she spluttered furiously. ''I was thoroughly enjoying my life exactly the way I was living it. For you to say otherwise is to—''

''State the facts,'' he finished calmly. ''I happen to know them, honey. Your father has been hounding you unmercifully to hook up with a husband with enough money to keep the Templetons in the style to which they've become accustomed. So you went through the motions of looking for Mr. Rich. You dated Quentin Ramsey's boy, Jed, and Cole Tremaine, to name only your most recent candidates.''

"Who are you? A member of some spy network? How do you know so much about my personal life?''

"Meticulous research. I used the same approach in choosing a wife that I do in my investments, Carly. There is little—if anything—about you that I don't know.''

"Is that so?'' She glared at him. No woman could listen to a man make such a smug, doggedly confident statement about her without feeling homicidal. Unfortunately, she would have to limit herself to verbally annihilating him.

"Yes. And I noticed an interesting pattern in your behavior. You seemed to have an uncanny knack of finding ways to keep the men you were supposedly considering as matrimonial prospects from considering *you* as one.''

She'd been mulling over the most insulting, vicious thing she could possibly say to him, but he threw her completely off balance with that observation. It was disturbingly close to the mark, and of course, she denied it. "I don't know what you're talking about, but it doesn't matter because nothing you say interests me anyway.''

He laughed. "You no more wanted to marry Jed Ramsey than you wanted to hike barefoot across the desert, but you pressured him, let him think that you and your father were cooking up a conspiracy with his father to drag him to the altar. Naturally, poor Jed took off—what self-respecting bachelor wouldn't? And you were saved from your father's expectations because Ramsey married another woman not very long afterward.''

She folded her arms across her chest and stared stonily ahead, pretending that she wasn't listening to him. But she was.

"And then there was Cole Tremaine," Kane continued. "Infinitely eligible, everything your father wanted in a husband for you. Wealthy, handsome, successful, from a good family. But did you even try to make him see you as a desirable, sexually eligible woman? No, you played it strictly as friends. A sexless, platonic, this-relationship-will-go-nowhere friendship. It came as no surprise when he married another woman, except to your poor, desperate father."

"And now look who I'm stuck with!" she burst out. "Anyone else I've ever dated would have been infinitely preferable to *you!*"

"Because I turn you on like no other man ever has and you don't know how to handle it?"

"Because you're the most conceited, revolting chauvinistic tyrant I've ever met!"

"That's not it at all. You can't help responding to me and you're scared to death of losing that icy control you've encased yourself in. But you're going to lose it. The barriers come down tonight."

"No!"

"Oh yes, sweet Carly." His grin was positively wicked.

"I won't even dignify that with a reply," she sniffed with a grand, self-righteous air.

"We're here," Kane announced a short time later, as he braked to a stop in a wide parking lot adjacent to a tall office building.

They walked inside, his hand resting on the small of her back in a proprietary fashion. This must be the way a condemned prisoner feels on his way to meet the firing squad, Carling thought bleakly. Hopeless, helpless, with all appeals for a reprieve denied.

A kind of merciful numbness set in, and as if in a trance, she went through the motions of filling out forms, getting a blood test and waiting the requisite few hours for a marriage license. Kane stayed at her side, alternately talkative and silent, frequently touching her, watching her, his gray eyes intense and blatantly sensual.

Finally, they were ushered before the judge who pronounced them man and wife and then wished them well. Carling stared down at the thick gold wedding band on the third finger of her left hand, the ring that Kane had placed there. Because she couldn't take her eyes off it, she was surprised when Kane cupped her chin with his big hand and tilted it upward.

Their eyes met. "Isn't this the part where the groom traditionally kisses his bride?" he asked softly.

He lowered his head and lightly pressed his mouth to hers.

She was too startled, too dazed to react the way she would have, had she not been so off balance. His lips were warm and full on hers, gentle and unthreatening. Her eyelids felt oddly heavy and dropped shut. He seductively increased the pressure as his mouth opened over hers and unconsciously, instinctively, she put her hand on his chest.

She could feel his solid, muscular strength and the steady thudding of his heart beneath her palm. When his tongue slipped into her mouth and massaged hers, a twinge of pure physical desire pierced her deeply.

Her eyes flew open at the same moment that he lifted his lips from hers. She was aware that her face was flushed and that her breathing had quickened. It was no use denying it, not even to herself: for one fleeting moment she had been oblivious of their surroundings, to the dull, institutional setting of the judge's office, even to the judge himself.

"Ready to go, Mrs. McClellan?" Kane asked huskily, taking her hand in his. "The sooner we get the celebration dinner with your parents over with, the sooner we can be alone together."

Carling made a strangled, incoherent reply. An aura of unreality enveloped her. This couldn't be happening! She was staring at the wedding ring again and the sound of "Mrs McClellan" was ringing in her ears. Mrs. McClellan—that was her!

She was married. Married! And to the one man she knew she could never control, could never keep at a distance, the one man who would never be content to let her go blithely on her way while he went his. She glanced wildly at him.

"This can't be happening," she whispered, vocalizing her thoughts.

"I made hotel reservations for tonight at a place near the airport," Kane kept talking as he walked her out of the room, out of the building, and back toward the car. "My plane is being serviced there and we'll fly out in the morning."

She couldn't let herself think about the two of them in a hotel room tonight. "Your plane?" she asked in an attempt to divert herself and him. Her throat was dry and her voice squeaked.

"It's a twin engine Cessna 310. Since I have a pilot's license, I flew it up myself. The ranch has its own small airstrip, so we'll be able to fly directly there tomorrow."

He had his own plane; his ranch had its own airstrip. He had been able to come up with a huge amount of money almost immediately and didn't look for repayment of the loan. For the first time, Carling realized just how wealthy Kane McClellan really was.

He was rich enough to buy the woman he professed to want for his wife, to marry her against her will. Rich enough to keep her for as long as he chose. Rich, strong and powerful enough to make her do whatever he wanted. It was a chilling observation and Carling shivered, despite the warm April sunshine.

The drive back to her parents' house was smooth and swift. Kane played the country-western station, sometimes whistling along with the music. Carling folded her hands tightly in her lap and rode in shaken silence. She couldn't waste her energy fighting with him, not now. She had to conserve every bit of her strength and her wits for tonight when she would successfully outsmart and outmaneuver her captor—her husband, Kane McClellan.

Four

Carling immediately recognized the caterer's van parked in her parents' driveway. *Capitol Affairs* was her mother's favorite catering service.

Kane read the logo printed on the van as he pulled up behind it. "So much for a home-cooked meal," he said, groaning. "I'd rather have gone to a restaurant than face this. Every catered meal I've ever eaten has tasted like warmed-over airline food."

"The food that *Capitol Affairs* serves has always been uniformly excellent," Carling retorted loyally. "They're the most popular catering service in the District."

"That's not saying a whole lot, especially since they're free to run over here on a moment's notice with their supply of edible plastics."

"It's a tribute to my mother that they're here on such short notice for a small simple family dinner..." Her voice trailed off. She'd just noticed all the cars lining the street, parked along both sides for as far as she could see. "Which might not be so small and simple after all."

Kane followed her gaze. "You don't think—" he began warily.

"That my mother has managed to throw together a party for us? That's exactly what I think."

"After I specifically said I didn't want a big society wedding?" Kane was frowning, clearly displeased.

His obvious displeasure, his disapproval, buoyed Carling's flagging spirits immensely. "We didn't have one," she reminded him. "And you made no objections to a large society reception afterwards."

"That's because it didn't occur to me to object. It didn't seem necessary. Who would ever suspect that anyone could put together an affair of this size in just a few hours?"

"That shows how little you know about Neva Templeton," Carling replied with a wry smile. "I should've known Mother was up to something—she gave up on the big wedding idea far too easily. No wonder she was so eager to get us out of the house. She must've started making phone calls before we were even in the car."

"Surely all those cars can't belong to your parents' guests?" Kane squinted at the seemingly endless lines of cars and scowled ferociously.

This was not at all what he had had in mind. He had considered even a quiet dinner with Carling's parents an intrusion, but he'd accepted it as a necessary obligation before commencing their wedding night.

"Unbelievable," he growled. "I hate big parties even when I know and like all the guests. Now I'm supposed to tolerate this extravaganza full of strangers?''

"They're not strangers to my family," countered Carling.

"Right. They're your thousands upon thousands of *close friends*."

"Well, since you insisted upon marrying a stranger, you might as well party with strangers, too."

He arched his eyebrows. "You're enjoying this, aren't you?" he drawled. "You didn't even try to keep the malicious glee out of your voice."

"If you're uncomfortable, unhappy or uneasy in any way, I'm thrilled. Although the idea of parading in there as Mrs. Kane McClellan is enough to make me break out in hives."

"Do you want to skip it and go directly to the hotel instead?" His smile was wolfish, his eyes challenging. As usual, he had completely ignored the insult, thereby putting her back on the defensive.

"No!" Carling hated the panic in her voice and hated Kane for putting it there. "I'd rather face any crowd, no matter how big or how curious, than be alone with *you!*"

Flinging open the car door, she rushed immediately toward the front door of the house. But by the time she'd reached it, Kane was already at her side, his long strides having easily closed the distance between them. He took her hand, interlacing his fingers with hers.

"Don't you want to present a united front to our well-wishers? We're supposed to be so wildly in love that we impulsively eloped, remember?"

Carling burned. That amused, slightly taunting tone of his was capable of driving her to mayhem. She, cool-as-ice Carling, never felt cool around him for very long, she admitted to herself. And instead of ignoring him with icy silence—her usual method of punishing those who angered her—she wanted to do something alarmingly physical to him.

Something like wiping that confident little smile off his face with the palm of her hand. Her mind conjured up another tantalizingly vicious possibility. She would give him a push with both her hands so that he lost his balance and fell to the ground; next, she would—

And then she felt his thumb begin to move over her palm, stroking in a slow suggestive rhythm, back and forth, up and down and around. The pad of his thumb was callused, abrasive against her soft, sensitive skin.

The caress affected her like an electric current, exploding in hot sparks in the deep, secret place between her legs. Carling drew in a sharp breath. The volatile pleasure made her head spin, and to her great shame she didn't gasp in outrage and jerk her hand away instantaneously. It wasn't until he lifted her hand to his mouth and pressed his lips against the palm he'd sensitized with his caress that a stunned Carling managed to summon enough willpower for the requisite gasping withdrawal.

"Don't!" she ordered in a voice far, far removed from the usual imperious tones she used to dissuade amorous would-be swains. Flushed and trembling, she found it impossible to look at him.

"Don't?" He pretended to be puzzled. "Why not? You liked it."

"I didn't!"

"You loved it, Carly. I was watching you. You were getting aroused from just that simple caress."

"That's purely wishful thinking based on your incredibly oversized ego!''

"It's a fact based on observation. I saw you squirming. You were squeezing your thighs together trying to—''

Carling uttered a strangled cry and pushed open the door. Her mother spotted her at once and proceeded to weave her way swiftly through the crowded vestibule toward her.

"Darling, you're here!'' Neva Templeton exclaimed joyfully, throwing her arms around her daughter. "Dixie Lee said that she thought she saw you and your handsome new husband coming up the walk. Oh, and here is that marvelous new son-in-law of mine!''

Carling whirled around to see Kane come up behind her. Neva instantly released her daughter to embrace him. "I can't wait to show you off to all our friends. Such a lovely couple!''

Linking one arm through Carling's and the other through Kane's, Neva purposefully steered them into the large living room, which was crowded to overflowing with guests. "Here are the bride and groom,'' she announced to everyone. "Mr. and Mrs. Kane McClellan.''

For just a fraction of a second, Kane's and Carling's eyes met. They exchanged mutual pained glances. He truly hated being in the spotlight. And while she usually thoroughly enjoyed being the center of attention, this time was the proverbial exception to the rule.

They were engulfed by swarms of people, and Carling reflexively slipped into her lifelong role as the gregarious, crowd-pleasing daughter of the perennial vote-seeking politician. She smiled and made the appropriate responses to the proffered remarks and remembered everyone's name. Her polished small talk was pleasant.

Kane, not a crowd-pleaser by birth or by choice, didn't even try to match his bride's performance. He stoically endured the endless introductions, but his expression remained serious and unsmiling as men shook his hand or slapped his shoulder, and women leaned up to kiss his cheek or hug him. The displays of faux affection were as disconcerting as the loud, meaningless conversations swirling around him. Did all the women have high-pitched voices that rose to eardrum-shattering decibels as they prattled on? Did all the men boom the guffaws which inevitably followed those spectacularly unfunny jokes?

One voice finally rose above them all—that of Senator Clayton Templeton. "Friends, we have a very special guest with us today and he is going to help us make this truly memorable day an absolutely unforgettable one."

Kane's lips twitched at the redundant hyperbole. The senator's speech writers must not have been available today. He glanced across the room at Carling, who was surrounded by a circle of excited, talkative young women.

"Carling, you sly dog, you!" squealed Marla Madison, who'd known Carling since their debutante days. "I can't believe you've been holding out on us! Keeping that *hunk* all to yourself until you grabbed the gold ring—literally!"

The women shrieked at the pun. Carling winced.

"Smart move, Carling," said Dixie Lee Shaw, the daughter of another southern senator. "The way

Marla has been drooling over the guy, she would've definitely posed a threat. You were right to see him on the sly until you nailed him.''

"What makes you think I'm no longer a threat?" Marla purred. "Husbands have been known to stray, you know. Kane McClellan would be worth waging an all-out campaign for. He's one of those *real* men that we city girls seldom get to meet. A man who can carry a woman to the bedroom without throwing out his back. A man who wouldn't borrow your mousse and blow-dryer to style his own hair. A man who can down a shot of whisky instead of sipping chilled white wine. A man who—''

"We get the idea, Marla," Debbie Marino, a long-time friend and neighbor of the Templetons, interjected dryly. "And your adultery plot—on Carling's wedding day!—goes beyond tastelessness, even for you."

"It's okay," Carling said hastily. A malevolent smile lit her face. "If Marla wants to make a play for Kane, let her try." What an ingenious solution to her dilemma! Marla was sultry and sexy. If she were to capture Kane's interest . . .

For one brief shining moment, Carling imagined herself gleefully agreeing to hand over her groom to the other woman. And as a condition to regaining his freedom, Kane would hand over the documents containing the records of his financial transactions on Senator Templeton's behalf. Her father would be free from the threat of investigation and she would be free from McClellan and the threat of life on his ramshackle ranch!

Her friends, completely unaware of her fantasy and the real reason behind her sudden marriage, totally misinterpreted her invitation to Marla.

"Carling is so sure that her man is crazy about her that she's challenging Marla to try to come between them!" exclaimed Cookie Loring, a Texas congressman's young second wife. "That's so sweet!"

"Every bride should feel such confidence in her new husband's love," Debbie Marino added warmly.

"Carling, do you plan to start a family right away or are you going to wait a few years?" asked Cookie.

Carling suppressed a groan. She couldn't take much more of this. She was grateful when Kim Hypes, one of her father's junior administrative assistants, joined them.

"Congratulations, Carling," Kim exclaimed with an approving smile. "Your father was beginning to worry that you'd never break out of the luncheon-shopping-party rut, but you did it! I hope you and Kane will be very happy. Of course, I know you will be! What could be more fun than living on a ranch?"

"I can think of at least three things," muttered Marla as Kim left to join another group. "Luncheons, shopping and parties. I'd rather be stuck in that rut than trapped in the wastelands of a Texas ranch."

"But she'll be trapped with a *real man*," Dixie Lee reminded her.

"True, but she can't spend *all* her time in bed with him," retorted Marla. "Carling, honey, what are you going to do with yourself when your sexy rancher is off roping steers? Will you take up quilting or churning butter or something?"

Carling felt sick. Hearing Marla outline the hellish existence awaiting her made her want to run screaming from the house. Living in isolation on a decrepit ranch, sex with Kane McClellan, quilting, churning... it was too awful to contemplate. What was she going to do?

"Carling, dearest, come on over here!" she heard her father call. "Reverend Wilkes has arrived and is going to perform the wedding ceremony, right here and now."

Reverend Wilkes from their church? *Wedding ceremony?* Carling was dumbfounded. She was pushed through the throng before she had a chance to utter a word. Reverend Wilkes was standing by the front window, holding the Templeton family Bible, an heirloom from three generations past. Kane arrived at the spot at the same time that she did. His face was devoid of expression, but there was a steely glint in his gray eyes.

"Your daddy and I respected your wish to have a very private wedding," Neva Templeton explained to her daughter. "But we couldn't bear not having your union blessed by the word of the Lord. Reverend Wilkes is here to marry the two of you all over again, this time in a religious ceremony."

She raised her eyes pleadingly to Kane. "I hope you don't mind, Kane. Of course, if you have any objections, Reverend Wilkes and the senator and myself will certainly understand."

"Of course I have no objections to a religious ceremony, Neva," said Kane. He glanced down at his bride's mutinous face. "I like the idea of being married twice to my beautiful bride. Makes the marriage seem airtight, hmm?"

That was exactly the way it struck Carling, too. She'd been able to distance herself somewhat from the unfamiliar judge and the brief, legal ceremony, which had been performed at the county building. But to have Reverend Wilkes marry them right here in her own house in front of friends and family, to have to listen to the familiar and meaningful biblical wedding phrases of the wedding ceremony...

A wedding like that combined the emotional with the intellectual, the spiritual with the secular. A wedding like that implied forever.

"Mama, there's really no need to drag Reverent Wilkes *or* the Lord into this," Carling whispered frantically. "I mean, what with—uh—everything going on in the world today, I'm sure they both have other more important things to deal with and—"

"I seem to recall that the Lord likes weddings," Kane put in. "Remember the one at Cana? And from the smile on Reverend Wilkes's face, it's obvious he's glad to be here too."

Neva beamed her approval. Carling shot Kane a black look.

"Reverend Wilkes," Senator Templeton exclaimed heartily. "Let's get on with it!"

"Dearly beloved," intoned the pastor, "we are gathered here today..."

It was adding insult to injury, Carling thought grimly. Rubbing salt into an open wound. Married twice to the same awful man. Forced to endure *two* marriage ceremonies against her will.

After the second ceremony was over, Carling was grateful for the multitude of guests. Their presence kept her away from her husband's side. During much of the boisterous reception, she and Kane McClellan weren't even in the same room—which suited Carling just fine.

It did not suit Kane at all. Ninety minutes of enforced socializing exceeded his tolerance by at least eighty minutes. He glanced at his watch, excused himself from the circle of people who surrounded him and moved purposefully from room to room until he spotted Carling. She was sitting in a corner of the den, engaged in conversation with an attractive young couple who were taking turns passing a fretful baby back and forth between them.

He immediately joined the group, barely glancing at the couple or the dark-haired infant currently being cuddled in its mother's arms. "We're leaving, Carly," he said without preamble.

Carling tried to swallow back the panic, which rose like bile in her throat. She couldn't leave yet. Leaving meant being alone with him and . . . She turned pale, unwilling to let herself consider exactly what that meant.

"Kane, you haven't met the Tremaines," she said quickly, in an effort to delay their departure. "This is Cole, Chelsea, and little Daniel. Daniel isn't having a very good time," she added with a smile at the baby, who was making small sounds of definite displeasure.

"He wants to go home and I'm in complete sympathy with him," Kane said. "I want to leave, too."

Carling winced. "This is my—my husband, Kane McClellan," she told the Tremaines. She watched the couple exchange frankly speculative glances and longed to sink through the floor.

"Cole Tremaine," Kane said thoughtfully. "You dated my wife before you married your own."

"That's true," Cole replied. He studied Kane with unconcealed curiosity. "Chelsea and I were astounded to read about your engagement in the paper today and even more astonished to receive Neva and Clayton's invitation to this party. We weren't aware that you and Carling were even—uh—dating."

Carling stared at the floor in embarrassed silence. She'd used her dates with Cole as a smoke screen in order to divert her father from his matchmaking campaign on behalf of Kane McClellan. Cole had been doing her a favor. There had never been a romance between them, and she'd been quite vocal in expressing to him her loathing for Kane McClellan— along with her determination to never marry the reclusive rancher. It was no wonder that the Tremaines were incredulous.

Incredulous *and* suspicious. Chelsea Tremaine shifted the baby in her arms and stared from Carling to Kane with questioning eyes. "Is everything all right?" Chelsea asked bluntly, the first person of the day to do so, the first one *not* to assume that this marriage was the culmination of a grand romance.

Carling was horrified to feel her eyes suddenly fill with tears and she gulped back the lump that swiftly lodged in her throat. Part of her, the pampered little girl who'd always been catered to and indulged, wanted to give into the tears and beg the Tremaines for help; Cole was a rich and powerful man and he could...

Could what? demanded the other part of her, the adult self, the one who'd taken on responsibility and recognized the irrefutable laws of cause and effect. Cole Tremaine couldn't help her father. She was the only one who could do that. There was no one who could help her.

"Carling, there's no need to pretend with us," Chelsea continued. Apparently, Carling's delay in replying had provided Chelsea with the answer. "If something's wrong, if you're in some kind of trouble, Cole and I will be glad to help you."

Cole nodded in affirmation.

"I'm sure my wife appreciates your loyalty," Kane replied dryly. He looked at Carling, his dark eyebrows arched. "Your friends are concerned about you, honey. Please tell them if there is anything wrong."

Carling held her head a little higher. How dare that snake bait her this way! But however vain or foolish it might be, she simply couldn't bring herself to admit to her well-meaning friends that she'd been literally trapped into marrying Kane McClellan. The Templeton pride, her own as well as her father's, was considerable—and deeply ingrained.

So much so that Carling forced herself to present a passable imitation of a smile and managed to ask gaily, "What could possibly be wrong? It's our wedding day. And we feel quite smug about having kept our—our relationship a secret from everyone. That's a major feat in this town where everybody knows everybody else's business."

Chelsea and Cole stared at her in patent disbelief. Kane was grinning, obviously amused by her performance. Carling longed to clobber him. But she didn't. Keeping up her performance, avoiding Cole's and Chelsea's eyes, she continued brightly, "And we can't leave the party just yet, Kane. It's too early and we're the guests of honor. We haven't even cut the cake yet or—"

"We'll cut the cake now and then you can go upstairs and pack a suitcase or two," Kane interjected. "I'll arrange for the rest of your things to be shipped to the ranch within the week." He nodded to the Tremaines, then placed his arm firmly around Carling's shoulders to lead her away.

"I want to stay. We *owe* it to everybody to stay," she insisted. She had to keep him at bay for at least a few more hours. Maybe by then she'd think up some plan of escape. She had to come up with something, but she needed more time. "My folks went to all the trouble and expense of giving this party for us and all these people cared enough to come and—"

"For the past interminable hour and a half, I've been heartily slapped and smacked. I've been joked with, fawned over, and even flirted with. Whatever I *owe* these good folks has been paid in full. As for the cost of the party, I fully expect your father to forward the bills to me as part of our agreement. So I feel no guilt about leaving while everybody stays and enjoys my hospitality."

Carling stopped short. "What do you mean, you expect Daddy to forward the bills to you as part of your agreement?" she demanded in a hoarse whisper.

"Your father asked me to pay all of your outstanding bills up to and including any incurred on our wedding day. I have no doubt that this party will be considered one of them."

"All my outstanding bills?" she repeated incredulously.

He nodded. "All your credit card bills, your phone bill, your car payments, your personal charge accounts at the local shops."

"No!" Carling felt her cheeks grow hot. She couldn't believe it—she wouldn't! "You're lying. Daddy isn't greedy. He wouldn't bleed you for money in any way and particularly not where I'm concerned."

"I try not to think in terms of greed and bleed, I prefer to take a more positive view," Kane said dryly. "So I looked upon acquiring your debts as a sort of dowry in reverse."

Glumly, she forced herself to face the facts. Kane wasn't lying; he was too frank, too outspoken, too *confident* to resort to that. Never had she felt so demoralized. Not only had her father sanctioned her sale to Kane McClellan, he'd stuck Kane with all her debts!

"I paid off your accounts but there was one bill I was curious about," Kane continued. His gray eyes were gleaming. "The three hundred dollars you charged at a store called *Her Secret*. Her secret what? And why did you need three hundred dollars worth of it?"

"I—I see my mother. I'll tell her about cutting the cake now," Carling said chokingly. She pulled away from him and fairly crashed through the crowd to reach her mother's side. She had to get away from Kane. Her whole body was one scarlet blush, right down to the dusky rose silk teddy she was wearing under her suit. Beautiful, feminine lingerie was her private weakness—and she bought much of it at *Her Secret*, an exclusive lingerie boutique.

But for Kane to know...for him to have paid for the very teddy and sheer silk stockings that she was wearing...Carling was horrified.

The cake cutting was accomplished in record time. Both Kane and Carling resisted the photographer's entreaties to feed each other a piece of wedding cake, an event which was to have been captured for posterity.

"I'm sorry but I simply can't eat a single bite of cake." Carling's voice was shrill with false gaiety.

"I've eaten entirely too much of all this wonderful food today." In truth, she hadn't touched a morsel; she was too nervous, her stomach too jumpy.

"I think I'll have dessert later," said Kane.

The jovial crowd found the sexual innuendo in his remark highly amusing and many ribald comments followed. Carling felt as if her smile was permanently plastered onto her face. She found none of the jokes even remotely funny; she vacillated from wanting to rage in fury at the jocular group to wanting to plead with them for help. But she did neither; she just kept on smiling.

"Upstairs," Kane murmured against her ear. "You have twenty minutes to pack and then we're leaving. I've had all the party fun I can handle."

It was a relief to leave the noisy crowd and escape to the quiet solitude of her room. For a few moments, Carling sat on her bed and stared out the window at the darkening sky. The earlier sunshine had been displaced by gray storm clouds, and the dismal gloom outdoors matched her mood. The unthinkable was about to happen, the unbelievable about to become reality. She was going to have to leave her home, her family and friends—to live with Kane McClellan.

But even that horror paled in comparison with her more immediate fate—going to bed with him tonight. Choking back a cry, Carling jumped up and sprang into action. Anything was better than passively sitting here and thinking about what awaited her. She retrieved her suitcases from a hall storage closet and began to pack.

She didn't stop until three suitcases and two canvas tote bags were stuffed to overflowing. Though the task was completed, she was loath to leave the peacefulness of her room. Carling grimaced as she recalled her mother stopping her on her way up the stairs and asking her if she was going to change into a "going-away outfit".

A "going-away outfit," indeed! What did a bought-and-paid-for slave wear when leaving for a life of servitude? She was tempted to slash a T-shirt and don her oldest pair of jeans in order to effect that holey, threadbare look, but she restrained herself.

What was the point? She'd learned enough about Kane today to know that he wouldn't care what sort of costume she chose to depart in. He would only laugh and make some maddeningly droll or suggestive remark. But her parents would be aghast, the guests titillated, and as for herself—her proper, always perfectly attired self—she would end up embarrassed.

Carling heaved a disgusted sigh. She would choose something appropriate to wear. Since she was leaving civilization, she might as well go out in style. Stripping to her dusky rose teddy and sheer stockings, which were kept in place with lacy garters, she stood in front of her open closet, surveying the contents of her wardrobe.

The door to her room opened—she hadn't given a thought to locking it—and Kane walked in. They stared at each other, silent and still, for a long moment.

Five

Kane's burning gray eyes slid over her, taking in her mane of champagne-blond hair, which tumbled over her shoulders, her full breasts with their pointed crests, her small waist and the womanly curves of her hips. The lace and silk confection she wore was as feminine and delicate as her small-boned frame and accentuated all her charms.

He dropped his gaze to her long, shapely legs. The stockings ended provocatively at the tops of her thighs, which were firm and rounded. He imagined the softness between them and desire stabbed at him. His loins grew taut and heavy in response to the alluring sight of his bride. She combined a compelling sexuality with a graceful elegance, and the results were challenging and irresistible. Never could he remember wanting a woman this much.

He found the incredible hunger raging through him more than a little unnerving. For the first time that day, the usually unflappable Kane McClellan felt himself in danger of losing his head. Immediately, he forced himself to tear his gaze away from her, to rein the wildness coursing through his body.

It had been a long, long time since anyone or anything had had such a powerful effect upon him and the realization unsettled him. He was not the kind of man who lost control; he managed his passion, his temper, his ambition, his intelligence with razor-sharp precision. He hid his feelings behind a cool, often glib facade; open displays of emotion were not for him. Those men who wept to demonstrate their sensitivity gave him the creeps.

Kane McClellan did not indulge in self-disclosure. A born introvert, he'd combined his deeply ingrained reserve with a quiet assertiveness to which others invariably yielded. It seemed natural for him to be in charge and so, naturally, he always was, in both business and family matters.

He'd planned his marriage with the same unerring dedication to detail that had earned him a fortune, choosing a wife who filled his requirements: intelligent but not involved in a career, of good moral character, from a stable family background, attractive, a woman who shared his traditional values that a wife and mother's place was in the home. Living on a huge working ranch, far from any urban area, it couldn't be any other way. Carling Templeton fit the bill perfectly, right down to her public declarations about wanting lots of babies and staying home to care for them.

But he hadn't let himself fully consider the physical impact she'd had on him, choosing to relegate that to the background as he engineered the marriage. Never had it occurred to him that the mere sight of her would leave him aching and breathless. That wasn't in his plans! Kane McClellan was invulnerable, in business, family and love!

He'd always possessed the ability to swiftly and thoroughly assess a situation, and that talent didn't fail him now. He had no illusions about his bride's feelings. Should she discover that she was capable of arousing these wild feelings in him, that she had the mystifying power to send him spinning out of control...

Kane clenched his jaw and swallowed hard. The results would be disastrous—to him. No sane man would allow a woman to know he was vulnerable to her, particularly not a woman who claimed to hate him, who would use that knowledge as power to hurt him in every way she could. He wasn't about to put that kind of a weapon in her hands!

He was aware that Carling saw him as her captor, as an iron man in absolute control of her and in absolute control of himself. He had no intention of disabusing her of that image.

"Get out of my room," Carling snapped. She was still shaking from his frank and intensely sexual appraisal of her. She'd seen the penetrating hunger in his eyes and had read the desire there. He wanted her and he meant to have her. His arrogance, his confidence, his masculine size and strength, his determination—all of it terrified her.

But she didn't dare let him see her fear. It was better he think that he infuriated her than for him to know just how scared she really was. She wasn't about to put that kind of a weapon in his hands! At least her anger and disdain for him gave her some illusion of power and she needed that power, however illusory, to hold her own against Kane McClellan tonight.

"I came up to ask if you needed any help with your suitcases," he said, pleased with the calmness of his voice. He was back in control again, the momentary madness safely at bay. "Perhaps you need some help getting dressed instead?"

"No, thank you." Carefully avoiding looking at him, Carling snatched an ultrasuede skirt in a soft pumpkin shade from a hanger. It was short and straight and very fashionable.

She pulled on the skirt and stepped into her pumpkin-colored suede shoes. The heels were very narrow and very high. Kane stood watching her, his gray eyes dark and burning.

The intensity of his gaze made her feel a little wild and that alarmed her. "Go back downstairs to our guests." She barked the order like a Marine drill instructor addressing the rawest recruit. "I'll be along when I'm ready."

"I'm sick of our guests. I'll stay here until you're ready to leave. And that's going to be momentarily." It was an order, not a statement.

Carling pulled on an ivory raw-silk blouse, her fingers fumbling with the delicate buttons. When Kane offered his assistance, she swatted his hands away. Undaunted, he slid one long finger under the thin strap of the teddy and lightly stroked her smooth white skin.

"So the Ice Princess has a predilection for sexy lingerie?" he murmured lightly. "What a pleasant surprise."

Carling shivered at his touch before she determinedly moved herself out of reach. "I chose my lingerie to please myself, not you!" she said fiercely.

"Isn't it fortunate that our tastes coincide?" His voice was low and deep. He watched her finish buttoning her blouse and put on a vest, which matched her skirt. A sudden smile crossed his face. "*Her Secret* specializes in lingerie, doesn't it? Sexy, feminine, expensive lingerie."

Carling pressed her lips together into a tight, straight line. It was humiliating to have to acknowledge the fact that he had paid for her lingerie, as if she were already his kept mistress.

"It affirms my belief in your passionate nature, Carly. If you were the dried-up prune you pretend to be, you would be wearing starched, opaque cotton underwear that contains and covers everything."

The intent in his eyes sent an unwilling, unwelcome heat rippling through her. Having him watch her dress made her feel positively lascivious. Worse, some primal, demented part of her actually wanted to preen under his hot gaze, to make her movements slow and sinuous...

Carling firmly suppressed the crazy and traitorous instinct.

She stormed over to her vanity table and grabbed her hairbrush, pulling it through her long, blond hair with quick, violent strokes. Her body language unmistakably reflected homicidal, not seductive intentions.

Kane watched her for a few moments, then turned to gaze around the room. It was a dainty, flowery feminine room, decorated in shades of pink and cream and mauve, with ruffled curtains and a canopied bed. He felt like an alien in it, as any male would.

And then his eyes focused on the corner cabinet, which was filled with... "Rabbits?" he exclaimed, walking over to investigate. All five shelves of the antique mahogany cabinet held small colorful rabbits, ceramic and porcelain and wooden ones in various poses and modes of dress.

"Good grief, a rabbit hutch!" He burst out laughing. "I've never seen so many rabbits in one place in my entire life!"

"A rabbit hutch?" Carling echoed. She decided that it would be useless to inform him of the cabinet's eighteenth century European origins. The barbarian could never appreciate the fact.

"I'm glad my collection amuses you," she said coldly. "I've been collecting since I've been six years old. Many of the figurines are antiques."

Kane was obviously not impressed. He was still laughing. "This is incredible. Pilgrim rabbits, Indian rabbits, rabbits wearing Hawaiian shirts and leis and holding ukeleles. And here's an entire school of bunnies, sitting at little desks with a teacher bunny standing by a little blackboard." He laughed harder.

"That wooden bunny school happens to be imported from West Germany. I fail to find anything funny about it or about my collection in general."

"The sight of a rabbit dressed like a Russian cossack or a Japanese geisha doesn't even bring a smile to your lips? A rabbit wearing a kilt and tam and holding a set of bagpipes doesn't strike you as hilarious?"

She raised her chin haughtily. "I have the complete set of twenty-four internationally costumed English bone china rabbits. It's twenty years old and priceless."

"Oh, it's priceless, all right!" His inflection gave the word an entirely different meaning. "Are you going to have the rabbit hutch and its inhabitants shipped to the ranch? Or keep them here—I hope."

"Oh, I'll definitely have them shipped to the ranch. In fact, I'll be sure to have the cabinet installed in your room. You'll hate that, won't you, Kane? All those cute little bunnies in your very own masculine domain."

"I've never been threatened with cute little bunnies before. You're really scaring me, honey." He chuckled, completely undaunted, making her feel even more foolish.

Her emotions roiling, she impulsively tossed her hairbrush at him. He caught it with one hand.

Kane stared at the brush, then at her, his dark eyebrows arched, his eyes narrowed to heavy-lidded slits. "Are you inviting me to use this on that saucy little bottom of yours?"

"Just try it." Carling's cheeks flamed a deep crimson. "Try it and I'll yell so loudly that everyone in this house will be up here to—"

"Watch me tame the shrew?"

"Oh, how I hate you!" she said breathlessly.

"So you keep saying. And I'm getting tired of hearing it." Still holding the brush, he advanced toward her, crossing the room in a few, long strides.

Carling tensed all over and began a retreat. She didn't know what he intended to do but whatever it was, she had to face the unpleasant fact that she'd driven him to it.

"No, Kane. Please don't!" She held up her hands to ward him off, but he merely used them to pull her close to him.

He stared down into her wide, apprehensive blue eyes. "Hmm, it seems that the shrew suddenly has been transformed into a scared little bunny rabbit. I guess this calls for a change in tactics." He dropped the brush and scooped her up in his arms. Holding her high against his chest, he headed for the door.

It was unsettling to be carried, to be high above the ground with no control over her own movements. Carling clutched at him in sheer self-preservation. "Kane, put me down. Where are we going? Let me go! I want to walk."

She kept up a running commentary as he strode from the room, through the hall and down the stairs, lapsing into mortified silence when he plowed through the cheering crowd, which had gathered to watch their departure.

"Her bags are upstairs in her room, if anybody wants to carry them out to the car," Kane announced with a charming smile.

His unexpected, previously unseen smile made an instant impact upon the guests. A group of both men and women trooped upstairs to do Kane's bidding.

With Carling still firmly ensconced in his arms, Kane swung open the front door. "Goodbye," he called cheerfully. "Y'all keep in touch now."

"Kane, we can't just leave!" cried Carling. "We didn't even say goodbye to Daddy and Mama yet."

"Sweetheart, I'm all for avoiding a big, tearful farewell scene. We'll call your folks tomorrow before we leave for the airport and say goodbye then."

But Clayton and Neva appeared in the front hall, having been notified by other guests of the couple's departure, and the tearful farewell scene that Kane had hoped to avoid began in earnest.

Neva and Carling embraced and wept openly. The senator hung behind, his blue eyes misting. Kane allowed for five full minutes of anguish and lamentations before he put his bride into the car, climbed behind the wheel and drove off with a jaunty honk of the horn.

"Alone at last," he said dryly, glancing over at Carling, who was sobbing into the lace handkerchief, which a thoughtful guest had pressed into her hand.

"How could you just drive away like that! My poor mother was—"

"Overreacting a bit. I did all of us a favor by leaving when she started into that 'what will Daddy and I do without our little girl?' stuff. You're twenty-eight, Carly, not fourteen. Most women your age have long since left the nest for their own homes and their own lives."

Carling's tears disappeared. Now she was too angry to cry. "I'm not interested in hearing your self-serving demographic statistics! Only an insensitive brute would fail to understand the distress Mama and I were feeling. And when I saw the stricken look on Daddy's face, I—"

"He looked relieved to me. When I told him to send me the bills for our wedding reception he looked downright ecstatic."

"Insensitive brute is too complimentary a term for a hard, cold, domineering tyrant like you." She was so infuriated with Kane that she forgot to be upset about leaving home.

Kane shrugged. "It's not the kind of compliment I especially enjoy receiving." He turned on the radio. "Shall we listen to my choice of music or do you have a station that you'd prefer?"

She wanted to ignore him, to brush him off with the cold-shoulder treatment. But if she didn't speak up, she'd be forced to listen to one of his country music tunes—and he'd have no compunction at all about *whistling* along. She decided to spare herself that.

She purposefully turned the dial to her favorite station, one that featured a format of "contemporary light rock, old and new." An old favorite from her college days was being played, and she settled back in the seat to listen.

Kane glanced at her. "You like that song?"

"Yes." She folded her arms across her chest and glared straight ahead. She had no intention of carrying the conversation any further, but midway through the song a kind of antagonistic curiosity forced her to ask, "Do *you* like it?" And to add, just to be contrary: "Because if you do, the song is ruined for me. I'll never listen to it again."

"I never particularly cared for it but Missy, my girlfriend at the time when it was popular, loved it. She played the song so many times that whenever I hear it, I think of her."

Carling considered what he had just said. And unexpectedly, her temper flared to flash point. "You're sitting here with your *wife* on your *wedding day* thinking about another woman? Boasting about an old girlfriend? That's—that's reprehensible!'' She leaned forward and changed the dial to an all news station.

Kane's lips twitched with amusement. ''I wasn't boasting. Looking back, Missy was more nightmare than dream girl.''

''I'm certainly not interested in hearing about her.'' Carling tossed her head. ''I couldn't care less about anyone in your past, present or future.''

But privately, she admitted that her actions belied her words. Why, *why* did he affect her like this? Why should hearing about a song that reminded him of an old girlfriend make her blood boil? Carling resolutely refused to consider an answer to either question.

They arrived at the hotel/motel complex near the airport and Kane checked in. He noticed her five bulging suitcases for the first time, as the bellhop loaded them onto a gurney.

''I said to pack a suitcase or two, not everything you own,'' Kane grumbled as they followed the bellhop toward the elevator.

''It's not everything I own, not even half. I had to pack enough to last me until the Wells Fargo wagon straggles the whole way out to your ranch—and that could be months!''

''Carly, the ranch is in Texas, not Outer Mongolia. Our mail is delivered daily and not by Pony Express.'' He sounded exasperated.

Carling was delighted that she'd managed to pierce his air of unfaltering implacability. She wanted him to feel as off balance as he made her feel. It wasn't fair that she should become irrational and overemotional around him while he always maintained his cool!

But her bravado abruptly faded the moment they stepped into the living room of the enormous suite. Kane handed the bellhop a generous tip and the man smilingly departed, leaving the couple alone.

Carling's breath caught in her throat and she clenched her fingers into fists. This was it. Somehow she'd managed to get through the day without fully accepting the fact that she would end up in a bedroom with Kane McClellan tonight. Always in the back of her mind had been the possibility, the *certainty*, that she would somehow escape. But such denial was no longer possible.

She stood stock-still, her eyes round, her mouth dry, watching Kane explore the suite.

"This is called the presidential suite," he said, examining the complimentary fruit basket and bottle of champagne. "I chose it over the bridal suite because hotel decorators sometimes have a tendency to run amok when it comes to bridal suites. Round vibrating beds, fur throws, mirrors on the ceilings ... I didn't think either of us would care for that."

Carling thought that if she were to walk into a bedroom and be faced with a round bed covered in fur and topped by a ceiling mirror, she would faint on the spot. As it was, she already felt dangerously lightheaded.

She sank into a chintz-covered chair, and like a mouse eyeing a stalking cat, she vigilantly watched Kane's movements. Then her stomach growled. Carling closed her eyes and groaned inwardly. This was all she needed. In addition to feeling weak and weepy with anxiety, she was also starving. She hadn't eaten a thing all day.

Her eyes flew open the moment she sensed Kane's approach. He stood in front of her chair, looking down at her with intense gray eyes. "Are you all right?" he asked quietly.

Had he made a glib or snide remark, she might have mustered the strength to fight back. But his tone was devoid of any flippant sarcasm and his expression was neither taunting nor amused. It was serious and concerned.

Carling silently shook her head, afraid that if she were to risk speaking, she might inadvertently burst into tears instead.

Kane got down on his haunches in front of her and took both her hands in his. "Your hands are like ice." He uncurled her fingers and interlaced them with his own. He stood up and slowly, inexorably pulled her to her feet so that she was standing in front of him.

Carling gasped sharply as a wave of panic assailed her. "No, don't! I can't go through with it! I just can't!"

He lifted her right hand to his mouth and kissed each fingertip. "I was going to suggest ordering dinner," he said mildly. "I noticed that you managed to avoid the dried-up canapés and the rest of that overpriced slop at the party, just like I did."

"*Capitol Affairs* does not serve slop," Carling rallied herself to say. "Their veal ragout is legendary. But you have a point about the overpricing. They do, outrageously. Wait until you get their bill."

"Something to look forward to," he said wryly.

"You'll be shocked at the cost of the reception," she added with relish, permitting herself to enjoy that small revenge.

"I suppose I should gallantly remark that money is no object when it comes to my wedding day."

His tone was so droll that Carling almost smiled in spite of herself. Almost. She opted for a cool, blank stare instead.

Holding her hand, Kane led her over to the small desk where a menu had been placed conveniently near the telephone. "Tell me what you want from room service and I'll call down our order."

Carling ignored the menu; her eyes darted nervously around the suite once more. Dining here, alone with him, was entirely too intimate. "Why don't we go out for dinner?" she asked with what she hoped passed for spontaneous ingenuous charm. She even managed a bright smile. "You wanted to go to a restaurant and I know all the good ones in the area. Just tell me what kind of food you feel like eating and—"

"We're eating here," Kane said flatly. He picked up the telephone receiver. "I'm ordering a steak for myself. Shall I order the same for you or are you going to tell me what you want?"

"I want to get out of here! I want to go home!" she burst out.

"I meant what you wanted from the menu," Kane explained patiently.

His deliberate obtuseness maddened her. Seething with anger, she snatched the receiver from his hand and slammed it back into its cradle.

"Does that mean you'd rather postpone ordering dinner... until afterwards?" Kane asked silkily.

Too late Carling realized the consequences of her outburst. He'd given her the ideal opportunity to stall for time by suggesting room service and she'd thrown it away. "No, I—uh—" She cleared her throat. "I just needed a little more time to study the menu," she improvised hastily. She grabbed the menu and pretended to study it, all the while carefully inching away from him.

His big hand reached out to take the menu away from her. He let it fall to the floor. "Are you afraid of me or of sex in general?" he asked quietly.

"I'm not afraid!" Carling refuted at once. She couldn't admit to fear, not to him! One must appear brave in the face of the enemy. "I just don't particularly care for sex. It's nothing personal against you," she added quickly, not wanting either to anger or challenge him at this point. Common sense had replaced outrage, making her nervously aware of her own vulnerability—a woman alone in a hotel suite with a man much larger and stronger than she was. "I don't want it or like it with anybody."

"And what brought you to that conclusion?"

Her blue eyes searched his face for any signs of mockery, but his expression was totally enigmatic. She swallowed. "I tried it once. That was enough for me."

"Once?"

"One time ten years ago. I didn't care to repeat—" she paused as a flush of warm color suffused her cheeks "—it."

"You really are repressed," Kane marveled. "You can't even say the word." He shook his head. "Now, let me make sure I've got this straight—after one adolescent sexual experience, you decided to put your sexuality on ice? And that's what you've done for the past ten years?"

His undisguised incredulity made her feel like a freak. "I tried to warn you that I wasn't...good in bed but you refused to listen." She scowled at him, her tone defensive. And then an idea occurred to her. She might just have a chance to escape, after all. "But it's true. I'm an icicle. Being married to me would be like—like being permanently stuck in the Arctic Circle. You're perfectly justified to seek an annulment and I'll gladly cooperate in any way I can to facilitate—"

"Baby, give it up." Kane sighed. "There isn't going to be an annulment. And your self-enforced chastity ends right now." He cupped her chin with one hand and swept his other arm around her to pull her close to him. "I'm here to set you free."

The swiftness of his actions caught her off guard and before she could utter a plea, protest or insult, his mouth had descended on hers. Startled, she arched her back and tried to wiggle out of his hold, but his grip was inexorable. His hard mouth had already closed over hers and was forcing her lips apart. She felt his warm breath filling her mouth and then his tongue thrusting into the moistness, probing, caressing, teasing her own tongue as her senses reeled.

Carling tried to pull away, but Kane ignored her futile attempts, deepening the kiss and tightening his hold on her. It was impossible to break free, she acknowledged dizzily, and it was becoming increasingly difficult to think her way out of her predicament.

Her eyes closed involuntarily and she couldn't seem to marshall the strength to open them again. Helplessly, she felt herself being drawn into a whirling vortex where sensation, not thought, reigned supreme. His seductive mastery was far beyond her level of experience. She grew languid and weak and for a moment she lay limply against him. It was easier to let him kiss her as intimately as he wished than to try to rally her defenses.

He slipped his hand inside her vest and cupped her breast in his big hand. The dual layers of her silk teddy and blouse offered no defense against the exciting warmth of his palm. His fingers caressed her, teasing the soft tip of her breast into a hard, throbbing little bead. Carling gasped at the hot surge of pleasure that flowed through her.

"You're so responsive," Kane said raspily, lifting his lips from her mouth to trail a path of fiery kisses along the slender curve of her throat. He pushed aside the collar of her blouse to seek the sensitive areas of her shoulder. "Too warm and passionate to live without loving. It's time for you to learn what you've been missing."

"I haven't missed a thing," Carling protested huskily as he swung her up in his arms.

"I'll get your opinion on that later, after you've been to bed with me," Kane said with a sexy male smile.

Six

He carried her into the bedroom, which was tastefully decorated in neutral grays and blues. The bed was a standard king-size, without mirrors, fur throws or anything else that might not fit with the room's conservative decor. He set her on her feet and began to unbutton his shirt with the natural ease of someone not at all uncomfortable about undressing in front of others.

Other *women*, Carling amended silently. The drugging cloud of passion, which had temporarily engulfed her, lifted and she found herself facing cold, hard reality. Kane McClellan was an experienced man, smooth and sure of himself, not at all the socially inept bumpkin he'd been portrayed as—and which she'd wanted him to be! She had needed the sense of superiority such an image of him provided for her.

But here in the bedroom, as she watched him take off his shirt, his boots, socks and wide leather belt, Carling grimly admitted that *she* was the inept one. She was inexperienced and scared. All her sophisticated polish, her skill in sparkling party conversation, her cool elegance were useless in an intimate situation like this. Was that part of the reason why she'd been avoiding just such an encounter all these years?

She sucked in her breath and gulped back a nervous whimper. She had to do something, but what? Her brain worked feverishly but with surprising acuity. Fighting him physically only increased his resolve, she thought. It excited him, too. She needed to try another tactic, one that discouraged instead of challenged.

Passive resistance? What if she were to lie as still as a corpse, cold and unresponsive? Surely any hot-blooded man, particularly one as passionate and demanding as Kane, would be completely turned off by such a—well—dead response.

A small mirthless smile curved her lips. A man with his confidence, which all too often bordered on arrogance, wouldn't tolerate a woman who didn't melt in his arms. He wouldn't be able to let her go fast enough! She'd have to make sure to have him promise to forward the incriminating financial documents before he hustled her out the door.

"You're grinning like a cat who's just noticed that the door to the canary's cage is open. Care to share the joke?"

Kane's voice jolted her out of her pleasant revenge-and-rescue fantasy. He was standing directly in front of her, close enough to touch, too close *not* to touch.

He was shirtless and the fit of his jeans had been altered by the insistent bulge beneath the heavy metal buttons of his fly.

"There isn't any joke." Her voice faltered. Unless it was on her, she said to herself, her eyes widening.

She wanted to look away from him, to run away, but she stood transfixed by the sight of him, by his sheer male power. His skin was smooth and golden from hours in the sun, his chest and shoulders broad and muscular. Dark hair covered his chest and arrowed downward, disappearing into the low-slung waistband of his jeans.

Kane's gaze followed hers. "Such great big scared eyes," he murmured softly. "Just like a quivering little bunny rabbit."

"Don't make fun of me!" It was supposed to be an order, but her voice didn't contain the necessary defiance to make it sound like one. To Carling's horror, she realized she'd sounded as if she were pleading with him instead.

Kane apparently thought so, to. "No, sweetheart, I won't hurt you. You're my wife, I'll never be cruel to you."

He stepped closer and took her hand, pressing it against his straining masculinity and holding it there when she reflexively tried to draw back. "Feel how much I want you." His voice was low and deep and almost hypnotic in intensity. "That's what happens to me when I look at you, when I kiss you and touch you. I want you, Carly."

He brushed her lips with his, lightly, provocatively, tantalizing and sensitizing, but not consuming her mouth with the ardent hunger of his previous kisses. "I want you."

A powerful combination of curiosity, confusion and desire burned within her, so intermingled that she couldn't begin to separate one from the other. But there was one emotion that was fast receding in the onslaught of the other three. And that was fear.

He felt hard and heavy under her hand, so foreign, so male. Hesitant but unwittingly fascinated, she relaxed her fingers and permitted herself to feel the rigid shape of him beneath the cloth.

Kane made a sound from deep in his throat. "Not yet, baby," he gritted out hoarsely. "Not now. We're going to have to go slowly this time." He carefully but firmly removed her hand and placed it on his chest.

It took sheer willpower for him to put on the brakes, but being Kane, he did so without hesitation. Her admitted sexual inexperience and apprehension evoked all his strong protective instincts. Carling belonged to him now. She was his wife and she needed to be soothed and taken slowly, regardless of the ferocity of his own needs. Those long years she'd spent in sexual hibernation made her much younger in terms of experience than her chronological age.

"There's nothing to be afraid of," he gasped. "I'm going to take care of you. I'll give you all the words and the kisses and the petting you need. It's going to be good for you, I promise."

He bent his head and kissed her.

This time she opened her lips to him automatically. His tongue delved inside to stroke her mouth, slowly, luxuriously. His hands moved over her back and then around and under her vest. He slipped it off her shoulders and let it drop to the floor. Carling barely noticed. The ribbon of heat uncurling in her belly claimed her full attention. It grew deeper and hotter as his hands rubbed the sides of her breasts through the cool silk.

Her fingers curled into the soft mat of hair, learning its texture, exploring the sinewy muscles beneath. She vaguely remembered her plan of not responding to him, but somehow neither active nor passive resistance seemed as compelling as it had earlier. A growing hunger for the feel of his hands on her naked breasts was overwhelming all rational thought. The double silk barrier of her clothing was becoming intolerable; her nipples were tight and tingling and aching for his touch.

When his fingers finally moved to the buttons of her blouse, she uttered a breathless, incoherent cry of anticipation. Kane's fingers immediately stilled. "Not yet?" he whispered, his lips against hers. "I won't undress you until you're ready, darling. We're not going to rush."

His hands resumed their torment, taking care to keep her clothing chastely in place while his mouth claimed hers in another deep, intoxicating kiss.

Carling twisted restlessly against him, wrapping her arms around his neck and running her hands through the springy thickness of his hair. She was acting on pure instinct, trying to get closer to him, aching with a growing need and emptiness she had never before experienced.

Kane felt her frustration build and a smile curved his lips as his mouth left hers to nibble on her neck. He had deliberately misinterpreted that wild little cry of hers; he wanted her to be more than ready, he wanted her to be burning for him. And if she was feeling frustrated, it was only fair because he felt as if the top of his head was about to come off from all those potent kisses. In fact, his whole body throbbed from the evocative force of the teasing, arousing caresses.

He hadn't indulged in a good old-fashioned necking session since his teens and now he knew why. It was murder on the nerves and required incredible stamina; any sensible adult male would choose to consign all of that to his past and proceed directly to intercourse. But he wasn't feeling very sensible right now. One could rightly say that he'd never been sensible when it came to Carling Templeton, beginning with his compelling interest in her from her pictures to assuming her father's large debt, the first unprofitable financial move in his life.

But it was all going to work out all right, Kane assured himself uneasily. He could absorb the senator's debts without economic hardship and he could control these excessive, inconvenient *feelings* Carling unexpectedly evoked within him. He felt sure that once he had sated himself in her creamy softness, the raging fever in his blood would cool. He intended to have sexual satisfaction in his marriage, but he had no intention of becoming absurdly besotted with his wife.

Still, his control was becoming harder to maintain. It took considerable restraint to slowly undo the first three buttons of her blouse. His instincts were to rip it off her, but he remembered his pledge not to frighten her. He paused, to bolster his flagging control. And when he did, Carling's trembling fingers finished the job of unbuttoning her blouse for him.

Their eyes met for a long, charged moment.

"Take them off," Kane ordered softly. "The blouse and the skirt. Now."

The rational part of her brain immediately registered a protest. Wasn't it enough that he'd blackmailed her into marrying him and was now intent upon exercising his full marital rights, despite her own objections to both? Now he expected her to aid in her own seduction?

It was all so calculating, so domineering, she thought wildly, an angry despair growing within her. He'd take everything, her freedom, her body, her self-control, but that wasn't enough for him. He expected her to hand over her mind and her will to him, too.

And she was almost on the verge of doing just that. She'd actually unbuttoned her blouse right in front of him! A flush stained her cheekbones and Carling caught the edges of her open blouse and held them together, to protect her breasts from his penetrating gray eyes. A civil war was raging within her, will-power and pride on one side, desire and need on the other.

She shook her head. "No."

"I should button up your blouse and resume the kissing and the petting-outside-the-clothes routine until you're sobbing with frustration. Then you'll strip for me without a murmur of dissent." His voice was as hard and hungry as his eyes.

That would be the ultimate power play, he knew, but he also knew that he wasn't up to it. The effect she was having on him, *he* might end up being the one sobbing with frustration, long before she did!

"But this is neither the time nor the place for game playing. If you won't or can't take off your clothes, then I'll do it for you." He slipped the blouse from her shoulders, then unbuttoned and unzipped her skirt and pushed it over her hips. This time Carling stood before him in the dusky rose teddy, the sheer stockings and the high, high heels.

She was immobilized by a combination of horror, anxiety and embarrassment. Yet battling that volatile trio of emotions was a suppressed excitement, so fierce in its intensity that holding back became more difficult than giving into it.

The internal conflict left her reeling. What had he done to her? What was she doing to herself? "You'll be sorry for this," she said shakily, and immediately suppressed a groan. She, Carling Templeton, noted for her quick, sharp repartee had been reduced to spouting a cliché straight out of a low-budget movie.

"No, I won't." Kane's lips twisted into a small, reckless smile. His eyes were gleaming. "And neither will you. I intend to make sure of that."

Carling wasn't ready to let him. Realizing that she didn't have enough time to run around the bed, she attempted to scramble across it. Was she running away from him or enticing him to follow, to catch her? She was too overwhelmed to venture a guess.

The king-size bed seemed as huge as a football field and any hopes she'd entertained of reaching the other side came to an abrupt stop when his fingers closed firmly around her ankle. She went sprawling flat on her stomach, her arms and legs outstretched. Before she could catch her breath, he'd rolled her over onto her back and straddled her.

Gasping for air, Carling stared up at him with glittering blue eyes.

Their gazes met and held.

"Stop fighting me," Kane ordered softly.

"I won't." She arched beneath him. "I can't."

"Yes, you can. And you will." He reached down to cup the soft swells of her breasts with his big hands.

His caressing fingers were deft and strong and she felt her nipples grow so hard and so sensitive that she cried out. She couldn't lie still, she twisted beneath his hands willing him to stop but praying that he wouldn't. She wasn't aware that she'd flexed her knees until she felt him lift her thigh and fit it snugly onto his hip. Instinctively, unthinkingly, she wrapped her other leg around him. The strength and tension vibrating from his hard masculine frame was as powerful an intoxicant as a gallon of moonshine.

His hands left her breasts to run along the smooth, long length of her legs. When he reached her feet, still encased in the pumpkin-colored suede heels, a rakish grin slashed his face. "Until I saw you in these, I never realized how sexy shoes could be. Do you want to leave them on?"

She shifted her leg, grazing him with the tip of the high, narrow heel. "They make an effective weapon," she murmured. She could certainly do some damage with them, so why didn't she? While she pondered her disturbing passivity, Kane slipped the shoes from her feet and tossed them to the floor.

"You don't need a weapon to use against me," he said, rolling down her silk stockings one at a time, then deftly divesting her of her garters.

Carling lay there, her breathing ragged, her heart pounding so wildly and so hard that the beats resounded in her head. His hands smoothed up and down her legs, and she felt the tight knot of desire growing, throbbing and burning in her abdomen and between her thighs.

She realized that somewhere along the line, she'd lost the inclination to escape and had begun to accept her fate. Was it because she was twenty-eight years old and tired of living a life of celibacy? Was it because she was a normal woman who had finally stopped repressing her normal urges?

It was a nice theory, but Carling was honest enough with herself to admit that it wasn't entirely true. Kane McClellan was the determining factor in her acquiescence. Though she'd tried to fight it, she had responded to him from the start; all her protestations were rendered irrelevant when she went wild in his arms. He was experienced and confident enough to separate her verbal hostility from her physical responses, abiding by the old axiom "Actions speak louder than words."

The thought galled her. Why, how, could a man she loathed make her feel this way, make her want... "It isn't right, it isn't fair," she blurted out.

"All's fair in love and war," Kane countered smoothly. He traced the circle of her navel through the cool silk of her teddy.

Just the touch of his fingertip sent shivers of desire rippling through her. Love. Merely hearing the word on his lips sent a bewildering surge of some unidentifiable emotion through her. It was anger, Carling decided resolutely. It had to be.

"This is war, all right," she snapped, struggling to sit up. It was impossible to do, given that his thighs were straddling her hips, but she kept trying. "Because the word *love* will never be used between you and me."

He put his hands on her shoulders and firmly pushed her down flat upon the mattress. "I'll keep that in mind," he said, lowering himself on top of her.

His lips took hers, teasing and coaxing until her mouth opened under his and when his tongue touched hers, she moaned. His body was covering hers; her softness absorbed the full, warm weight of him. She felt the seductive abrasiveness of his hair, the smooth, muscled hardness of his skin. Instinctively, her arms encircled him and she drew him even closer.

They kissed. Slow, ardent, hungry kisses, which grew longer and deeper and more intimate. After a long while, his lips left hers to draw the tip of one of her tightly budded breasts deeply into his mouth. He sucked it hard and the sound of Carling's moans of pleasure, of arousal filled the room. She felt lost in a world of pure sensation, the likes of which she had never even imagined.

And then he moved away from her, sitting up on the bed and leaving her lying alone and bereft across the mattress. Without thinking or caring what she was giving away or giving into, Carling gave a desperate little cry and reached out her arms to him. "Don't leave me," she begged in a throaty, sexy voice, speaking words she had never spoken before in a tone she had never heard herself use.

Kane smiled at the sound of it. "I won't," he promised. "I'm not."

Her eyes opened a slit and she watched him shuck off his jeans and briefs. Completely nude, he moved toward her again. Carling's eyes opened wider. Her only other sexual experience had been in the dark, with clothing hastily rearranged, not removed. This was her first sight of a fully aroused, mature naked male.

Her mouth went dry and when he came down beside her, she stiffened. He was so big, so strong, so nerve-shatteringly masculine. A wave of panic swept over her. What was she doing here? And how was she going to get away?

Kane propped himself up on one elbow and gazed intently at her. "Scared?" He stroked her cheek lightly.

Carling gulped. "I—I guess it's too late to holler 'rape.'"

He smiled. "I guess it is." His big hand slid caressingly over the curves of her body and came to rest at the juncture of her thighs. Still holding her eyes with his, he moved his hand between her legs.

"Then how about 'help'?" she asked breathlessly, trying to cross one leg over another in an attempt to avoid his long, probing fingers.

Her efforts were futile. He moved his thigh between hers, effectively opening her to him. Carling blushed as he reached for the hidden snaps of her silk teddy, which was moist with evidence of her desire.

"Why don't you try saying 'I want you,'" Kane suggested as he swiftly, deftly undid the snaps. He eased off the garment, his eyes studying her nakedness. "You're beautiful, Carly," he murmured. "So soft and feminine. So—*beautiful*," he repeated, his voice husky.

The word somehow seemed inadequate, but his mind was spinning too fast to run through a list of synonyms. She was all softly rounded curves and hollows, her skin smooth and white, the tips of her breasts pink, the dark, downy thatch hiding the secret folds of her femininity. And she was his. His woman; his wife. He felt proud and possessive.

A fierce, unexpected tenderness welled up within him, surprising him. It was all so foreign to him. He knew himself to be responsible and dependable, he would admit to being dominating and aggressive at times, and passionate, too, when the circumstances were right. But tender? He was amazed by the feelings sweeping through him, by the words he suddenly wanted to say to her, by the things he wanted her to say to him.

Somehow it was no longer enough that he had her in his bed, physically ready to admit him inside her. He wanted more. He wanted to hear her say the words. He needed those words, he realized, his astonishment growing.

Carling felt hot all over. The intensity of his gaze felt as heated as a flame. That he should have such intimate knowledge of her was as daunting as it was thrilling. She didn't understand how it was possible to feel so weak and languorous, yet so vibrant and alive, all at the same time.

"Say it, Carly. Tell me that you want me." It was a command, and Carling instantly rebelled. He was poised over her, watching her with hooded eyes.

"No." Who was she fighting, him or herself? a nagging little voice in her head taunted. She had no secrets from Kane McClellan, not now. He had seen her, touched her...he knew. Oh, he knew exactly how aroused she was and how much she wanted him. But, dammit, she wasn't about to tell him so. He couldn't have it all his way. "No," she repeated stubbornly.

Unexpectedly, Kane laughed. "You're a feisty one, bunny rabbit. Your body has already surrendered and we both know it. You're hot and wet and ready for me. Why won't you admit it?" His voice grew coaxing and seductive. "Say that you want me."

It was the voice of the serpent suggesting that Eve take just one tiny bite of the shiny red apple, Carling thought grimly. She closed her eyes. "I won't ever say that."

"You will," he said with his usual confidence.

Or was it determination? Carling wasn't sure; with Kane they sometimes seemed one and the same.

And then he touched the feathery softness between her thighs. Her body arched spasmodically against his hand and he smiled with pure male satisfaction. She wanted him, and badly, even if she wouldn't admit it. Yet.

He continued to caress the soft, swollen warmth of her, exploring the secret folds, delving deeper, rubbing, pressing, stroking rhythmically. Heat waves of pleasure spiraled from deep within the feminine center. Carling clutched his shoulders, her nails biting into his muscled flesh. She moaned and tossed her head back and forth, consumed by a fierce, delicious urgency she had never experienced before. Her eyes were closed, her lips parted, her breath came in short, sharp gasps.

Her mind seemed to be splintering away as she surrendered to the unbearably wonderful sensations pulsating through her. Her whole body began to quiver and a fine sheen of perspiration covered her skin.

"You want me. Say it, Carly."

Kane's voice swirled in the velvet mist surrounding her. Once again, it was a demand, but this time a demand from him did not incite her to rebel. Instead, she wanted to give to him, she wanted to please him. It was all so new to her, the flowing passion, the dependence, the soft need to yield. She gave into it, into him.

"Yes," she whispered, clinging to him. "Yes, I want you."

She was out of control and it was exciting, exhilarating, as if she were breaking out of prison. Her body tensed and then went rigid as a hot shower of sparks exploded within her. Her moans turned into cries of ecstasy and she convulsed helplessly around his fingers.

Tears of release stained her face and Carling lay nearly insensate with bliss, wanting nothing more than to lie alone in silence and savor the languid glow radiating through her. Kane's voice, coming from somewhere above her, was an unwelcome intrusion into her pleasurable state of erotic solitude.

"Open your eyes, Carly."

She did so, reluctantly. He was poised over her, his mouth twisted into a wry smile. "Your nap will have to wait, sweetheart. You're not through for the night yet."

She felt the hard thrust of his manhood against her. She couldn't look at it or at him. "I'm afraid," she murmured. But she lay still, her legs apart and open, making no move to get away from him.

"I know, baby." He acknowledged her anxiety, but didn't offer to end it by letting her go. Nor did she suggest it. It was time; his possession was inevitable. An odd relief surged through her as she acknowledged it.

He entered her easily. She arched upward, expecting pain but there was none. She could feel him filling her with his masculine power and strength. She could feel her body reflexively accommodating him. And still there was no pain.

He moved within her, slowly at first as she adjusted and accepted all of him, then deeper and faster and harder as her body instinctively matched his rhythm.

In and out, over and over again. Each time he withdrew from her she ached with an emptiness that only his hard male heat could alleviate. She felt the exquisite tension build inside her again, felt the incredible pleasure flare through her once more.

She wrapped herself around him and clung to him, crying his name. She didn't know what was happening to her or how or why, she only knew that she wanted him inside her, again and again, deeper and harder, more of him, all of him.

The wild, savage passion surged through her, expanding in hot rhythmic waves, sweeping both of them into the tumultuous seas of rapture. When the final shimmering tremors of release ebbed, Kane collapsed on top of her in a state of unadulterated satisfaction. Carling held him tight. She felt weak and utterly replete, too dreamy and dazed to do anything but lie beneath him, clinging to him.

When Kane finally pulled away from her to lie on his back beside her, she had to force herself to swallow a cry of protest. She was shocked to realize how much she still wanted him on her, and in her.

The golden afterglow began to fade and the first unsettling twinges of reality set in. Carling made herself open her eyes. The sight of her naked body lying across the big bed, flushed and damp from the passionate consummation of their marriage, struck her as shockingly wanton. Vivid, sensual memories filled her brain, so real that she could actually taste his kisses, feel his hands on her, feel him moving inside her.

Carling sat up, her face crimson. Kane rolled over onto his side, watching her intently. She had to drag her eyes away from his long, hard body. *That* part of him looks so very different now...after. She drew in a ragged breath.

He traced the straight, sensitive line of her spine with the tip of one long finger, and sensual shivers rippled through her.

"Lie down with me." His voice was huskily inviting.

"I just did. Now I—I want to take a shower." Her mind was mired in a bog of confusion. She needed to be alone to clear it. But when she tried to move out of his reach, his hand snaked out to seize her wrist.

"I'll overlook your lack of bedroom etiquette since all of this is so new to you." With one easy movement, Kane pulled her down and over his body, then held her there with arms of steel. "But you can definitely use a couple of basic lessons. Bedroom Etiquette Lesson One—don't go racing off to the shower immediately after making love. Your partner is liable to think that you can't wait to wash away all traces of him."

He shifted her slightly, to better absorb the cushiony softness of her weight. "Makes a bad impression, you know?" He grinned at her, inviting her to share the humor.

She wasn't in the mood to be playful. Carling tried to twist free, but his grip remained firm. Lying on top of him like this gave her an entirely different view of his virility and she was finding it increasingly difficult not to savor it and revel in it.

What was the matter with her? she wondered bleakly. How could she still respond to him, still want him when her body hadn't yet recovered from his first powerful possession of her? Worse, he was her avowed enemy, the man she hated most in the world!

"Let me go," she said desperately. Then she swallowed hard and forced herself to add, "Please. I just need a little time and space. To be alone for a while."

He appeared to consider it. "You want time and space to start rebuilding those walls that came tumbling down tonight. To convince yourself that I'm a treacherous, manipulative villain who made you do all kinds of things you didn't want to do."

"You did! You are!" she exclaimed. And then, to remind herself as well as him, she added wildly, "I hate you!"

She tried to fight him for her freedom, but he easily subdued her by simply rolling over and pinning her beneath him. He was so strong, so big. Her breathing began to grow rapid and shallow. He was so virile and hard. Not to mention treacherous and manipulative.

She squirmed as her body began to tighten and throb in response to his nearness. The wiry-soft mat of hair on his chest tickled her breasts, her thighs were entangled with his. She moved again, but he didn't loosen his hold. Her insides were melting. How could she be expected to fight him and win? He was bigger and stronger and far more experienced than she was. Of course he could make her do all kinds of things she didn't want to do. He was making her feel like doing them right now! It was so easy to blame him for her acquiescence instead of herself and she gladly did so.

Kane glanced down at her. Her eyes were heavy-lidded and starting to close. Her body had begun to move sinuously against his. She might be too stubborn to admit it or even to realize it, but she wanted him as much as he wanted her. But her words rang unpleasantly in his ear. I hate you! Not exactly what a man wanted to hear from his bride on his wedding night, particularly not after what they'd just shared.

Frowning, he suddenly levered himself up. "I'm going to order that steak dinner now," he announced, padding naked into the sitting room of the suite. "I'll order the same for you," he called out.

Carling lay alone, too startled by his sudden departure to say a word. With effort, she raised herself on her elbows and stared vacantly into space. She knew it was absurd, but she felt like bursting into tears.

Kane appeared in the doorway a few moments later. She was sitting on the edge of the bed, wondering what to do next, trying to keep her tears and her thoughts at bay. She saw him survey her with cool gray eyes.

"Now might be a good time for Bedroom Etiquette Lesson Two," he said with enviable smoothness and calm. "Saying 'I hate you' in bed tends to alienate rather than entice a lover. A useful fact to keep in mind." He walked into the bathroom and closed the door behind him.

A moment later, she heard the sound of running water. "I said *I* wanted to take a shower first," she muttered aloud. It occurred to her that if they were a normal couple sharing a normal wedding night, she might slip into the shower and join him there. She'd seen enough movies to be able to picture the scene— the two of them standing under the spray of the water, making a rich lather from the soap and running caressing hands over each other's bodies. But in light of her newly acquired experience, she carried the fantasy a step further... Closing her eyes, she pictured him reaching for her, lifting her, entering her....

Carling's eyes flew open. She didn't know how, she admitted, her body vibrating with frustration. Was it actually physically possible to make love standing up? The more she tried to envision it, the more frustrated she became. Furious with herself for even considering it in the first place, Carling grabbed her indigo silk kimono from her suitcase and jerked it on, tying the sash firmly around her.

If she kept this up, she would be ready for a room with rubber walls, she thought crossly. And she'd be bouncing off every one of them. Kane chose that moment to emerge from the bathroom, a white towel tied around his waist.

Carling's heart jumped into her throat. If he came near her—if he tried to touch her—

He didn't. "The bathroom's all yours," he said with sickening cheerfulness. "Better make it snappy, though. Dinner should be here any minute." Whistling, he dropped the towel and strolled over to his canvas overnight bag.

Carling watched him, her eyes focused on his nude, muscular frame. She took a small step toward him and cleared her throat. Kane appeared to be oblivious of her presence as he rummaged through his bag.

It was as if he were alone in the room. He pulled on a pair of briefs, walked to the window and adjusted the curtains, then went back to search through his bag. He never glanced once in her direction. Tilting her chin at an imperious angle, Carling stalked grandly into the bathroom. She slammed the door so hard that the mirror shook, and she made sure to turn the lock with a loud click.

From the other side of the door, she heard that damn tuneless whistling of his. Kane hadn't reacted at all to her burst of temper. He hadn't come after her, hadn't even *looked* at her! Well, what had she expected? A terrible chilling wave of despair washed over her. Since he'd already had her, he felt no need to pursue her. He wasn't interested in what she was feeling or why.

Carling stepped into the shower and turned on the taps full blast. The water sluicing over her face, over her body effectively masked the tears streaming down her face. She didn't know why she was crying or why she felt so miserable. It certainly wasn't because she wanted Kane McClellan to come after her, to hold her in his arms and comfort her, to soothe away her tears and anger and confusion. Never that!

If he dared to break down the bathroom door and snatch her from the shower, she would hit him and kick him and bite him . . . Her stomach lurched. She'd bitten his shoulder tonight while caught up in the full throes of passion. She could remember the wildness coursing through her as his bold fingers worked their magic. She could remember writhing and moaning and finally sinking her teeth into his hard flesh because the urgency and fire were driving her out of her head. It was scary to think she'd been so out of control.

Carling felt hot and flushed, despite the cool temperature of the water. What was even scarier was that she wanted to feel that way again.

Seven

"**W**e'll be landing in a few minutes." Kane leaned over to give Carling's shoulder a gentle shake.

She jerked awake and stared around the cockpit of the small plane with dazed, drowsy eyes. It had seemed as if only moments ago they'd boarded the Cessna 310 with Kane at the controls. All the way to the airport she had protested the arrangements, reiterating her fear and dislike of private planes, casting aspersions on his abilities as a pilot.

At first Kane had attempted to reassure her, citing a study of safety statistics involving small planes and telling her the number of hours he'd flown during the fifteen years he'd had his pilot's license. When she had continued her litany of complaints, he had pointedly ignored her, bundling her and her luggage into the plane in his customary high-handed way.

During takeoff and their first fifteen minutes in the air, Carling waited with a kind of fatalistic dread for the plane to plummet in flames to the earth. When it didn't crash, she went on to anticipate a horrible bout of airsickness. But she didn't get sick, not even mildly queasy. Kane handled the controls with competency and ease. The plane flew smoothly, and her thoughts had turned to other things.

Like last night. Her cheeks turned pink and she glanced covertly at Kane, who was reading the instrument panel, unaware of her scrutiny.

Last night, her wedding night. . . .

She had emerged from the shower, appalled that she'd cried and determined to never succumb to tears and weakness again. Kane might have won a victory of sorts by taking her to bed, but she hadn't lost the war yet. Nor would she! Before she could formulate any sort of plan, before she even had a chance to decide what clothes to put on, Kane had called from the other room that their dinners had arrived.

Carling flushed at the memory. She'd been starving, so hungry that she'd reacted without thinking, simply dropping her bath towel and slipping into her indigo silk kimono to rush to the table. Looking back, it was embarrassing that she'd been governed by such a common, elemental urge as hunger. It seemed so primitive, so physical, and she was *not* a person controlled by physical urges, she assured herself.

Still, to her discomfiture, she had to admit that she hadn't given a thought as to how Kane might interpret her appearing at the dinner table in nothing but a short, skimpy robe. At the time, her thoughts had been fixed solely on the steak dinner and her hunger pangs, which were so strong that they actually caused her pain.

If she closed her eyes now, she could visualize the small table set up in the suite with the snowy white tablecloth, the candlelight, the bottle of wine chilling in a sterling silver ice bucket. Carling nearly groaned aloud at the memory. It was a setting for seduction and she'd been the proverbial sitting duck. The food had been delicious, her wineglass had been liberally refilled throughout the meal and Kane had been attentive. So very attentive...

She'd felt so mellow after they'd finished the meal that she hadn't even offered a token protest when Kane had scooped her up in his arms. If he had taken her into the bedroom, she might have marshaled a defense, but instead he'd sat down on the long, cushioned sofa with her on his lap, talking to her, stroking her hair.

He'd caught her completely off guard. After all, one would expect a conservative, traditional man like Kane McClellan to confine his lovemaking to a bed in a bedroom. Not on a *sofa!* And by the time he'd begun kissing her, by the time he'd slipped his hands inside her kimono to touch her quivering, aching flesh, it had been too late. Her willpower had melted in the heat of his caresses, her resolution to resist him obliterated by the force of her desire.

Behind her burning eyelids, she could see herself shrugging the open kimono off her shoulders. In a kind of mental instant replay, she watched herself, naked and languorous, lying down on the sofa. She could almost feel the thick, chintz-covered cushions against her bare back and the solid weight of Kane's hard body upon her...

"We're down." The sound of Kane's voice startled her so much that she jumped. She'd been completely lost in those potent, erotic memories.

Blushing, she looked out and saw that they were on the ground and taxiing along a paved runway—in the middle of nowhere. Resentment flared anew. "I can't believe we're really here," she said. "I don't want to believe it."

"In a snit because all your dire predictions about flying in a small plane with me as the pilot didn't come true?" He took her hand and lifted it to his mouth, pressing his lips against her palm. "The flight was so smooth and I'm such a capable pilot that you relaxed completely. You slept for most of the trip."

She jerked her hand away. "I still have no faith in your rattletrap plane and even less in your so-called piloting abilities. And I didn't fall asleep because I was relaxed. I slept because I was totally exhausted. You kept me awake half the night!"

Kane laughed. Carling covered her mouth with her hands, aghast at her outburst. Why on earth had she brought up last night? The last thing she wanted was to rehash *that* with *him!*

"I was in top form last night, wasn't I?" He grinned wickedly. "Four times, hmm? Five, if you count this morning."

"You were relentless, and I don't mean that as a compliment!"

"Well, I'm taking it as one because you were with me all the way, baby. And that's what's driving you crazy, isn't it? All your convictions-set-in-concrete crumbled last night. You're neither the frigid ice princess nor the prim, fastidious maiden lady you thought you were. You're earthy and sexy and passionate and you loved everything we did together. In bed and out."

She sat stiffly in her seat, his words hitting her like stinging slaps. "Stop this plane. I want to get out!"

It was an effective exit line, only because the plane was already grinding to a halt. Scowling fiercely, she fumbled with the metal latch keeping the door shut.

"Wait a minute." Kane pulled her back to face him, and her traitorous nervous system went into overdrive at his nearness. The last time she'd been this close to him, she had been nude and so had he.

She blocked the thought and started to struggle. "Let me go!"

"Not until I tell you that my little sister is meeting us here to drive us back to the house. I radioed her shortly before landing. For Holly's sake, I'd like you to try to look more like a conventional bride and less like a combative prisoner."

"I am a prisoner! Stop trying to trivialize what you've done to me!"

"Maybe you could enlighten me," he said mildly. "Exactly what have I done to you?"

He was smiling, the snake. Carling wanted to scream with rage. "You bought me, as if I were a commodity on the open market. Do you know how it feels to know that you—you own me?"

"Judging from your responses last night—and this morning—I'd have to guess that it feels wonderful."

He'd struck a nerve, so Carling struck him. But he was expecting it and moved so lithely that she managed only a slight cuff to his shoulder. "You've ruined my life!" she cried, panting with fury. "And now I'm going to do my best to ruin yours!"

"Thanks for the warning. I'll be sure to be on guard. And as much as I'd like to continue our discussion, we're going to have to postpone it for now. There's Holly." Kane reached across her, unlatched the door and pushed it open.

"Kane!" cried a slender brunette with short dark hair and big gray-blue eyes. She was standing near a green station wagon. She jumped up and down and waved her arms when the plane's door swung open.

Carling stared at her. Kane's twenty-two-year-old sister Holly was about five feet eight inches tall, definitely too tall to be described as pixieish, but she had a certain elfin quality all the same. She was wearing jeans, boots and a blue and white checked Western-style shirt, proper ranch attire to be sure.

Carling smoothed the pleats of her short, red knit skirt, which, along with her red, white and blue cotton sweater and red high heels were as far from proper ranch attire as one could get. She looked ready to hit the mall, not ride the range.

Holly ran to the plane and stuck her head inside. She was beaming. "You have to be Kane's wife, Carly!" she exclaimed joyfully. "Oh, I'm so thrilled to meet you. And so surprised. I didn't know Kane even knew you. And he never mentioned that he was getting married. He never even mentioned that he was seriously dating anyone! I just screamed when he radioed me that he was arriving with his wife. Wait until Scott and Tim find out!"

Carling felt her mouth arrange itself into a smile. "Hello, Holly. It's nice to meet you, too," she heard herself say with the credible sincerity of a seasoned political campaigner.

Why? some submerged, rebellious part of her howled. Why did she always, always act as if she were seeking votes for her father? Why did she smile when she felt like spitting with rage? Why did she invariably utter polite, conventional phrases when she was thinking something else entirely? Only with Kane had she ever been able to express what she was really thinking and feeling. Terrific, she thought glumly. I can only be myself with my worst enemy.

"Let's get her bags into the car, Holly," Kane said, as he began to unload the luggage from the plane. Holly good-naturedly grabbed them and began to stuff them into the back of the station wagon.

Carling watched. She supposed that she should help, but loading and unloading bags was not her particular forte. As a senator's daughter, she'd always had someone around to handle such tasks. There had always been someone around to help her in and out of vehicles, too, but when Kane came to lift her from the plane, she quickly brushed him off and hopped down, unassisted.

Holly took the wheel of the car and Kane sat in the back seat, so close to Carling that his shoulder touched hers and his leg pressed against her thigh. His arm was firmly around her, and every time she tried to inch away from him, he moved right with her, as if he were glued to her. Her wriggling caused her skirt to creep slowly up her thighs.

When she saw Kane staring at her legs with *that* familiar gleam in his eye, she tugged the skirt down, feeling flustered and vulnerable. He had watched her dress this morning, had seen her don her red lace bra and panties, the red garter belt and sheer stockings. Carling shifted uneasily in the seat, feeling hot with shame. She hadn't tried to cover herself then; it was as if she'd *wanted* him to watch her.

She straightened abruptly and pulled her skirt down farther, primly arranging it over her knees. She hadn't wanted to entice him, she insisted stubbornly to herself. She'd simply been too tired to indulge in the fight she knew would ensue if she'd tried to send him out of the room while she was dressing.

"Tell me everything!" Holly cried, as she drove them away from the airstrip and small hangar. "When you met, how you met. When you decided to get married. Oh, Kane, this is the most exciting, romantic thing you've ever done." She paused and added incredulously. "Actually, it's the only exciting and romantic thing you've ever done."

"I'll let my beautiful bride fill you in on all the romantic details, Holly," Kane said, leaning down to brush Carling's temple with his lips.

"If I had any talent for creating romantic fiction, I'd be writing romance novels," Carling muttered in a low voice meant for Kane's ears only. "Although this marriage falls more into the realm of the horror genre. *You* tell her our bloodcurdling story."

Kane merely smiled and launched into a bare-bones recital of their first meeting at a political rally for Senator Templeton and their alleged long-distance secret romance, which had culminated in their elopement yesterday.

"It's wonderful," said Holly, sighing. "I'm so happy for you both. And now I don't have to worry about moving into an apartment in town and leaving you alone at home, Kane."

Carling felt Kane's body tense. "Holly, we've already discussed the idea of your moving into town and decided that—"

"*We* didn't discuss it. You said I couldn't and refused to discuss it any further," Holly interrupted quickly. "But that was before you got married. Things are different now. Oh, Kane, I really want to be on my own. I found a perfect little apartment in Stanton that I can move into right away. In fact, I should go as soon as possible. After all, you'll want to be alone with your bride. This is practically your honeymoon and you don't want your kid sister hanging around!"

"The house is certainly large enough to accommodate all of us," Kane said with a finality in his tone that Carling had come to know very well. It meant that his mind was made up and the issue wasn't open for further discussion.

Holly must have recognized it, too. She made a sound that was a cross between a groan and a wail. A tense silence settled over the car.

Carling bit her lower lip nervously. She was totally unaccustomed to sibling tension. The need to maintain a socially smooth facade was so deeply ingrained that she took a deep breath and asked politely, "Uh, where *is* Stanton?"

"It's the nearest town, about forty miles from the ranch," Kane replied. "You were sleeping when we flew over it."

"It's small and safe and there's absolutely no reason why I shouldn't live there," Holly interjected bitterly. "Except that Kane chooses to view it as the Texas version of Sodom and Gomorrah, just as he continues to see me as a dizzy teenager, who needs to be under Big Brother's constant surveillance. Carly, surely *you* can understand why—''

''Don't bother appealing to Carly for assistance, Holly,'' said Kane, as implacable as ever. ''She's never lived alone. She's twenty-eight years old and has lived with her parents all her life. And was perfectly content to do so, weren't you, sweetheart?''

Carling cleared her throat. She opened her mouth to speak, then closed it again. She wasn't about to be dragged in as a goody two-shoes role model.

''Well, that's fine for her, but not for me!'' wailed Holly. ''You expect me to live at home until I marry Joseph Wayne? Why can't you understand that I want—I *need*—some freedom and independence? I'm old enough to run my own life, Kane!''

The car braked to a sudden stop. Holly threw open the front door and jumped out of the car, crying. There was a long moment of silence.

''Well,'' Kane finally said, shrugging. ''Welcome to the family. I'm sorry you had to be exposed to Holly's histrionics during your first fifteen minutes here at the Triple M.''

Carling arched her brows thoughtfully. Apparently, relations between the McClellans weren't quite as idyllic as Kane had led her to believe. And all her sympathies lay with Holly, another apparent victim of Kane McClellan's unyielding dominance.

''It's not unusual for a twenty-two-year-old to want her own apartment,'' she pointed out. ''You told me that Holly has graduated from college. She's of age and she's used to being on her own, so why can't she live in town if she wants to?''

''But why should she?'' argued Kane. ''Holly has a nice suite of rooms here, her own bedroom, bathroom and little sitting room. She'll be marrying young Joe Wayne and moving in with him soon, so why does she need a place in Stanton?''

Carling frowned. "Poor Holly. How does one explain the need for freedom and independence to a dictatorial tyrant like you? Look at it this way—your brother Scott has his own place, doesn't he? Why shouldn't Holly?''

"The circumstances are completely different. Scott works in Dallas. He *has* to live there. He can hardly commute two hundred and fifty miles to the bank each day. If Holly had a job in Stanton, it would make sense for her to live there, but she isn't interested in any employment the town has to offer. She prefers to work here on the ranch as sort of a girl Friday. She does as much or as little as she feels like on any given day. It would be absurd for her to live in Stanton.''

Carling thought about that. It seemed Holly wanted to have her cake and eat it, too. She wanted a cushy job on the ranch, as well as her own place in town, which Kane would have to subsidize. When she considered the situation objectively, she realized his stance wasn't unreasonable.

But Carling wasn't in the mood to be reasonable. It was far more satisfying to view him as the implacable oppressor. "I don't think you'd find it so absurd if Holly were male. This is just another example of your overbearing sexist—''

Kane laughed slightly. "Can we skip this part of the argument if I agree that I'm a male chauvinist pig? Or whatever the current term happens to be?'' He opened the car door and stepped out. Then he reached inside for Carling's hands to pull her from the car. "I don't want to fight with you, honey. I want to welcome you to your new home.''

Carling blinked owlishly. The abrupt switch in topic, and in his tone and attitude as well, was disorienting. Then she saw the house and gasped. It was not the rundown, ramshackle dump she'd been dreading. Far from it. The McClellan home was a big, sprawling Spanish-style ranch house, with white stucco walls and a red-tiled roof. It was surrounded by tall trees, whose green leaves provided welcome shade from the sun. Flowering bushes and shrubs abounded and the gravel path to the long porch, which fronted the house, was lined with azalea of all colors.

Carling's jaw dropped. "It's beautiful," she said, stunned.

"I knew you'd like it." Kane smiled. "Come inside." He slipped his arm around her waist. He kept it there, chaining her to his side as he walked her to the massive front door, which was made of carved dark wood. And like a traditional bridegroom, he picked her up in his arms and carried her over the threshold.

Inside, Carling glimpsed thick white walls accented with dark walnut wood and shiny brick-colored floor tiles before Kane's lips took hers in a deep, possessive kiss. Conditioned by the long, passionate night they'd shared, her mouth opened instantly under his and she responded to him before she had time to remind herself not to.

He ended the kiss and set her on her feet just as unexpectedly as he'd picked her up. Dazed, already weak with arousal, Carling clung to him and buried her face against his chest.

She was stunned to hear cheers and a round of applause. Lifting her head, she swiftly turned around to see a line of people standing before her. They were grinning, cheering and clapping. Carling was mortified.

Incredulity followed as Kane proceeded to introduce her to his house staff. He had live-in household help? She could hardly take it all in. The Templetons' domestic help had been limited to a part-time cleaning lady. In Kane's employ were Juanita the cook, Clara and Lena, the maids, Will the gardener, Tony the jack-of-all-trades, and Marcella the housekeeper.

"You'll meet Webb Asher, the ranch manager, and the ranch hands later," Kane told her. "Webb and the hands live in bunkhouses on the property and have their own separate kitchen and mess hall. I'll take you around the spread tomorrow. Today, I want you to get acquainted with the house and the staff, especially Marcella. She'll be leaving at the end of the week. She's retiring to live near her daughter in Houston."

Marcella was petite and graying, somewhere in her late sixties or early seventies, Carling guessed, as the small woman came forward to fill her in on the housekeeping details.

"Marcella oversees the running of the house," Kane said, smiling at the older woman. "She tells Clara and Lena what housework needs to be done, works with Juanita on the weekly menus and sends Tony to the store for groceries and whatever else is needed from town. She's been with us for the past twenty years and we all consider her a member of the family," he added warmly.

"But it's good you have a wife to run your house now," Marcella said, smiling fondly from Kane to Carling. "That's as it should be."

"Come along, sweet, I'll give you a tour of the place." Kane took Carling's hand in his and guided her down the long, cool hall.

Electricity seemed to vibrate through her at the feel of his big hand engulfing hers. She was excited at the prospect of being alone with him and the reluctant admission set her teeth on edge. "I'm beginning to see why you decided to marry in such haste." Her caustic tone was the only defense she could muster. Her body had turned traitor and had begun to respond to him almost of its own volition. "Your housekeeper is retiring and you needed a replacement."

"Believe me, I could've hired twelve housekeepers at Marcella's salary for the sum I paid your father," Kane said coolly. "I thought you could take over running the house if you wanted to, but it is by no means a requirement. I can easily hire another housekeeper. I'd expected that I would have to eventually, when you're busy with our children."

Carling gaped at him. He was always one step ahead of her, keeping her off balance with unerring precision. "Children?" she repeated weakly. "I'm not even p-pregnant."

"Aren't you?" He stopped and took her by the shoulders, turning her to face him. "We haven't been using any type of birth control, Carly."

Carling blushed. Birth control had been the last thing on her mind when Kane had stirred her blood with his hot kisses and caresses. It was an additional shock to realize that the possibility of pregnancy did not fill her with horror. Rather, the thought of a baby of her own filled her with a kind of sweet, melting warmth. For the first time in her life, she imagined herself pregnant, fantasizing about the feel of a child growing in her womb, visualizing herself cuddling and feeding a soft, pink infant.

She conveniently skipped over the labor and delivery part, just as she didn't bother to dwell on the fact that her adorable, lovable baby would be Kane's child, too. Why put a damper on a perfectly delicious fantasy?

"When is your next period due?" Kane asked with his typical bluntness.

Carling blushed to the roots of her blond hair. She knew it was ridiculous to be shy with him—they'd already shared every intimacy—but she was. She stared at the gleaming tile floor, unable to look at him. "In two or three days," she mumbled.

"Looks like our timing is off this month." Kane grinned, his eyes gleaming wickedly. "But in a few weeks, you'll be in the ovulatory cycle and conception can occur—"

"Will you shut up! You're not talking about breeding cattle!"

"I like teasing you and watching you blush, Carly. You're an entertaining paradox—completely uninhibited in bed and so straitlaced out of it." He cupped her chin with his hand and leaned down to kiss her lips lightly.

After that, she was too bemused to offer any defense at all. She walked quietly with him through the house, admiring the large, spacious rooms with their Southwestern decor, the sturdy wooden furniture and Navajo rugs and earthenware ceramics perfectly complementing the stucco, wood and tile interior.

The house was cool, the air conditioning providing welcome relief from the already hot April afternoon sun. Summers, even when outside temperatures soared to unbearable highs, would be pleasant inside the house, Carling realized. She was delighted with the interior courtyard, which was filled with lush plants and a fountain with fat goldfish swimming in it.

There was even a swimming pool in the back of the house, its bright blue water shimmering in the sunlight. Cushioned chaise longues and chairs and a glass table with a striped umbrella filled the walled patio surrounding the pool, along with a variety of flowering trees and shrubs.

And she'd thought he lived in a hovel! Carling mocked herself for her earlier assumptions, and felt more than a little intimidated as well. He was very rich and very powerful while she…wasn't. Being here and observing the extent of his wealth drove home anew the cold, hard facts: he owned her and was in the position to determine the future of her father's career as well.

She gulped when she thought of the things she'd said to him, the way she'd behaved. Angering him was not a very good idea, Carling decided with growing apprehension. She would be helpless against the wide scope of his retaliatory wrath. Marrying him wasn't enough; she was going to have to make sure she pleased him as well. After all, a man with Kane McClellan's resources could do anything he wanted, to anybody.

"You don't have to hire another housekeeper when Marcella leaves," she said suddenly, as he led her inside from the pool area. "I can certainly run the house."

He stared at her thoughtfully. "Can you?"

"Of course. From what Marcella said, Juanita does the cooking, Clara the cleaning and Lena the laundry and ironing. My job will entail making lists and giving orders, and I happen to excel at both.'' She managed what she hoped was a sufficiently pleasing smile.

''And what brought on this sudden change of heart? I had the distinct impression that you saw yourself as Marcella's replacement and thoroughly resented the idea.''

''Well, your distinct impression was wrong. After all, I have to do something here to—to pass the time, don't I? I live here now, I have to earn my keep.''

Kane frowned. Her answer had clearly annoyed him. ''You're my wife, Carly, you don't have to *earn your keep*. If you'd rather have a housekeeper to run the house, then say so. You don't have to do anything that you don't want to do.''

He took her into the master bedroom suite, which was as large and luxurious as the rest of the house, perhaps even more so. Their private sitting room had its own compact disc player, large-screen color TV and VCR, just as the big family room did. The bathroom was tiled in white, green and black and had an enormous state-of-the-art Jacuzzi, along with a tile and glass shower stall, mirrored walls and triple sink.

Back in the bedroom, Carling stared at the huge oak platform bed, which was piled with pillows and covered with a colorful native woven spread. ''I don't have to do anything I don't want to?'' she repeated, her tongue moistening her lips. Her mouth was suddenly dry.

''Don't try to tell me that you don't want to sleep with me,'' Kane said, pulling her over to the edge of the bed, anticipating the remark before she could make it. ''Because you do, and we both know how much.''

Carling said nothing. There was an odd fear shadowing her face and he didn't like it. He couldn't understand it, either. Discounting her near virginal apprehension about sex, she'd never been frightened of him but she was unmistakably wary now. His frown deepened. He preferred her feisty and outspoken. He certainly didn't want her to hold back what she was thinking just to placate him.

"What's going on in that conniving little mind of yours?" he demanded. "This sudden capitulation of yours doesn't ring true."

"If you want me to fight with you, I will. I'll do anything you tell me to, say anything you want me to." A ghost of a smile lit her face. "We slaves aim to please. It's written in the terms of sale."

"The martyr role doesn't suit you, Carly." He pulled her into his arms and she felt him nibble sensuously along the sensitive curve of her throat. "Not that you'll be able to sustain it."

She might be a slave but she did have a modicum of pride left. "I can so," she insisted. "I'll do whatever I have to do to keep you from ruining my father's career."

His hands slipped under her sweater. "You've already done it, sweet baby. Our marriage wiped the slate clean. It's just you and me from now on."

He unclipped her bra and gently strummed over her nipples with his thumbs. Carling tried and failed to stifle a moan. "It's not that simple. We're not an equal match. You own me."

She whimpered as he inserted his thigh between hers, molding her to the hard, masculine planes of his body. Desire, primitive and insidious, was growing inside her. She wanted to cling to him as much as she wanted to fight him.

"You belong to me," Kane corrected softly. His hand smoothed over her back, then glided around to cup her breasts possessively. "There's a difference between ownership and belonging. A subtle one to be sure, but a difference all the same."

And then his mouth was on hers and he was kissing her with an ardent hunger that evoked her own wildly impassioned response. Raising the hem of her short, pleated skirt, he put his hand between her legs and the feel of his long, hard fingers against the warm, moist silk of her panties sent shock waves crashing through her.

They sank onto the bed, their bodies entwined, their breathing ragged, at the very moment that a loud, insistent knock sounded on the bedroom door.

"Kane, is Carly in there with you?" Holly called from the other side of the door. "I wanted to know if she wants to come to the barn to see the horses with me."

The abrupt cessation of passion was dizzying. Frustration, the force of which she'd never before experienced, surged through her, leaving her flushed and trembling and emotionally volatile. Carling slowly opened her eyes. She was wrapped around Kane, her body arched into his. She would have been humiliated at her obvious loss of control if she hadn't noticed that Kane didn't appear to be in any better shape than she was.

Groaning, he rolled onto his back and lay there, staring at the ceiling through slitted lids and breathing heavily, his chest visibly rising and falling. "Holly," he said through clenched teeth. "Go away."

Holly banged on the door again. "After Carly and I see the horses, I thought maybe she'd like to drive into Stanton with me and see the town." She jiggled the doorknob vigorously. "Hey, the door's locked." A giggle. "What's going on in there, anyway?"

Kane jumped off the bed. "Holly, if you don't get lost by the time I count to three—"

"No, Kane, wait." Carling sat up and placed a restraining hand on his arm. "She's just trying to be friendly. She's trying to make me feel welcome and I should—"

"She's deliberately making a pest of herself. She's set on making her presence here intolerable, so I'll be happy to pack her off to Stanton."

Carling had to concede it was an ingenious plan. But whatever Holly McClellan's motives, Carling felt obliged to offer the correct social response. She unlocked the door and opened it.

Holly stood in the hall looking quite pleased with herself. "Gee, I'm sorry if I interrupted anything," she said, grinning.

Carling tried and failed to keep from blushing. "It's—um—all right," she murmured, keeping her eyes fixed on the ground.

"No, it's not all right," Kane came up behind her and wrapped his arm around her waist, pulling her back against him. "We're going to have to lay down a few ground rules right here and now, Holly. You—"

"You're too dressed up to visit the stables, Carly," Holly put in brightly. "Why don't we do that another day? We can drive into Stanton this afternoon instead."

"Carly does not want to make the round-trip into Stanton today, Holly," Kane said tightly. "She's tired from the long flight."

Holly smiled sweetly. "Why don't we let Carly answer for herself, Kane? Are you too tired to drive into town with me, Carly?"

"I feel as if I'm caught in the cross fire here," said Carling, with an uneasy smile. Kane's arm was strong and warm against her middle. If she tilted her neck slightly, the back of her head would be resting against the solid muscular wall of his chest.

No, she didn't want to drive into Stanton, but she didn't want to reject Holly's overture of friendship, either. Vaguely, she thought that it would be a fitting revenge to leave Kane aching and frustrated in the bedroom while she flitted off to town with his little sister. Yesterday, she'd have done it in a minute. But now...

She was pondering this unfathomable turn of events when Kane growled, "Quit trying to stir up trouble, Holly. Carly is staying here with me. Now find yourself something to do and leave us alone."

Holly shrugged. "Well, I could drive into Stanton myself, I guess. I'm supposed to meet Joseph there for dinner, anyway. We're going to the movies later tonight, too."

"Fine. Good. Leave now and get an early start," Kane said and closed the door.

He turned to Carling. "Now where were we?"

"You were very impatient with your sister, Kane. In fact, you were downright rude. I think I should go after her and—"

"I think you should stay here, where you belong."
He picked her up and carried her over to the bed, setting her on her feet to stand closely in front of him.

"Don't worry about Holly's tender feelings being bruised, she's as tough as a ranch hand." He laughed slightly. "Maybe tougher. It's a miracle that she fell in love with a quiet, sweet guy like young Joe Wayne."

"Opposites attract, so they say," Carling murmured. Of course, it was not the case between her and Kane, she assured herself.

Kane shrugged. "I'm so pleased about Holly and Joseph getting together, I try not to delve too deeply, always keeping in mind that old adage about never looking a miracle in the mouth."

She grinned in spite of herself. "I hadn't heard that one. Is it a corollary to the one about the legendary gift horse?"

It occurred to her that she and Kane were actually carrying on an amicable conversation as they stood beside the bed, about to make love. Suddenly, it was all too cozily domestic for her. After all, it wasn't as if they were a pair of congenial, infatuated newlyweds. He was a domineering, blackmailing snake and she was the property he'd purchased. Based upon that line of thinking, she was *compelled* to revive the hostilities.

"Of course you wouldn't—" she began.

"Don't." Kane cut her off immediately. "No arguing, not now."

And before she could move, speak, or even breathe, his mouth opened over hers, hot and wet and seeking. Carling felt the steely length of his arousal pressing insistently against her. Her body was melting into his, already ahead of her mind in its urgent capitulation to the passion flaring between them.

She wanted him. That is, her body certainly did, Carling amended giddily. Her rational mind certainly did not! She tried to fight the languor sweeping through her which was making her dazed and dizzy with erotic hunger. It was much too threatening to think that she—cool pragmatic Carling—was becoming emotionally involved with this autocratic, arrogant man.

But if emotions were ruled out, then her responses to him were based on pure lust and that made her nothing but a shallow, carnal creature lacking the finer, higher feelings . . .

The thought was appalling, even more threatening than the outrageous notion that she was falling for him. Hard. It was better not think at all. Moaning, clinging to him, she let her senses take over, banishing inhibition and intellect into the dark mists engulfing her.

Eight

Dressed in fashionable designer jeans, an apricot-colored silk blouse and a spotless pair of aerobic shoes, and with her hair neatly French-braided, Carling was ready to tour the ranch operations with Kane and Holly.

The sister and brother exchanged amused glances as she joined them in the sun-filled breakfast room. "Maybe we should go into Stanton and do a little shopping before we go near the barn—or anywhere else on the ranch," Holly suggested, grinning. "One misstep, and her clothes will be totally ruined."

"I see your point." Kane's gaze traveled lazily over Carling. "Carly, don't you have any old clothes? And a sturdy pair of boots?"

"Old clothes?" Carling repeated incredulously.

"You know—clothes that weren't purchased within the past three months. Or even the past three years."

Kane gave a wry grimace. "I realize it's an alien concept to someone whose hobby and full-time occupation was shopping. What we're trying to tell you is that the clothes you're wearing aren't suitable for tramping around the barn and out on the cattle fields."

He was definitely patronizing her! "I happen to own some old clothes," she said haughtily. "Some of my cashmere sweaters and wool suits and gowns are classic styles so I kept them. But they're still at home. I couldn't put everything I owned into your little tin plane, remember?"

Holly chuckled. Kane shrugged. "Never mind," he said, rolling his eyes heavenward. "You couldn't ride in a wool suit or a gown, anyway. Incidentally, I called a transportation company this morning and arranged to have the rest of your things shipped down here immediately, including your car. I also called your mother and she agreed to supervise the packers."

Carling was on the verge of thanking him when she remembered that he wasn't doing her any favors. If it hadn't been for his insistence upon marrying her, she wouldn't need to have her belongings shipped down here in the first place.

Instead of responding, she slipped silently into a chair and helped herself to the breakfast of freshly baked cinnamon rolls, eggs, bacon, fresh fruit, juice and coffee. She was hungry and sampled everything, surprised at the amount of food she consumed. She'd never been much of a breakfast eater, preferring only half a piece of toast and a cup of coffee or tea in the morning. But then, she'd never spent her nights the way she'd spent last night, her second one as Mrs. Kane McClellan....

As she reveled in the memories of the night before, her hand shook and coffee sloshed over the rim of the cup.

"Okay, we'll go to Stanton and buy a pair of boots, a hat and a more practical shirt and pair of jeans," Kane's voice cut in on her reverie. "But, Carly, we don't go shopping every day around here," he added in a tone which set her teeth on edge. "I don't believe in running up big monthly bills on charge accounts. Here at the Triple M, shopping is for provisions, not a way of life. We buy things we need when we need them, but—"

"Yessir, life is tough here at the Triple M State Prison," Holly interjected dryly. "We inmates are only allowed out of our cells to work the ranch and we get a couple bucks a week to spend at the cell block canteen. Don't expect to do anything but hard time here, Carly."

Kane frowned reprovingly. "Stay out of this, Holly."

"On the contrary, I appreciate her filling me in on the rules and regulations, Warden," Carling said coolly. "Of course, I realize that she's not a lifer here, so she has certain privileges that I could never hope to have. For example, I don't expect you to spend a cent on me. I'll make use of whatever I already have. You'll *never* have to worry about me running up bills by spending your precious money!"

She tossed down her napkin and would have stormed from the table if Kane hadn't seized her arm. "Sit back down," he ordered. "You've deliberately chosen to misinterpret everything I said."

"I didn't have to misinterpret anything. You spelled it all out quite clearly," Carling said tightly, trying to wriggle away from him. "You think I'm an irresponsible, extravagant spendthrift who will blithely run you into bankruptcy."

A sudden hot flood of tears burned her eyes. Good Lord, wasn't that what she and her mother had almost done to her father? The insight was shattering.

Kane saw the haunted look shadow her face and almost cursed aloud. He could guess what she was thinking, some nonsense about being responsible for her father's financial woes when the senator's own pride and fiscal foolishness was the cause of that mess.

He stared at her thoughtfully. He'd never been renowned for his sensitivity, far from it. But he was beginning to understand Carling in a way he would have never thought himself capable. He'd quickly become attuned to her, to her emotions and her moods...

His body began to tighten. It was incredible, impossible, after their fevered coming together last night and their slow, languid early-morning passion just a few hours ago, but he was starting to want her again.

He thought of his plans, marrying her and bringing her here to share his home and raise a family. It had been such a convenient and practical idea, sparing him all the time and effort of a stupid courtship which might not have ended in the marriage he'd wanted anyway. But something had gone awry. His feelings for his bride were anything but convenient or practical; they were raging, ferocious. She was swiftly becoming an obsession.

And she professed to despise him. Actually, she had every right to. He had barged into her life and irrevocably changed it, completely against her will. Kane frowned. This would never do. Second-guessing himself was wildly out of character for him. He'd never been plagued by ruminations and self-doubt; he did what he felt was right and was invariably proven correct. Pushing aside his troubling thoughts, he resorted to action, his usual panacea.

"We're going into Stanton, Carly," he said decisively. "I'll buy you the clothes you need."

"I'll buy them myself!" Carling snapped. "I have my own money with me."

"I said I'll buy them and I will. The fifty dollars you have in your wallet won't even buy one boot, let alone a pair of them, not to mention a Lady Stetson and a few pairs of jeans and shirts."

"How do you know how much money I have in my wallet?" demanded Carling.

"I looked," he replied without the slightest trace of an apology.

"You went into my purse?" Carling was incensed. "You had no right, that's a blatant invasion of privacy."

"There is no reason for secrecy between us, Carly," he said tautly. "Not now, not ever."

"Privacy isn't the same as secrecy, you—you blockhead!" Carling cried.

"You two have an interesting marriage," Holly remarked, and the couple turned, startled, to face her. Both had completely forgotten her presence.

Holly smiled devilishly. "Yeah, I'm still here. And since you two are so fascinating to observe, you can be sure that I'll *always* be around. Don't count on any privacy *or* secrecy as long as I'm living in this house." She left the table, humming.

Carling and Kane stared at each other, nonplussed. And then Carling's lips curved into an irrepressible smile. "So this is what it's like to have a little sister?"

She laughed in spite of her determination to stay angry. Somehow, her indignant rage had dissipated. "And to think I desperately wanted one for years!"

"Yeah, well," Kane rubbed the nape of his neck with his hand. "You know what they say... be careful what you wish for—"

"Because you may get it," they chorused. Their gazes met and held.

Then Kane rose from his chair and held out his hand to her. "Let's go into town, Carly," he said quietly.

Carling gazed at him, feeling suddenly breathless. Standing there, so commandingly masculine, so virile and strong, he was more attractive than any man she'd ever known. Her pulse began to race and her legs felt wobbly. She'd never simply *looked* at a man and felt this yearning, this temptation to forget about everything but him and the way he made her feel.

She gave her head a shake, as if to clear it. This would never do. He was beginning to dominate her thoughts as well as her body and her life. She couldn't let it happen. "I don't want any new clothes," she said, her voice as frozen as an ice floe. "I'll take my chances with these, thank you all the same."

"You'll go with me and wear what I buy you, thank you all the same," Kane mimicked rudely. He scooped her up in his arms and stalked across the room, down the hall and out the front door.

He was ready to deposit her into the front seat of the station wagon, when they were approached by a darkly tanned, blond man with a tall rangy build and startlingly green eyes. He was the quintessential cowboy, from his wide-brimmed hat to his dusty boots. "Kane, I understand you got married. Is this the new missus?" he drawled.

"She is." Kane turned around so the other man could get a better look at Carling.

Why, he was inspecting her—and Kane was showing her off—as if she were some prized piece of livestock! Carling seethed at the unspoken, mutual machismo going on here. "Put me down," she ordered Kane.

He didn't, of course, so she was introduced to Webb Asher, the ranch manager, while being held high against Kane's chest.

"Let me get the door for you," Webb said with exaggerated politeness, flinging open the front door of the station wagon.

Kane put Carling inside. "We're heading into Stanton," he said to Webb. "Don't expect us back at any particular time."

"Right." Webb nodded. "It was a pleasure to meet you, Mrs. McClellan," he added with a smile that Carling found insolent.

"I don't like your ranch manager," she announced, as Kane steered the station wagon away from the house.

"You don't have to like him. He does a helluva job and that's all that matters."

She folded her arms across her chest and scowled. "I don't like you, either," she added, throwing down the gauntlet.

Kane did not pick it up. "Yes, you do. It's killing you, but you're liking me more and more, Carly."

What could she say to that? His confidence was virtually unshakable. No, she corrected herself. It wasn't confidence, it was arrogance, damnable, detestable arrogance. Because she still couldn't come up with a suitably scathing reply, his invitation to find a station on the radio was a welcome diversion. They listened to her favorite music all the way into Stanton.

Stanton, Texas, was a small town, but not as small as Carling had been expecting—and dreading. There was a two-block shopping district where most all necessities—and even some luxuries—could be purchased. There was a movie theater, several bars, a small hotel and a family-style restaurant. One of the ubiquitous fast-food chains had a franchise there as well.

Kane took her on a brief driving tour of the town, pointing out the churches, the post office, the library and the two schools, Stanton Elementary for kindergarten through eighth grade and the four-year Stanton High.

"Our kids will go there," he said casually, as if it were the most natural thing in the world for them to be discussing their future offsprings' education. "A school bus will pick them up and drop them off at the end of the road leading to the house."

"It's a long commute, especially for small children," Carling said witheringly, not wanting to foster the illusion of compatibility in any way. Bad enough that the drive into town had been completed without an argument or cross word, now he wanted to prolong the period of peace.

"It's an easy trip," replied Kane. "The road is straight and flat, and you saw how little traffic there is on the highway between the Triple M and Stanton. The school bus makes good time."

Carling arched her brows. "So in addition to sending little children to a school forty miles from home, there is the added danger of a speed demon bus driver who is determined to make 'good time.'"

Kane laughed. "You're very quick," he said approvingly. "You're always ready with a good comeback."

He thought she was teasing him, just kidding around to make him laugh! Carling was nonplussed. Should she tell him that she wasn't, that she'd intended to fire the opening salvo in the resumption of their own private war? Somehow, an explanation seemed laborious and beside the point, like trying to explain a joke to someone who didn't get it.

She glanced at him. He was still grinning. More disconcerting was the involuntary smile beginning to twist the corners of her own mouth. It was difficult to stay angry at someone who thought you were witty and entertaining. He'd said she was quick, always ready with a good comeback.

Wouldn't some of her less-than-enthusiastic former dates be surprised to hear that description of her? They'd described her as cold, starchy and humorless—to her face. Her feelings had been terribly hurt, but she'd never let them know....

Kane bought her the practical clothes, boots and hat, and she politely thanked him, promising herself that these were the first, last and only things he would ever buy for her. She might be a slave, but she was a proud one, she reminded herself. And though her father had managed to garner a chunk of the McClellan fortune, she would not attempt to follow suit, even if it meant never shopping again!

Spring roundup was in full swing at the Triple M, and the calves were culled, branded and separated by

the cowboys under the supervision of the ranch manager. Carling watched as hundreds of calves were vet-
ted into a chuted corral with gates opening into neat
paddocks where they were branded. It was noisy and
dusty, with cowboys shouting and calves bawling.

Carling shuddered. She found the whole process
extremely distressing. "I feel so sorry for them," she
said, staring anxiously at the scene. "First dragged
away from their mothers and then hurt with that hot
branding iron. Can't they at least be given a local an-
esthetic before they're branded?"

Kane, Holly, and Webb found her comment hilarious and howled with laughter. Carling walked away
from them and climbed into the pickup truck, where
she waited for Kane and Holly to join her.

"We have over one hundred thousand head of cattle on the Triple M," Holly said proudly as Kane drove
the truck away from the corral. "Kane has a com-
puter in his office with records on each one and Webb
is the best ranch manager in the county, maybe even
the whole state."

Carling had already visited Kane's office, which was
located in the house. A big, antique mahogany desk
shared space with all kinds of modern electronic
equipment, an incongruous combination she'd found
amusing. He was as much businessman as rancher,
she'd learned, when he mentioned his other investments, stocks, bonds, oil leasing and real estate hold-
ings, which comprised the McClellan wealth.

"The key is diversity," he'd explained, pulling her
down onto his lap.

Remembering what had happened next brought a
flush of color to her cheeks. The man was not only
creative in monetary matters, he was also incredibly

creative when it came to making love. Carling knew she would never be able to look at his wide, polished desk without remembering that late afternoon interlude they'd shared.

"You'll like visiting the stable," said Kane, his voice breaking into her intimate recollections. "We have several newborn foals that—"

"You're not going to brand *them* too, I hope?" she asked archly.

He shot her an amused glance. "No, honey, we don't brand pure-blooded Arabian horses." He and Holly exchanged wide grins.

Carling smiled politely and pretended to understand the ranch humor they were enjoying. She was not looking forward to visiting the horses, not even the baby ones. Once in the barn, someone was bound to assume that she was dying to ride one of the horses and then make the suggestion. In truth, Carling had absolutely no desire to ride a horse. She'd managed to postpone the dreaded visit to the stables her entire first week on the ranch.

But now the moment was at hand, and she dutifully admired Kane's prize Arabian stallions, though she privately found them wild-eyed and terrifying. She exclaimed over the foals as they suckled their mothers, but she preferred the young barn cats who chased each other through the wood chips that littered the floor. They were small and close to the ground, unlike the horses who seemed to tower above it.

Inevitably, Kane and Holly eagerly offered to saddle up one of the quarter horses for her to ride, a sturdy, frisky mare called Lady Slipper.

Carling eyed Lady Slipper, who seemed to stare back at her with a fiendish glee. "I'd better get back to the house," she said quickly. "I told Juanita that I'd look over the menus and write up the grocery list."

"That can wait," Kane was already saddling his own mount. "The horses need to be exercised. We haven't ridden together since you came to the ranch, Carly."

"There's a reason for that," Carling mumbled.

Holly was already on her horse, which whinnied spiritedly and kicked up its hooves in anticipation of leaving the barn. Carling's heart leaped into her throat. She watched Kane lead the prancing Lady Slipper toward her and she began to slowly back away. "I'm not going to ride," she announced.

"Of course you are," Kane countered calmly.

He assumed she was being contrary simply to rile him, Carling realized anxiously. Hardly an unusual course of action for her, but this time she wasn't trying to annoy him. She was trying to save her life!

"Let me put it another way. If you want to get me on that horse, you're going to have to knock me unconscious and tie me to the saddle." Lady Slipper gave a snort and Carling's eyes widened. "She knows I don't like her and she doesn't like me, either," she added nervously. "Take her back and let me go to the house."

"You don't ride?" Holly appeared thunderstruck. "You don't like horses?"

"I had a bad experience with a horse once," Carling said, her eyes fixed on Lady Slipper, who never seemed to stop moving. The young horse was the essence of animal strength and power, one Carling knew she couldn't hope to control.

Her stomach churned with anxiety. "When I was six, my father and I went to a rodeo rally fund-raiser and someone put me up on this gigantic horse. It was jittery from the noise of the crowd, and it started to buck. It threw me off. I broke my collarbone and my arm and had a serious concussion. I saw double for days and was in the hospital for two weeks.''

''Wow!'' Holly was clearly impressed. ''I've been thrown lots of times, but I was never hurt badly enough to be taken to the hospital.''

''You can see why I've avoided horses ever since,'' Carling concluded. She turned to Kane to find him watching her intently.

''You tried something once, it turned out badly and you made a vow to never do it again,'' he drawled. ''That whole scenario has a familiar ring to it.''

Carling's breath caught in her throat and she had to gasp for air. He was alluding to her attitude toward sex! Until he'd come along and changed it completely, that is. ''There is no similarity whatsoever,'' she insisted.

''Isn't there?''

''No!''

''I think there is. And we both know what happened when I insisted that you break your mule-headed vow of abstinence, don't we, Carly? The same rules apply here.''

''What are you talking about?'' Holly demanded.

''This is a private conversation that doesn't concern you, Holly,'' Kane said, exasperated. ''Kindly make yourself scarce.''

''It might not concern me, but it interests me,'' Holly shot back. ''And if I had my own place in Stanton, I wouldn't be here invading your privacy. Right, Carly?'' She turned to her sister-in-law for confirmation.

"That's right," Carling agreed succinctly. "And I'm not going to let you bully me into riding that horse, Kane McClellan. It wants to kill me, I can see it in her eyes and—"

Kane laughed. "I concede that Lady Slipper is a bit too frisky for a beginner. We'll start with good old Lucky Charm. Get down and saddle her up, Holly."

"No, don't, Holly," countered Carling. "I don't care if old Lucky Charm has one shoe in the glue factory, I'm not riding her. I refuse to get on any horse and no one is going to make me." Straightening her shoulders, she stalked determinedly toward the house.

She turned her head at the sound of prancing hooves. Holly had ridden up alongside her. "He's taking Lady Slipper back into the stable," Holly exclaimed. "Looks like you won this round, Carly. I can hardly believe it—nobody says no to Kane and makes it stick."

"Well, there has to be a first time for everything," Carling said with satisfaction. "Enjoy your ride, Holly."

"I will. I just wish that..." The girl's voice trailed off as a thunder of hooves sounded from behind them. "Uh-oh! Looks like you're going riding after all, Carly."

Carling saw the huge, chestnut-colored horse with Kane astride, heading toward them. She wanted to scream and run, but she resisted the impulse. She should have guessed that saying no to an aggressive male like Kane had presented him with an irresistible challenge. Well, she wouldn't back down. She would stand her ground and state her case reasonably and rationally.

Kane slowed the horse to a trot and reined in beside her. "There's nothing to be afraid of, Carly," he promised in soothing tones. "I'm going to put you up on the horse with me, just to get the feel of it. You'll be perfectly safe."

"Kane, I've already explained why I—"

"I want you to learn to ride, Carly."

"But why? It's possible to live a rich, full life without getting onto the back of a horse, you know."

"When you live on a ranch with a subspecialty in horse breeding, you have to know at least the rudiments of riding."

"You make it sound like a law or a religious obligation or something. That's ridiculous! Forget it, Kane."

"Sorry, honey." He didn't sound sorry at all as he suddenly bent down to grab her and pull her up to sit on the saddle in front of him. "You're going to enjoy riding, Carly. I guarantee you'll thank me for this."

Carling clutched the pommel with both hands. She was balanced precariously between Kane and the front of the saddle. The ground seemed miles below them and the excited horse was making all kinds of alarming movements. This time she *did* follow her instincts. She shrieked.

"I'm going to fall off!"

"No, you're not. Sit still," Kane ordered roughly. He had one hand on the reins to control the horse while he wrapped his other arm around Carling's waist to control her frantic wriggling. Neither effort succeeded very well.

"Let her down, Kane. She's scared to death!" Holly shouted.

The high-strung horse required gentle handling, and when Carling's struggles made Kane accidentally jerk hard on the reins, the animal panicked. It bucked and reared like an unbroken bronco in a Wild West show. Kane, who'd successfully ridden unbroken broncos before, managed to hang on, but there was no way he could keep a terrified novice like Carling in the saddle when her violent struggling thwarted his every attempt to do so.

Moments later, she fell from the horse, hitting the ground with a thud. Holly screamed and Kane's horse became even wilder. It took all his strength to keep the animal from trampling Carling's inert form. After he'd guided it safely away from her, he quickly dismounted and slapped the horse's rear, sending it dashing toward the barn.

"Carly!" He raced over to her, a sickening combination of horror and terror surging through him. The accident replayed crazily in his head and once again he could feel her slip from his grasp, see her fall from the horse and hear the hard force with which she'd struck the ground. Then came the added nightmare of the horse kicking dangerously near her, of watching her lying in the dust, so still. So very still.

Holly was already crouched over Carling when he knelt down beside her. "Oh, Kane!" was all his sister could exclaim in dismay. "Oh, Kane!"

He filled in the unspoken part. How could you let this happen? How could you do this to her? She'd been terrified of horses and he'd forced her onto one. "It's all my fault," he said thickly. He felt as though he'd been kicked in the gut. He couldn't swallow, couldn't breathe.

"You're damn right it is," Carling muttered darkly.

"She's conscious!" squealed Holly. "Oh, thank God! Carly, can you hear me? Do you know where you are?"

"Of course. I never lost consciousness." Slowly, gingerly, Carling raised herself to a sitting position. "I landed on my stomach and had the wind knocked out of me, so I couldn't breathe. Believe me, you don't feel like moving or speaking if you can't breathe."

"She's okay!" cried Holly exultantly. "She sounds just like her old self!"

Kane, pale and shaken, immediately began to run his hands over Carling's body. "Can you move your arms? Your legs?" His voice was hoarse. "Are you in pain?" His fingers examined her head, her neck. "Do you—see double?"

Carling stared at him. No, she was not seeing double; there was only one of Kane and he looked distraught. His face was white and his hands were shaking. *Kane McClellan!* It was amazing to see him in such a rattled state.

"Carling, I'm so sorry."

He'd actually said her name correctly. Carling gazed at him, perplexed. Surprisingly, it didn't sound right, coming from him. She'd gotten used to his nickname.

"I'm going to carry you to the car and drive to the airstrip," Kane continued. He looked and sounded positively shattered. "We'll fly into Dallas immediately and have you seen at Parkland Memorial Hospital."

"The hospital in Dallas?" Carling said incredulously. Since she'd hit the ground with a solid wallop, she would probably have some bruises. It certainly hadn't been pleasant to lie stunned and breathless for those first few moments. But she knew she wasn't badly hurt.

"I'm all right. I don't even need to see a doctor, let alone go to a hospital," she declared.

Kane picked her up and strode toward the house with lightning speed. "Sweetheart, I know you're being brave. I'll make this up to you, I promise. After you get out of the hospital, I'll take you anywhere you want to go. If you want to visit your parents in Washington, we'll fly up there, commercial, first-class, if you want and—"

"Kane, I'm all right. I don't need a doctor. And if you don't put me down right this minute, I—I'm going to scream."

To her astonishment, he set her on her feet immediately. When had such a paltry threat ever worked with Kane? But he looked terrible, tormented.

"Carly, I never wanted you to get hurt," he said.

It came as a distinct shock to her that she didn't like seeing him this way. Gone was his unflappable confidence and maddening arrogance. He thought she was hurt and he blamed himself. At this point, *he* was hurting more than she was.

"You think you know what's right for everyone," she began.

He flinched. For reasons she didn't even want to think about, the stricken look on his face affected her.

"I know you didn't mean for me to fall," she said quietly. "But I'm okay." Hesitantly, she reached out her hand and laid it on his forearm. "Honestly, I am. It was an accident, it's over and let's just forget about it."

He covered her hand with his. "When I saw you on the ground—" He took a deep breath and swallowed hard.

"The accident wasn't your fault, Kane, but I really am afraid of horses."

He pulled her into his arms and hugged her hard. Carling let him, not even objecting to the pressure on her bruised rib cage. She was aware that some invisible, intangible line had been crossed, but she didn't want to dwell on what it all meant.

"You never have to go near a horse again if you don't want to," Kane promised fervently. "I promise I'll never again suggest that you ride."

He knew it was a most un-Kane-like declaration, but he wasn't feeling at all like his normal self. Despite Carling's generous disclaimers, he knew he'd helped cause the accident. That she was unhurt didn't lessen the seriousness of what he'd done. He had made the decision for her to ride, certain that it was right because he'd come to believe that he inevitably made the right choices, for himself and everyone else.

But this time he'd been wrong! He'd always had difficulty in admitting he was wrong. Since his parents' deaths when he'd taken over the ranch and began to build the McClellan fortune, when he'd assumed guardianship of the kids, he'd abandoned the notion that he ever could be wrong. He didn't dare be wrong, not with so much depending upon him.

But he'd definitely been wrong this time and Carling had paid the price. He never should have pulled her onto that horse. He had been arrogant and blindly stupid. Carling could have been critically injured or killed. He gazed down at the warm, vital woman he held in his arms and thought what his life would be like without her. The prospect was infinitely chilling, much harder to bear than the revelation that he was not infallible.

She'd been his wife for ten days, but he couldn't seem to remember life without her. Now he couldn't even envision a life without her. It worried him that she should have so much power over him. No woman ever had before. And it was a relentless, all-consuming power, so much more than the sexual power of a desirable woman. He'd begun to suspect that his feelings for her went far beyond sex. Today's incident confirmed that suspicion.

They were a quiet, reflective pair as they walked slowly toward the house, his arm around her shoulders.

"About the trip to Washington to visit your parents," he said, as they entered the house.

"The one where I fly commercial, first-class, instead of in your toy airplane?" Carling's blue eyes sparkled mischievously. "Let me guess—the offer has been rescinded."

"No, no, of course not!" Kane hastened to reassure her. "I wanted to know when you wanted to go so that I could make the reservations."

Carling considered it. Back to Washington. Home to Mama and Daddy. Lunch and shopping with the girls, lunch and shopping with Mama, lunch and entertaining, visiting constituents and colleagues with Daddy. Dinner with whomever happened to be available.

She frowned thoughtfully. Somehow, her former life had lost some of its allure. The thought of shopping particularly palled when she considered the state of the Templeton finances.

"I guess I'll stay here," she said, carefully avoiding Kane's eyes, not wanting to give away...what? She wasn't sure. "All my things are due to arrive here any day now and I ought to be around to unpack. It seems a bit foolish to go home when all my stuff will be here."

"*This* is your home, Carly," Kane corrected with a definite, dogmatic trace of his usual self. "Your parents' place is your former home."

To their mutual amazement, she didn't deny it.

Nine

The middle of May was warm and sunny and free of the high humidity that would later make the summer months so sticky and oppressive. Carling took advantage of the pleasant weather and slipped outside to the pool after she'd organized the house and staff for the day.

Her swimsuit was a one-piece, modestly cut, black and strapless, with a white ruffle across the top. It was a suit that would draw complimentary glances from women without inspiring lust in their husbands and sons. Always aware of her role as a senator's daughter, Carling had always chosen such suits.

It wasn't until she'd come to the ranch that she had even thought of wearing something like the peacock-blue string bikini she'd seen in one of the mail-order catalogs that were delivered to the house. She allowed her mind to drift, visualizing herself in that same bikini, sunning herself by the pool...

She would be drowsy, lulled into sleepiness by the warmth of the sun, and wouldn't hear Kane approach. He would tell her that she needed to apply more sunscreen, that she was so fair-skinned that she must take extra precautions against sunburn. He would have the lotion with him, of course, and would begin to apply it, with long, slow, sweeping strokes. She would feel herself becoming aroused, feel her nipples tighten to pebble hardness, feel the syrupy warmth between her thighs. She would try to lie still, try to disguise her arousal, but Kane would know. He would continue to tease her, not touching her where she wanted to be touched until she was moving sinuously beneath his hands, until she was flushed and moaning and out of control. She would unclip the bikini top and cast it to the ground and Kane would look at her, with that sexy, hungry smile on his face...

Carling's book slipped through her fingers and hit her foot. The jolt of pain catapulted her out of her daydream into full awareness. She glanced furtively around her, embarrassed by how completely she'd been involved in the fantasy. She'd never had a sexual fantasy in her life, until she'd married Kane, and now...

Carling pressed her hands to her hot cheeks to cool them. Now when she wasn't making love with Kane, she was daydreaming about it. She waited half-expectantly for the wave of rage and shame that should follow this confession. After all, he'd bought her, practically kidnapped her, for heaven's sake, and if she had any pride, she should continue to protest her enslavement and diabolically plan his downfall.

Though she couldn't seem to work herself into a full-fledged vengeful fury, Carling did manage to achieve a state of righteous indignation.

Scowling, she stretched out on the yellow-and-white chaise longue and opened her book, a thick historical romance that Holly had highly recommended. By page five the heroine had been kidnapped by a lusty pirate captain who, to her, bore a startling physical resemblance to Kane. By page fifteen, the heroine was in the hero's bed helplessly succumbing to his virile charms—and Carling was no longer scowling.

Lena, the maid, appeared on the patio in the middle of a particularly intense scene on page seventeen, to announce the arrival of a visitor, Edie Wayne, from the neighboring Wayne ranch. Carling sighed inwardly and closed her book.

"Carly, my dear, it's wonderful to meet you! I've heard so much about you from my son Joseph!" Edie Wayne greeted Carling effusively, giving her an affectionate hug. "I was delighted to hear about Kane's marriage and I had to restrain myself from coming over any earlier. I know how newlyweds value their privacy!"

Carling smiled. She was pleased that she didn't blush. These days mere references to sexuality didn't make her lose her cool. "I'm delighted to meet you too, Edie. I understand your Joseph and Kane's sister Holly are—"

"Oh yes, Joey and Holly! Such an inseparable pair!" Edie shook her head in a gesture of maternal indulgence. "You must be sick of seeing that son of mine around here every evening. I tried to explain to *him* about newlyweds and privacy but he's too wrapped up in Holly to think of anything else. You've been very kind to invite him to dinner so many times. Why, he hasn't spent an evening at home in weeks!''

Carling was silent. Maybe she hadn't heard right. Had she had too much sun? She'd never even met Joseph Wayne, much less invited him to dinner. Holly mentioned his name frequently and she was forever driving to the Wayne ranch to have dinner and spend the evening with him there or meeting him in town.

Except that Joseph Wayne's mother said that her son hadn't spent an evening at home in weeks. Carling chewed her lower lip thoughtfully. She'd never had a younger sister but she recognized a masterful piece of sibling deception going on here. Kane thought his little sister was visiting the Waynes and the Waynes thought their son was visiting the McClellans.

Loyalty to Holly kept her silent on the subject of the couple's alleged whereabouts. She and Edie Wayne sipped tall, cool glasses of lemonade and chatted. When Edie mentioned that she would like to throw a big party to welcome Carling to the county and to celebrate the McClellans' marriage, Carling was delighted and immediately agreed. She wanted to meet her neighbors and although she hadn't missed the intensive socializing of her past, she was ready to enjoy a big, friendly party.

"There is one problem though, my dear," Edie said, frowning a little. "If you tell Kane we're having a party, he won't come. He hates them."

Carling thought of the tales of the reclusive rancher she'd heard before she had ever met Kane; then she remembered how much he'd enjoyed their wedding reception—not at all. She nodded. "I see you know him well."

"Everybody who knows him thinks the world of Kane so he's always invited to everything, though he rarely comes." Edie paused, then brightened. "Suppose we engage in a little creative deception? You could tell Kane that I invited just the two of you over for dinner next Saturday. Oh, and tell him that Holly and Joseph will be there, too. Kane enjoys very small gatherings and he's as enthused about the kids' romance as my husband and I. I'm sure he'll come."

"Yes, I'm sure he will," Carling agreed. Kane was extraordinarily pleased with Holly's romance with young Joe Wayne and he was eagerly anticipating their wedding.

Edie Wayne left shortly afterward and Carling turned to page seventeen of her book. She'd read two paragraphs when Holly, slim and lithe in a lime green swimsuit, bounded out onto the deck.

"Kane'll be out in a few minutes," Holly announced. "He's changing into his suit."

Carling's heart did a funny little somersault. The mere mention of Kane's name could create that effect. She was exhibiting a lot of peculiar signs and symptoms these days: like not being able to take her eyes off him when he was in a room with her, like hanging on his every word, like thinking of him when she was alone and starting to ache for his kiss, to throb and burn for his ardent caresses. Squirming and shifting her legs, she was starting to feel that way now.

Both to divert herself and also to satisfy her curiosity, she turned her attention to Holly. "Edie Wayne came by today to invite us to a party. Kane thinks it's just us and the Waynes, but Edie plans to invite everybody they know who knows Kane."

Holly chuckled. "Kane will hate that." She paused. "Did—uh—Edie happen to mention Joseph?"

"She thanked me for having him over to dinner all these weeks. She remarked how inseparable you two are, how he spends all his time over here and is seldom home in the evenings.''

Holly sank into the chair beside Carling. ''Did you tell her—otherwise?''

''That you've been telling us that you spend most of your evenings over there? No, I didn't.''

Holly let out a heartfelt sigh of relief. ''Oh, thanks, Carly. I owe you one, a big one!''

''Then I'd like to call it in now, Holly. What's going on? Why did you lie, to the Waynes and to Kane and me? Where are you and Joseph really spending your time?''

Holly blushed fiercely. ''Oh, Carly, please don't ask me that!''

And then Carling understood. As someone who'd only recently become involved in an intense sexual relationship, she recognized the young woman's constraint. Holly's neighbor-boyfriend was also her lover and since both lived at home with their families, they were meeting in clandestine places. But where? she wondered. The small hotel in Stanton? The barn? The field? The back seat of a car?

Carling shuddered. No wonder she had been such a poor candidate for an affair. All of the aforementioned places struck her as either embarrassing, uncomfortable or inconvenient. Or all three!

''I'm not going to press you for details, Holly,'' she said soothingly. ''But maybe you and Joseph should think of getting married sooner rather than later? If you had your own place and your own—'' she cleared her throat ''—bed, you wouldn't have to—'' she lowered her eyes discreetly ''—go searching for—um—privacy.''

''Yeah, sure.'' Holly giggled nervously. ''Thanks a lot for understanding, Carly. You're a terrific sis!''

She raced to the edge of the pool, dived gracefully into the water and began to swim laps.

It went without saying that Carling wouldn't mention this little talk to Kane. Anyway, she didn't want to be the one to tell him that his little sister was sneaking around having sex. She knew Kane well enough to know that would truly rankle, no matter how much he liked Joseph and the Waynes.

Kane joined her a few minutes later, wearing black swim trunks. His chest was bare, his legs long and muscular. Even his walk was sexy and pure male. The sparks, which had been kindled by her earlier thoughts of him, burst into a full blaze.

She wanted him. Her body tightened in anticipation and delicious shivers tingled through her. She was no longer the inhibited young woman she had been just six and a half weeks ago. Kane had released the passionate woman within her, introducing her to the pleasures of her own burgeoning sexuality.

"I thought you had some business in your office to attend to," she said, trying to sound nonchalant. But her pulse was racing and there was a buttery warmth seeping through her limbs.

"I took care of it. Made a few calls to Dallas and to New York. Now I'm free." He smiled, a rather dangerous, predatory smile which stirred her senses.

"See you two later!" Holly shouted, as she climbed from the pool and headed into the house. "I'm having dinner at Joseph's tonight. Don't expect me back till late."

"Holly is being considerate and letting us alone?" Kane said mockingly. "I can hardly believe it. Maybe she's finally given up on the idea of moving into Stanton."

Carling was surprised by how much she wanted to tell him the truth. Keeping secrets from Kane didn't feel right. But wasn't Holly entitled to her privacy? She was an adult, capable of making her own choices and decisions. And there were some things that a young woman might feel uncomfortable sharing with an overprotective older brother, her sex life being one of them. Though brotherless herself, Carling could certainly understand that.

Kane traced his finger along the smooth skin just above the white ruffle of Carling's swimsuit. "You're very fair. You have to be very careful in the sun to avoid a bad burn."

Carling's eyes swept over her demure suit and she wished she'd ordered that outrageous peacock-blue string bikini. "Are you going to insist on putting more sunscreen on me?" she asked huskily, gazing at him from beneath lowered lashes.

"Later. After we've had a swim." Unexpectedly, he caught both her hands in his and jerked her to her feet. "Let's go. Last one into the water has to—"

"I don't want to go into the water. I'll get wet."

"Water will make you wet. An interesting theory," Kane said drolly. He picked her up in his arms and strode purposefully to the pool. "Let's test it out right now."

He was going to drop her in the water! "Kane, don't!" she squealed.

He ignored her, walking to the deep end of the pool and teasingly swinging her over the water. "One—two—"

"Kane, please listen! If you're going to throw me in, at least do it in the shallow end. I—I can't swim!"

Kane's game came to an abrupt stop. He immediately set her on her feet. "You can't swim?" he echoed incredulously.

"I fell into a neighbor's pool when I was four years old. By the time someone noticed me, I was already on the bottom and had to be revived. Mama and Daddy were hysterical—they wouldn't let me near water again."

Kane groaned. "You're too smart not to see the pattern here, Carly. I'm not going to force you into the water, but I think you should try to overcome your fear of it and learn to swim. You're not a scared little girl anymore. You're an adult. We have a pool here, we'll have children who will be using it and—"

"I'm not afraid of the water. I haven't been for years," she interjected swiftly. She didn't want him to think she was a hopeless phobic! "I wanted to learn to swim, especially when I was a teenager, but by then all my friends already knew how and I felt stupid admitting that I didn't. So I would always say that I didn't want to go into the water because I didn't want to get my hair wet."

"And no teenage boy ever took that as a challenge and tried to toss you into the pool anyway?"

Carling smiled wryly. "No. Not a single one dared."

"Even as a teen, the Ice Princess could freeze a guy at twenty paces?"

"Oh yes."

"It's a good thing I wasn't around then." He smiled a daring, challenging smile. "You know what I would have done to you, don't you?"

"Made me go into the water despite my protests, telling me that it would be good for me? That I needed it? That I'd feel more content and calm after I'd worked off all my high-strung energy…in the pool?"

Her smiles, her words were deliberately provocative. So was the tilt of her head and the subtle thrust of her hips. The Carling of six weeks ago would have been shocked at her own brazenness, the Carling of today reveled in it.

Kane's eyes swept over her and he growled softly, "Oh baby, you're asking for it."

"Somewhat of a cliché, but still a perfect cue." Carling laughed seductively. "What else can I say but, 'Am I going to get it?'"

Tension vibrated between them, but there was also genuine warmth and affection in his eyes and in hers as he reached for her. "Most definitely, honey. Right here. Right now." He picked her up again.

"In the water?" she asked with languid interest.

"That's a more advanced course. You'll take it later." He laid her down on the chaise longue and lowered the bodice of her swimsuit. The sight of her breasts, so white and soft and beautifully shaped, peaked with taut pink nipples stirred his blood. He knew he would never tire of looking at her, never stop wanting her. Had he not been half-drunk with desire, the thought might have worried him as bordering on the obsessive.

But when he took her nipple in his mouth, she arched and cried out, holding his head close, stroking his nape, his hair with her slender fingers, Kane could think of nothing but how good it felt to hold her, to taste her, to pleasure her.

He sucked first one breast, then the other until Carling was writhing and twisting and shuddering for release. She wanted him now, deep inside her; an empty throb ached between her thighs. Insistently she pressed herself against the muscular column of his hair-roughened thigh.

"Kane, please," she gasped. Her hands slipped inside the waistband of his swim trunks and she found him, smooth and hard and pulsing with virile strength.

"Yes, baby. Yes, love," he muttered hoarsely and helped her pull off his suit.

When he tried to remove hers, the tight spandex material seemed to cling to her like a second skin. He pulled and tugged, his usual dexterity impeded by the consuming force of his desire. "Is this thing glued on or what?" he gasped with exasperation.

Carling joined the struggle. Why hadn't she ever realized how ridiculously impossible it was to get out of this suit? She felt like a fat lady struggling out of a too-tight girdle, hardly an alluring image!

When they'd finally worked the suit off, Kane flung it to the ground with a muffled oath. "The damn thing could serve as a modern-day chastity belt!"

Carling began to giggle. She was excited, her nerves humming, her emotions very close to the surface. "I guess a bikini would be a bit more conductive to—uh—poolside romance."

"Definitely. Wear one next time." He laid her back onto the chaise and lowered himself over her.

"Sorry, I don't have one." She smiled up at him, opening her legs to him, for him.

"Then we'll have to buy you one, won't we?" His finger penetrated her, testing her readiness.

Carling closed her eyes and moaned. She felt as if she were on fire there, ready to explode with the wildness coursing through her body. "Kane, now. Please!"

She felt her body being stretched and filled. She clung to him, enveloping him. The emptiness was gone, he was part of her now. The pleasure was so intense it obliterated her awareness of everything else.

He thrust into her with increasing power, faster and harder and deeper until he felt her body convulse around him and she was whimpering soft, sexy sounds that she couldn't control. Her climax triggered his and he felt explosive shock waves jolt through him as he gave in to the wild, surging pleasure.

They lay together for a long while afterward, their bodies still joined. Carling felt the heat and hard weight of his body upon her, inside her. She smelled the musky male scent of his skin, and the heady aroma of sex. She sighed, savoring the supreme contentment, the sublime glowing warmth.

"Kane," she whispered his name, just to say it, just to hear it on her lips. She wanted to say something more, something profound that would convey the way she was feeling. Alas, her verbal creativity seemed to have taken a leave of absence. She didn't know what words she wanted to use. She really wasn't sure what she wanted to say.

Kane slowly sat up, and she had to force herself not to beg him to stay with her.

He stared at her, his eyes intent. Her eyes were heavy-lidded, her lips moist and parted. She wore the expression of a woman who had been loved to rapturous satisfaction. Just knowing that he could make her feel that way, could make her look like that, made him feel like the most potent, desirable male on the planet. He wanted to say something to convey the way he felt when he was with her, the way he felt about her, but he couldn't. He didn't know what words he wanted to use. He really wasn't sure what he wanted to say.

For a few long moments, they stared at each other, saying nothing. Then Kane heaved a ragged sigh, picked up his swim trunks and put them back on. "Ready for your first swimming lesson?"

"Now?"

"Now."

"I guess so." Languorously, Carling stretched and sat up, her movements slow and sensuous. She was very aware that he was watching her. And then she noticed her suit, all rolled up and tangled on the ground.

"Uh-oh," she said with a grimace. She didn't want to go through her fat-lady-and-the-girdle routine again. It had been ungainly enough when Kane's eyes had been clouded with passion. To have him view the performance now was out of the question.

His gaze followed hers to the suit. A wicked smile slashed his face. "Perhaps you'd like to take the lesson nude? It can be easily arranged. Your instructor is very obliging."

"I'm sure," Carling said dryly. "If you'll excuse me for a moment, I'll go inside and find another suit to put on." She reached for her canary-yellow terry cloth cover-up and slipped it on.

"While you're inside, take a minute and order the bikini from that catalog you were poring over."

She looked at him with surprise. "You noticed?" She was slightly unnerved. It wasn't as if she'd been drooling over the pages. In fact, she thought she'd been rather subtle.

"I notice everything about you, Carly."

His tone, firm, quiet and exceedingly seductive sent tiny ripples of heat tingling through her. But she remembered her vow not to spend his money on anything for herself but necessary health-care products. "I have more than enough swimsuits, Kane. I don't need a bikini."

"If your other suits are all like that rubber armor lying there on the ground, you definitely do need one,

Carly. Anyway, you wouldn't have mentioned it if you hadn't wanted one. Order it.''

''I can't.''

''You can't? Why is that?''

She took a deep breath. ''Kane, we'll never be able to pay back the thousands and thousands of dollars that you gave to my father. I have no intention of adding to the Templeton debt.''

''The Templeton debt,'' he repeated carefully. ''You're really hung up on that, aren't you? I've already told you—how many times?—to forget it. There is no debt.''

''I can't forget it,'' she said. ''How can I when it's changed my whole life?''

If Kane hadn't given her father that money, she wouldn't be married to Kane, she wouldn't be standing here right now, warm and wet from his loving, she wouldn't be wondering if she was pregnant with his child—because she was already a week late.

She could never forget how she happened to become Kane's wife, because it was a fact of their history. But it was a fact that was beginning to matter less and less, she realized with a start. What seemed important now was that they were married. She was his wife and maybe nine months from now, the mother of his child!

But Kane wasn't privy to her thoughts. He reacted strictly to her words—and they were fighting ones to him. ''So we're back to that, hmm?''

His eyes blazed with sudden, fierce anger. He'd come to hate it when she threw up to him the conditions of their marriage. Perhaps his methods had been—well, a bit unorthodox—he was forced to concede. Still, the end result had been a marriage that was working out very well, so didn't the successful result justify the means?

He wasn't an avid proponent of the "end justifies the means" school of thought but, in this case, there was a valid argument to be made for it. Carling was happy as his wife and he knew it, though she might be too proud and too stubborn to admit it. And he . . . well, he was happy too. Happier, in fact, than he'd been in years. Maybe even in his entire life. *He* wasn't too proud or stubborn to admit it, at least to himself, he added with silent self-righteousness.

And then it hit him—what he wanted, what he expected from her. The impossible. He wanted her to forget the peculiar history behind their wedding, to consider their marriage as one which had been entirely, mutually voluntary. To act as if they'd met, fallen in love and decided to marry, just like any other couple.

Kane scowled. What an idiot he was! Carling had made her feelings about this marriage—and him— perfectly clear from Day One. Sure, she responded to him physically. After all, she was a passionate young woman whose warm and loving nature had been suppressed for too long. He was good in bed, he was skilled in the arts of arousing a woman, he had sexually awakened her. There was definite chemistry between them, but he was foolishly deluding himself if he thought that his wife was a willing partner in this marriage anywhere else but in the bedroom.

A surge of fierce primitive rage coursed through him. That he knew his anger was unreasonable made him even angrier. His mouth tightened. "Since you seem determined to wallow in the image of yourself as a bought-and-paid-for slave, I won't try to argue you out of it anymore. From now on I'll speak to you as

your master, not as your husband. When I tell you to
buy something, you'll damn well buy it, just as you'll
do what I tell you to do, wear what I tell you to wear."
He smiled coldly. "Need I continue or do you understand the concept?"

Carling stared at him nervously. He was furious!
This was the first time she'd ever seen Kane truly angry, and it was more than a little scary. No matter what
she'd said or done previously, he had reacted with in-
souciance or amusement or occasional mild exasperation, but never this rage she now saw burning in his
eyes. He was so big and strong. The size and strength
of him coupled with his anger underscored her own
weakness and vulnerability.

The caustic retort she would normally have flung at
him died on her lips. His wrath had a definite dampening effect on her own. Instead of exploding in rage
at his infuriatingly chauvinistic declaration, she decided to beat a strategic retreat.

"I'd like to go inside now," she said, striving hard
for a detached composure she was far from feeling.
Implicit in her cool withdrawal was the fact that she
wouldn't be back out for a swimming lesson.

"Then go inside," Kane said harshly. "And think
about what I told you."

Carling fled into the house. Even his tone scared
her. What a wimp she'd become, she thought dispir-
itedly. The old Carling would have never let anyone
speak to her so imperiously.

But she was no longer the old Carling, she admitted, as foolish tears misted her eyes. Worse, she didn't
want to be the old Carling again, and that revelation
was scarier than anything Kane could have said or
done to her.

* * *

They avoided each other for the rest of the day, meeting only at dinner which they ate in cool, tense silence. Afterward, Kane tossed down his napkin and rose decisively from his chair.

"I'm going over to the Wayne ranch to talk to Sam Wayne about a foal he's interested in buying from me," he said, heading out of the room.

Carling felt her heart stop, then start again at triple speed. He couldn't go to the Waynes; Holly was supposed to be there with Sam and Edie's son Joseph. She wasn't, of course. Edie Wayne's disclosure that afternoon made Carling certain of that.

The scenario unfolded unpleasantly in her imagination: Kane, already in a bad mood would go to the Waynes, expecting to find Holly and Joseph. He would make some remark and the loquacious Edie would mention how much time the young couple spent at the Triple M. She might even mention having thanked Carling for tolerating their presence. Then Kane would know that she had helped Holly deceive him.

Carling shivered. She didn't even want to think about what kind of a mood he would be in when he returned home. There was something more, too, something she wasn't ready to acknowledge: she didn't want Kane to think that she'd betrayed him. She wasn't yet up to facing what that said about her feelings for Kane.

"Kane!" She blurted out his name as she scurried after him down the hall.

He paused and turned to face her. "Yes?"

Carling was really nervous now. Anything she said would plunge her deeper into this stupid, involuntary conspiracy with Holly. "I—I don't think you should go."

"And why not?"

"Because... people shouldn't go storming away in anger. It's not—" She paused, frantically searching her brain. What was the word she was looking for? "Very nice."

This was a sophisticated public speaker? Carling mocked her own insipidity. But an angry Kane Mc-Clellan unnerved her more than a raucous political audience numbering in the hundreds.

"Too bad," Kane said coolly. "As a slave you have no input concerning any of my actions."

"Would I have some input as your wife?" she shot back.

He started walking toward her. "What are you trying to say, Carly?" He came to a stop directly in front of her.

"I—I'm not sure. Maybe that I want to be a wife and not a slave?" Her words surprised herself as much as they surprised Kane.

"That would mean that you'd have to stop all that nonsense about adding to the Templeton debt." He put his hands on her shoulders and she raised her head to meet his eyes. "You'll have to—"

"Spend your money?" she interrupted, a teasing glint in her eye. Their fight—or whatever it had been—was over. She knew it, and she suddenly felt giddy and lighter than air.

"You'll need it for such necessities as bikinis and lingerie and bunny rabbits for that infernal collection of yours that's taken over the den." A slow smile curved the corners of his mouth. "But we'll have to negotiate the amount which—"

"Oh, I know, I know, you've already explained the McClellan Rules of Shopping to me." She lowered her voice, mimicking his. "Shopping is not a vocation to us. We buy what we need when we need it but—"

"Maybe my lecture was somewhat patronizing and paternalistic," Kane conceded.

"I think obnoxious and offensive are the words that best sum it up."

"Is that so?"

She nodded. "Kane?"

He took both her hands in his. "Hmm?"

"Is it too late to have a swimming lesson now?" She forgot all about the Waynes and Holly and why she couldn't let Kane go there. Foremost in her mind was mending the rift between them—and just being with him. If that also included learning to swim, so much the better.

"The pool is heated and lighted. We could do it if you wanted to."

"I do."

"Okay, then. Let's go." He flung a casual arm around her shoulder and they headed to their bedroom to change.

Halfway down the hall, Carling's arm crept around his waist and her head came to rest lightly in the hollow of his shoulder. It seemed natural for the two of them to walk together that way, normal for them to glance at each other and spontaneously smile. And oh-so-right for him to draw her into his arms as they stepped inside their room for a long, deep, passionate kiss.

Ten

Kane was delighted when his younger brothers, Scott and Tim, arrived for an impromptu weekend visit the following Friday, the day before he, Carling and Holly were scheduled to have dinner with the Waynes. Carling and Holly weren't at all surprised by the visit. They knew that the Waynes had invited the boys to the enormous party they were throwing to honor the newlyweds and to welcome Carling to the county. Wisely, the logistics and the size of the party were being surreptitiously kept from Kane.

Carling couldn't remember exactly when she'd begun to consider Kane's aversion to big, bustling social events amusing rather than annoying. Her change in attitude seemed to have evolved naturally. After all, she reasoned, Kane wasn't a genuine misanthrope. He had friends he enjoyed seeing, either one-on-one or in small groups. However, he was selective about whom he chose to spend his time with—and she knew that she was one of the chosen.

Kane would rather be with her than with a roomful of guests, regardless of how charming or illustrious or useful they might be. That appealed to her, although she wasn't ready to put a label on why and how she found his attention and preference for her so affecting. And stirring. And arousing.

Kane proudly introduced Carling to Scott and Tim, indulging in some big-brotherly bragging. In just a few weeks, Tim would be graduating with highest honors from Rice University, and a trip to the graduation ceremony was already scheduled. Immediately afterward, Tim planned to move to New York, where he'd been accepted into medical school.

"I wish you could take some time off and relax here at the ranch for a while, Timmy," Kane said, eyeing his youngest brother warmly.

Tim laughed. "I couldn't sit around with nothing to do any more than you could, Kane," he teased. "I'm ready to get moving. I can't wait to get into my new apartment and start my classes."

"Kane's clone, the boy wonder," Scott muttered under his breath, too low for Kane to hear. But Carling was near enough to pick it up. She knew Holly heard too, because the young woman gave Scott a sympathetic smile and nodded her head.

Carling watched the brothers closely after that. Kane was obviously as proud of Scott and he was of Tim. She listened as Kane talked on at length about Scott's job at the bank in Dallas, about the fascinating ins and outs of the financial world. But it seemed to be a one-way conversation. Scott volunteered only a word or two about his job or about banking and finance. He seemed to have nothing to say about his social life, either.

Of course she had had no experience with sibling relationships, Carling reminded herself. Maybe it was the norm for the eldest brother to do all the talking. She noticed, though, that it wasn't that way between Tim and Kane. Tim was bursting to tell Kane everything, about his classes, his dates, his interests and activities, while Scott shared virtually none of the details of his life in Dallas.

Different personalities, different styles of relating, Carling told herself, as she walked to the stables where the horses were kept. She'd taken to visiting there every other day or so, though she kept her visits a secret from everyone. She had no intention of getting on one of those four-legged snorting giants but she'd decided that she ought to at least learn to tolerate their presence. Anyway, she thought the baby horses were cute, even petting them if their mothers kept a respectable distance.

Her determination to conquer her fear of horses had nothing to do with any desire to befriend the species or to learn to ride, even at a slow trot. But she was *not* going to be one of those mothers who infect their children with their own foolish fears and hang-ups.

And she was going to be a mother! Carling wavered constantly between awe and disbelief at the realization. She was eight days late—an extraordinary phenomenon in a body that had always been as regular as clockwork—and so she'd purchased a home pregnancy testing kit at the drugstore in Stanton. The results had been positive, but Carling hadn't quite believed it. A baby growing inside her? She thought of how badly she'd wanted a baby sister or brother throughout her childhood. Now it seemed she was to be gifted with a baby son or daughter of her own.

After two weeks, she'd bought another testing kit, just to be certain. Once again, the results were positive. She really was pregnant!

Now she was three weeks and four days late, well into her first month. It was time to think about making an appointment with an obstetrician. Carling laid her hand on her abdomen. It had become an automatic gesture lately, as if she were protecting and comforting the tiny new life growing inside her. She was filled with a serene contentment, a peace and calm that she'd never before experienced in her peripatetic life as a Templeton.

She hadn't told Kane about any of this. She was consumed with the wonder of having a baby inside her, so very proud of that amazing accomplishment. But every time she thought of telling Kane she grew anxious and uncertain. It was *her* baby and something in her balked at sharing her secret with him.

There was no use pretending that they were a normal married couple or that Kane was a husband madly in love with his wife, pregnant or not, Carling reminded herself bleakly. Though she'd ceased to refer to herself as his bought slave, the facts hadn't changed. Because her father's political future was completely in his power, Kane McClellan owned her. She was a hostage, held in exchange for her father's career—and so was her unborn baby.

Carling quickly put the thought from her mind. It was too painful to think about a child hostage, a baby of blackmail. Her eyes filled with hot tears. She was so emotional these days, so confused. Only one thing seemed inviolate: as long as she kept her secret, her child was free.

The barn door was open and Carling walked inside, heading automatically for Winsome's stall. Winsome seemed less threatening than the other horses; she didn't glower and make menacing noises when Carling approached, the way some of the others did. One time she could have sworn the horse had nodded with maternal approval when Carling had stroked and cooed to Winsome's beautiful little foal.

She passed the stall of her nemesis Lady Slipper, and jumped when the horse made a sudden movement toward her. She was annoyed with her own skittishness and when Lady Slipper emitted a jeering whinny—yes, it was definitely a jeer—Carling stuck her tongue out at the horse.

She stopped when she heard Holly's voice, and then Scott's, and was about to call out a greeting when she heard them mention her name. Immediately, she fell silent. There was an old saw about eavesdroppers never hearing anything good about themselves, but Carling doubted that it had ever hindered a potential eavesdropper from listening in. It certainly didn't hinder her. She leaned against the side of one of the stalls, out of sight, and proceeded to listen shamelessly.

"I just don't know how to tell him, Holly!" Scott exclaimed. There was genuine anguish in his voice, and resentment as well. "Since he's married to Carling, I was hoping he would concentrate exclusively on her, but he's as involved in our lives as he's always been."

"That's Kane for you," Holly said gloomily. "Always ready, willing and able to run the lives of the people he loves. He simply added Carly to his list."

"I never thought Kane would marry. He must be crazy about her," Scott said thoughtfully. "Can she get around him? Could we use her as an ally?"

"I'm not sure. She's crazy about him, too. Right now I'm living in mortal fear that she'll tell him what she thinks she knows about Joseph Wayne and me."

Scott and Holly thought that she and Kane were crazy about each other? Carling felt another ridiculous rush of tears fill her eyes and she mocked herself for her own stupid sentimentality. It was true what they said about emotions running amok in pregnant women, she decided. Otherwise, why should she feel like crying because Holly's and Scott's supposition *wasn't* true?

"Oh, Scott, what's the matter with us anyway?" Holly was wailing when Carling tuned back into the conversation. "We're nothing but spineless cowards! We deserve to have our lives run by Kane because we let him do it. We never stand up to him."

"How do you tell someone who's devoted his life to you, who gave up all his own plans and dreams for you, who wants only the best for you and is absolutely certain that he knows what will make you happy..." Scott paused to draw a deep breath. "How do you tell him to butt out and let us live our own lives?"

"We don't." Holly sighed. "Instead, we lie and sneak around behind his back. We're worse than cowards, Scott. We're genuine creeps. It would serve us right if somehow Kane were to find out the truth. In fact, I almost wish he would."

Living in the political arena wasn't unlike life in the theater, and Carling had learned the value of good timing and the merit of a dramatic entrance. She used both to full advantage when she stepped from her hiding place to join Holly and Scott. "How would you like your wish to come true, Holly?"

Holly shrieked. Scott jumped. Both gaped at Carling as if she were an apparition.

"Were you spying on us?" demanded Scott. "Did Kane put you up to it?"

"How much did you hear?" Holly wanted to know.

"I'm not a spy and all I heard was that you two consider yourselves a couple of lying, sneaking creeps." Carling shrugged. "I don't happen to agree with you, but if you feel that way, why don't you tell Kane whatever it is you can't bring yourself to tell him and stop the lying and the sneaking."

"Oh yeah, right." Scott laughed sardonically. "Tell Kane, who thinks banking is the world's greatest career, that I despise it? Sure, Carling. Kane pulled all kinds of strings to get me that job and I know some ambitious banker type would kill to be in my position, but every day I spend in that bank is like doing time on death row."

Carling thought of how proud Kane was of Scott's budding career at the bank. Hadn't investment banking been Kane's first choice of a career for himself before his parents' fatal accident had compelled him to return to the ranch and raise his younger brothers and sister?

"Surely it isn't written in stone that you have to be a banker, Scott," she said reasonably. "That might've been Kane's aspiration for himself, which he transferred to you, but if you tell him how you feel, don't you think he'll understand? There are so many careers and you—"

Holly and Scott interrupted her with laughter. It wasn't a happy, full-of-fun kind of laughter, either. Carling swallowed. She was seized by a sense of ominous foreboding. "What career do you have in mind, Scott?"

"I'm a rock singer with a band," Scott exclaimed eagerly. "The lead singer. I play guitar and keyboard and have written some songs. We've been booked at college parties for the past three years and have started getting regular weekend gigs at clubs in Dallas and Fort Worth. We want to go to L.A. But I have to grow my hair," he added, running his hand through his short, banker-style cut with a look of genuine disgust on his face. "And I need to get at least one earring. You can see how having to look the part of a staid banker is really hurting my rocker image. I have to wear a wig when we play!"

Though Carling wasn't an expert on the latest heavy metal rock bands, she knew enough about them to know that they were undoubtedly the antithesis of the conservative sedate banker, style-wise, personality-wise, in any and every way.

"You want to be a rock star," she said flatly. She remembered when she was five or six years old, she'd wanted to grow up to be a princess. It struck her that Scott's career goal was on a par with that. And he was twenty-four!

"It's not like this is some wild pipe dream and I don't have a prayer of making it!" Scott argued, as if reading her mind. "I have talent and I work hard at my music. All I need is one good break. And I'm gonna make it happen. I quit the bank yesterday and I'm heading for L.A. this weekend, right after the Waynes' party. I—I'll tell Kane then."

"Oh no!" Holly exclaimed in dismay. "Why didn't you give me advance warning? I could've arranged to be visiting my college roommate in Atlanta and missed what's going to be an explosion that'll rival a hydrogen bomb.''

Carling tended to agree with her. She knew only too well that Kane was used to having things go the way he'd planned them to go. And he was accustomed to having people do what he wanted them to do. Having Scott trade a promising banking career for an electronic guitar and an earring was not viable in the world-according-to Kane McClellan.

"How will you support yourself in L.A., uh, until your big break, Scott?'' Carling asked politely. She fervently hoped he wasn't expecting Kane to foot the bill. Because she knew he wouldn't and she didn't want to see the brothers' relationship ruptured.

Strange, she'd once wished Kane a life of misery—she'd even promised him one!—but now that he was facing disappointment and possible estrangement from his brother, which she knew would make him truly miserable, she could hardly bear the thought. She wanted to protect him—a ludicrous notion since Kane was so tough and so strong that he seemed to need protection from no one.

Scott heaved a sigh. "Don't worry, I'm not counting on my big brother to subsidize me. Not that he would, anyway. Kane believes in hard work and making it on your own. Our father was in debt and the ranch was going to hell when Kane took it over and made it profitable—and made a fortune from his sideline interests, too. He could've easily kept it all to himself, but he set up trust funds for Holly, Timmy and me. We're financially secure, but we won't get a penny of the money until we turn thirty. Kane wanted us to *have* to learn to support ourselves, not be rich kids living off money we hadn't earned ourselves.''

"That was very wise of him," Carling said thoughtfully, remembering how aimless she'd been. She'd had too much time on her hands and no goals, responsibilities or ambitions. She wouldn't want her child to lead such a life.

"Of course you'd think so," grumbled Holly. "But if Scott had his money now, he could go to L.A. and live in style out there."

Scott shook his head. "No, Kane is right about the money. Besides, I can't buy myself a recording contract. I have to be good enough to get an offer. I figure I have six years to make it. If I haven't hit it big by the time I'm thirty, I'll go back to the bank and make my money work for me."

Carling smiled. Either she was getting accustomed to the idea of Scott as a rock musician or she was beginning to feel that his plans weren't quite as insane as she'd originally thought. She told him so.

"I wish Kane would see it your way, but there's not much chance of that," Scott said dolefully. "Will you help me break the news to him, Carling? Not until after the party, though. Let's keep it a secret till then."

Carling agreed and tried to think of ways to present his plan in the most favorable—or least horrifying—light as she walked back to the house with Holly and Scott.

"There is one question I'd like to ask, to sort of prepare myself, since you McClellans seem to have a penchant for secrets," she said. "Are Tim's graduation and plans for medical school for real? Or are they bogus? Does he have an undisclosed alternative ambition, something along the lines of living in a tent on the beach and becoming a full-time surfer?"

"Not Tim," Scott assured her. "He's not leading a secret double life. Tim has always been the most like

Kane. Successful at whatever he tries. Up-front, honest, open and frank.'' He gave a self-deprecating grimace. ''Unlike Holly and me, who want to please Kane but then end up double-crossing him.''

''Not wanting to work in a bank is hardly a double cross,'' Carling said soothingly. ''And just because Holly and Joseph want to be alone but are too embarrassed to—''

''Holly and Joseph Wayne?'' Scott interrupted with a hoot of derisive laughter. ''Don't tell me you bought the trumped-up tale, too! I thought you knew that—''

''Shut up, Scott,'' Holly cried fiercely. ''If you say one more word, I'll go straight to Kane and tell him that you quit the bank.''

''And I'll tell him that you've been carrying on with his ranch manager for the past ten months and using a phony romance with Joseph Wayne as your cover,'' snapped Scott.

Carling's jaw dropped. ''The ranch manager?'' she echoed. Webb Asher and Holly? She could hardly take it in. ''But what about Joseph Wayne? His own mother said that he, that you—''

''Joseph and I worked out an arrangement because we both needed to get out and we knew our families would never object to a romance between the two of us,'' Holly said sullenly. ''We could go out every night and stay out as late as we wanted, no questions asked, because Kane and Sam and Edie Wayne are positively enraptured with the idea of Joe and me as a couple.''

''And all those times you were supposed to be with Joseph, you were really with Webb Asher?'' Carling stared at the young woman in disbelief. ''But why the subterfuge, Holly? Kane speaks highly of Webb

Asher. He likes him. I can't believe that he wouldn't approve of your dating him.''

"Dating him?" Holly repeated with a sneer and then promptly burst into tears. "I'm not *dating* him, Carly! I'm sleeping with him, every chance I get. He lives in the bunkhouse, but there's a partition around his bed so—''

"The bunkhouse?" Carling was appalled. She'd seen the bunkhouses, including the largest one with the paper-thin walls partitioning the ranch manager's sleeping area from the ten other bunks in the building. No wonder Holly had been so desperate for her own place in Stanton. Making love in the bunkhouse? Carling shuddered. "Holly, that is *not* a place anyone could ever consider conducive to romance.''

"Romance?" Holly laughed hollowly, through her tears. "Webb isn't offering me romance, all he wants from me is sex. He doesn't love me and he's never pretended to. He sees other women and flaunts them. He doesn't ever want to marry and settle down.''

"Webb is a throwback to the cowboys of the Wild West," Scott explained. "He likes to drink and fight and roam from place to place. He's been here for five years and is terrific at his job, but he'll probably move on just because he doesn't want to put down roots.''

"He'll end up putting down roots in the cemetery if Kane finds out he's been using Holly," Carling said grimly. "At the bunkhouse!" She grimaced. The lack of privacy, the seediness, the smell . . .

Her mind was truly boggled. "Holly, why? I'll concede that Webb Asher is good-looking in a hard, rough sort of way, but you're so pretty and bright, you have everything going for you. Why would you accept such shabby treatment from any man?''

"Not any man, Carly. Just him, just Webb." Holy cried harder. "I love him, Carly. I love looking at him, I love touching him, I love the way he makes me feel. I'll do anything to be with him, whenever he wants me. Think of the way you feel about Kane... what if he didn't love you in return, what if he only wanted you for sex? Loving him the way you do, wouldn't you go to him whenever he called? Wouldn't you—"

"I have a strong feeling that if Kane were to invite Carling to the bunkhouse for sex, she wouldn't have any difficulty refusing his call," Scott interrupted dryly.

Holly stopping crying long enough to give her brother a sharp jab in the ribs with her elbow. Carling didn't blame her. This was hardly the time for humor. For Holly's words had stuck a paralyzing nerve within her: *I love looking at him, I love touching him, I love the way he makes me feel.* Didn't that accurately describe the way she felt about Kane?

Carling began to tremble as the revelation hit with full force. Oh God, I'm in love with him! She wanted to laugh and cry at the same time. Of course she was in love with him! There could be no other explanation for the feelings and changes within her, feelings and changes which she had refused to examine and acknowledge on anything but the most superficial level. But she admitted them now. Kane had become the center of her life; she loved him so much while he...

He didn't love her. Carling forced herself to face reality. The pain to her psyche was shattering, far worse than any physical pain she had ever suffered.

What if he didn't love you in return, what if he only wanted you for sex? Holly's description of her depressing relationship with Webb Asher also defined her marriage to Kane, Carling thought, and despair surged through her.

Kane didn't love her; he owned her and controlled her. At least when she'd thought she hated him, she had the strength and spirit to fight back, but now... Now she was pregnant and had admitted to herself that she was deeply in love with him. Now she ran the risk of being completely subjugated under his domination, because her love would make her weak, no match for the indomitable Kane.

She pictured her lost self, weak and cringing with no will of her own, afraid to speak her mind to Kane, to tell him when he was wrong—and dammit, he *was* wrong at times! What kind of a mother would such a shadow figure be? Her children might very well end up like Scott and Holly, mixed-up and deceitful, because they perceived Kane as an unapproachable tyrant, however well-meaning his motives might be.

She reflexively covered her still flat abdomen with both hands. Her child deserved a happy family with two strong parents, who respected and loved each other. Instead, it faced being stuck with a lovelorn wimp for a mother and an unchallenged dictator as its father! Her poor baby!

"Oh, Carly, don't cry." Holly put her arms around Carling and hugged her. "It's so kind of you to care so much."

Carling knew that Holly thought she was crying tears of empathy, not realizing that she was crying for herself and her baby and the unholy mess they were in. She'd fallen in love with Kane, a man who didn't love, a man who owned and controlled and always, always made things go his way.

"Well, you'd both better stop blubbering before Kane sees you," Scott said with brotherly scorn.

"Because then we'll have to cook up a reason why you're both crying and I don't know about you, but I'm not feeling very creative at this particular point in time."

"We could always say that Joseph Wayne dumped me," Holly said, brightening a little. "Maybe then we could get out of the party tomorrow—because it's going to be awful. For the first time in my life, I'm going to hate a party as much as Kane will. Webb will be there flirting with every single woman in the county. And Joe and I will supposed to be pretending we're in love, when nothing could be farther from the truth."

"Since Joseph agreed to your charade, did he need a cover for a secret lover, too?" Carling asked. She didn't really care, but she'd always found making small talk was easier than having to face her deepest feelings. Particularly when they were so dismal.

"Poor Joey. His situation is even worse than mine," Holly said sadly. "He's in love with an American Indian girl named Maya, a full-blooded Apache. She's a social worker on the reservation about a hundred miles southwest of town."

"And the Waynes hate Indians, especially Apaches," continued Scott. "I mean they really *hate* them. Prejudice is too mild a word to use to describe their feelings. They'll disown Joseph if he marries Maya and he really loves her. She loves him too, but I think their relationship is doomed."

"That's terrible!" Carling cried, forgetting her own misery for the moment.

"Tom Wayne, Sam's great-grandfather got scalped during a fight with an Apache, so the story goes," said Scott. "According to Kane, the rest of the story is that Tom Wayne was a murdering, thieving cattle rustler, who got exactly what he deserved. Of course, the

Waynes don't see it that way. They've been born and bred to hate Indians down through the generations.''

"That's revolting!" Carling was indignant. "These are the 1990s, not the 1890s. There is absolutely no excuse for such misplaced animosity.''

"Try telling that to the Waynes," Holly said grimly. "You can see why Joseph was glad to work out a cover story with me. But we're both buying time and we know it. Sooner or later, the truth will have to come out.''

"How about delaying it, till I'm far away in California?'' suggested Scott.

Holly glared at him. "Do you have to be so damned flippant?''

They began to bicker. Carling felt too drained to care. What a day this was turning out to be! She felt as if she were living in a maze of mirrors, which distorted everything. Nothing was as it seemed. Kane thought that Scott was happily employed in a Dallas bank and that Holly was in love with Joseph Wayne. He didn't know about their baby or that she loved him. He was existing in an entirely different reality and Carling found it difficult and confusing to maintain the pretense. There were too many things to keep straight!

It was easier to avoid Kane, and she did so, pleading an upset stomach and going to bed immediately after dinner. She pretended to be asleep when he came in to check on her several times throughout the evening. And when he climbed into bed beside her later that night, she kept her eyes closed and her breathing deep and even.

Kane moved closer and touched her arm. He felt the soft warmth of her skin and inhaled the feminine sweetness of her body. Every muscle in his body tightened; he was ready, willing and able to take her immediately. No one but Carling had ever affected him so intensely. All of his senses responded to the sight and sound, the smell and the feel of her. And his desire kept growing stronger, the longer they were together.

Desire had become need and he knew it. There was no use denying it. He was in love with her; there was no use denying that, either. But telling her... Did he dare? He was accustomed to examining and analyzing all sides of a situation before making an investment and he did so now. Tell her he loved her? When she didn't love him, when he'd forced her into marriage, disrupted her life....

It was all so new to him, being in love and feeling uncertain. It was unsettling to realize that he couldn't control Carling's emotions or his own. It was more than unsettling; it was downright terrifying! He resolutely tried to think about something else, anything else: the price of oil, the young bull he'd been wanting to purchase from Bobby Killeen's stud farm, Juanita's incomparable chicken-fried steak and milk gravy. But nothing diverted him for long. Carling claimed his thoughts as well as his heart and his body.

Was she pregnant? he wondered. He was fairly certain that she was. He was an observant man and as a result of his vested interests in cattle and horses, extremely knowledgeable about breeding. A slight smile curved his lips. He'd better not put it in those terms to Carling; she would definitely be insulted.

He wanted her to tell him that she was pregnant. Every day he waited and every day she didn't mention it. Was it possible that she was unaware of her condition? It seemed unlikely. Still, he'd rather believe that than face the fact that she was deliberately keeping the news from him.

Tonight she'd eaten a full meal, then said she felt sick. She'd looked fine but he hadn't questioned her when she insisted on going right to bed. He knew that fatigue and nausea were both common symptoms of pregnancy.

She was carrying his child! The thought filled him with such pride and love he thought he would explode. In fact, his aching, throbbing body was already perilously close to doing exactly that. Tonight was the first night since they'd been married that they hadn't made love and he wanted her so much he was shaking, from the urgency of his passion for her.

"Carly?" he whispered her name. When she didn't respond, he said it again, a little louder. Still, she appeared to be deeply asleep, not stirring at all, her breath coming in a slow deep rhythm.

And he knew then that she was faking. He knew that she awakened easily and quickly. He'd certainly awakened her often enough deep in the night, his body hard and burning for her. Now she was deliberately pretending to be asleep, not realizing that her comatose act had given her away.

"What's going on?" He hadn't realized that he'd spoken his thoughts aloud until he heard his voice break the silence in the room.

Carling's heart thumped and she rolled onto her stomach and buried her face in her pillow. Had Kane found out about Scott or Holly and their convoluted dilemmas? He would view her prior knowledge as complicity and she dreaded his disapproval as much as his wrath. She simply wasn't up to quarreling with him tonight. Even a calm discussion was too arduous to contemplate. She was exhausted, from the demands of pregnancy, from the emotional upheavals of the day—and from pretending to be asleep while lying there alert and tense.

"You can stop faking, Carly. I know you're awake. Do you feel like telling me why you felt the need to enact this little charade?"

She continued to lie still and made no reply.

"Coma victims are more responsive than you are. Give it up, Carly," he said roughly. His growing anger was a welcome diversion from the passion which still shook his body. "If you don't want sex, then say so. One thing I can't tolerate is dishonesty."

Carling's heart plummeted. If you don't want sex, he'd said. *Sex*. Not making love, but sex. That's all he wanted her for, for sexual release. He was like Webb Asher summoning Holly to the bunkhouse for a quick roll in the ... bunk.

Which brought her to another sickening realization. One thing I can't tolerate is dishonesty, he'd said in a tone that meant it. And she was dishonesty personified, deceiving him by omission by not sharing her knowledge of Scott and the rock band, and Holly and the ranch manager, and Joseph Wayne and his Apache girlfriend. Not only did Kane not love her, he would find her presence intolerable when the truth came out.

It was too much to bear and her emotions were too fragile from the stress of early pregnancy. Hating herself as a weak-minded nitwit, Carling nevertheless gave into the sobs that racked her body. Tears streamed down her cheeks. She kept her face firmly buried in the pillow, swiftly dampening the pillowcase.

"Carly, what's wrong?" Kane sounded truly alarmed. He sat down on the bed and tried to take her in his arms.

She fought him, pulling away from him. She was too dishonest to deserve his comfort. But there was much, much more. She absolutely refused to be soothed by the man who had sex with her but didn't love her, who'd made her pregnant but didn't love her. Who'd made her fall irrevocably in love with him but who didn't love her.

"Go away, leave me alone," she sobbed. She managed to sound both fierce and heartbroken at the same time.

She was pregnant, Kane was sure of it now. He stared at her bleakly, and reluctantly withdrew from her. At any other time, he would have stayed and held her and petted her and aroused her until she was moaning and clinging to him, and the tension and hostility between them had been melted in the heat of their passion.

The rough, never-give-up-or-give-in part of himself urged him to do that now. But the protective, paternal part of him won out and he bowed to her wishes. She was pregnant and she knew it and she hated him for it. He was certain of that. It explained her withdrawal, her tears and rage. Never had he felt so low.

"I'll leave you alone," he said quietly. "I'll sleep in one of the guest rooms tonight."

He left the room noiselessly, closing the door behind him. Carling sat up in bed and stared around the empty room in shock. He'd left her! This was the first night of their marriage that he hadn't made love to her. No, it was the first night that he hadn't had sex with her, she mentally corrected, but as quickly as she'd had the thought, she discarded it with a shake of her head. Whatever it meant to Kane, to her it was making love. She was so in love with him.

She climbed out of bed and walked to the window, staring out at the moonlight and willing him to come back to their room. He wouldn't have to say a word; she would gladly give herself to him. She faced the unthinkable—that she would even make love with him in a *bunkhouse* if he asked her to!

She went back to bed and lay down. If he hadn't returned in fifteen minutes, she decided she would go to him, even if it meant searching all through the house to find him. Her eyes drifted shut. Fifteen minutes, she promised herself. And promptly fell asleep in five.

Eleven

She had attended her first party at the tender age of two weeks old, and had gone to countless others for the subsequent twenty-eight years, but none in Carling's memory came close to equaling the Waynes' party. It was by far the most traumatic, miserable, wretched event of her life, almost enough to make her detest parties as thoroughly as Kane did.

The day had started out badly enough. She'd awakened, alone in her bed, and learned that Kane had flown to Dallas. He'd gone without telling her he was leaving or when he was coming back, although he'd left word with Juanita, the cook, that Carling was to go to the Waynes for dinner with Holly and the boys and he would join them later.

By the time he arrived, the party was in full swing, with cars lining the entrance to the Waynes' house, instantly tipping him off that this was a social extravaganza, not the quiet family dinner he'd been anticipating. He hadn't seen Carling all day and he barely got to nod to her before he was swept away by a jolly band of well-wishers, leaving her to make mindless small talk with her new neighbors.

They were welcoming and friendly and eager to fill in Kane's lucky new wife on all the details of Kane's premarital life. "I can't believe that Kane finally tied the knot," a man named Bobby Killeen, about Kane's age, exclaimed incredulously. "I never thought he'd get married, not when he didn't marry Missy Howser. Now *that* was one hot and heavy romance! The whole county was keeping tabs on that one." He chuckled and rolled his eyes heavenward. "Did Kane ever tell you about the time he and Missy were in the midst of one of their humongous fights and to get even, she arrived at a party wearing one of those flouncy dresses and no underwear? And proceeded to take part in a square dance?" He grinned broadly at what was obviously a fond memory.

"No," Carling said with a tight smile. "He never shared that particular anecdote with me."

"Bobby, just hush up!" Bobby's wife glowered at him. "We're all sick to death of that story and Carling isn't interested in what is now ancient history."

Carling managed what she hoped was a lighthearted little laugh. Wasn't Missy the same old girlfriend who had constantly played that former favorite song of hers she was never going to listen to again? "Whatever happened to that Missy person, anyway?" she asked, feeling curious in spite of herself.

"Why, she got married and divorced and returned to Stanton earlier this year," Bobby replied. "There she is, over there, across the room. The great-looking brunette in the slinky black dress. Um, looks like she's just spotted Kane and is going over to talk to him.''

Carling turned in time to see a voluptuous dark beauty slither to Kane's side and gaze up at him with worshipful black eyes. From the way the woman had been poured into her eye-popping, tight-fitting dress, it was obvious that she'd forgone her underwear tonight, too.

Carling glanced down at her own dress, which was bright red cotton with white polka dots, had a fitted bodice, shirred elastic back and full swingy skirt. She didn't dare compare herself and her outfit to the sexy, sultry Missy; her ego wasn't up to such a challenge.

She escaped from the effervescent Bobby and his wife and moved on. T. R. Wayne, Joseph's older brother, and his wife Janie were eager to chat. They had nothing much to say about Missy Howser except, ''We knew Kane would never marry that little tramp,'' but reminisced fondly about Robin Sue Taylor, with whom it seemed, Kane had shared another equally compelling ''hot and heavy romance.''

''Kane and Robin Sue broke up because she resented having to share him with the younger kids, and of course, Kane wouldn't hear of giving them up or sending them away,'' Janie said with a sigh. ''I never thought he'd marry after that. From then on, he just sort of dallied with lots of different girls.''

''Is Robin Sue here tonight?'' Carling asked resignedly. Undoubtedly, she was, and looking gorgeous and sexy to boot. It was that kind of night, that kind of party. A party from hell.

''She sure is!'' T.R. said heartily. ''That's Robin Sue, over there, across the room. The knockout redhead.''

"The one heading toward Kane," observed Carling. She felt jealous and depressed. There was no one in her dull, uneventful past whom she could claim as a former great love. Kane was the one and only true love of her life.

Standing here, watching two of Kane's ex-loves jockeying for his attention, was definitely one of the low points of her life, she decided miserably. She had to *do* something! She glanced desperately around the room and spied the Triple M's ranch manager, Webb Asher, necking with a giggly young blonde who had obviously had too much to drink.

Carling looked over at Holly, who was sitting beside Joseph Wayne on a corner sofa. Both looked so young and so hurt. Joe was probably wishing the woman he loved was here, accepted by his family. And Holly's eyes never left Webb, who was indeed flaunting his pretty young companion.

Carling's blue eyes narrowed to slits and her mouth tightened into a firm, straight line. She'd been looking for something to do and taking the perfidious Webb Asher to task filled the bill perfectly.

"I want to talk to you," she said imperiously to him, then turned to the blonde and said in a tough, impolite tone that she'd never used during her years as the senator's perfect daughter: "Get lost."

The blonde stopped giggling and promptly disappeared into the crowd. Webb Asher smiled his insolent smile. "So what can I do for you, Carly? Get you a drink? Name your poison, babe."

The insect actually thought she was coming on to him! Carling stared at him with distaste. "First, you will refer to me, *always*, as Mrs. McClellan. And second, unless you're prepared to marry my sister-in-law, you will stop seeing her immediately."

Asher's jaw dropped. "You—you know about Holly and me?" He looked totally disconcerted.

She'd taken him by surprise and Carling homed in on her advantage. "I know everything. And the only thing stopping me from telling Kane right now is that it'll take a couple weeks to institute a search for a new ranch manager. As soon as—"

"Mrs. McClellan, I don't want to leave the Triple M." Webb Asher was perspiring now and had turned a chalky white. "It's the best job I've ever had and the closest thing to a home I've ever known."

Carling was not moved. "Then you know what you have to do, don't you?"

"I can't get married. I'm not a marrying man!" he exclaimed, clearly in a panic at the very thought.

"Then break it off with Holly," Carling said coldly. "I'll be watching you carefully and if I find that you dare continue to use her for your—your own selfish pleasure, I'll fire you on the spot." She paused, to heighten the effect of her words. "And then I'll tell Kane everything and he'll make certain that you'll never work on a ranch anywhere, ever again."

She wasn't sure if Kane could actually carry out her threat, but Webb Asher seemed to think so. He lowered his eyes and stared at the ground, his shoulders slumped in defeat. "Yes, ma'am," he mumbled without out a trace of his usual bravado.

Carling watched him walk away, knowing that Holly was going to be hurt by his rejection, yet feeling convinced that she'd done the right thing. Because she cared about her young sister-in-law, she just couldn't stand idly by and let her be used by an unfeeling rake.

She felt a hand close around her upper arm and gave a startled gasp. Threatening Webb Asher had been

such a successful diversion that she hadn't noticed
Kane desert his fan club and join her.

"We're leaving," Kane growled, "as soon as we say
good-night to Sam and Edie."

"Surely you haven't finished catching up with Missy
and Robin Sue?"

Kane groaned. "I have great friends, but they talk
entirely too much."

"But then, you've given them so much to talk
about," she said sweetly. "Your reputation as a reclusive rancher is totally misleading—you're a ro-
mancing rancher. How many other former sweethearts
do you have roaming around the county? And are they
all here tonight?"

He frowned, his gray eyes darkening with controlled anger. "If you're trying to be funny, you might
take note that I'm not laughing."

"I'm beginning to understand why you aren't too
crazy about big parties," Carling continued, undaunted. "It must be extremely inconvenient to have
all the players in your romantic past mingling
with—"

"Forget Sam and Edie. We're leaving now." He
pushed his way through the crowd, his grip on her arm
never slackening.

Ever well-mannered, Carling automatically smiled
and made her goodbyes as he dragged her along after
him. No one seemed to mind that the guests of honor
were leaving early. The other guests all kidded and
laughed, as if they'd expected it.

It was a silent drive home. Carling studied Kane
covertly, trying to gauge his mood. How angry was
he? She tried to emulate his cool withdrawal but she
couldn't sustain it. By the time they reached the Triple M, her nerves were tightly strung. This was not

good for a woman in her condition, she scolded herself. She had to take care of herself and the baby, and having an anxiety attack was hardly prenatally ideal.

"Kane, this is making me crazy," she announced, as they entered the dimly lit foyer. "I'm not spending another night like last night."

"You slept like a baby last night," Kane retorted. "I know that for a fact because I came in to check on you ten minutes after I left the room." He grimaced wryly. "It was a resounding blow to my self-esteem to find you sound asleep instead of fretting over my absence."

She stared at him, her blue eyes wide. "Oh."

"Yeah." He shrugged. "Oh." He started down the hallway. "Come into my office." It was a command, and she followed, too bemused to rebel.

When they were inside the paneled office, he handed her a thick portfolio. "Everything is in there," he said in a cool, gruff tone. "The complete record of the financial transaction between your father and me. There is only one copy and when you destroy it, there will be no evidence of any questionable financial dealings concerning Senator Clayton Templeton."

She stared from the portfolio in her hand to Kane's hard, unyielding profile. What did it mean? Her mind clouded. She tried to think but couldn't.

"You're free, Carling," he said, as if in answer to her unspoken question. His voice was as forbidding as his expression. And he had called her Carling.

"Why?" she whispered. "Why are you doing this?" Her hand settled on her stomach, just above the place where their child nestled within her. Destroying these documents had been a dream and a goal of hers, but now that she had them in her hands, she couldn't decide if she wanted them or not. It all depended on what Kane's motives had been in giving them to her.

Pain shot through her sharp as an arrow as a horrible thought struck her. What if his offer of her freedom was really a ruse to get rid of her? "Did seeing Missy or Robin Sue tonight have anything to do with—"

"Oh, give me a break!" he snapped, glowering at her. "I flew to Dallas today to retrieve these documents. I intended to give them to you before I saw either Missy or Robin Sue at that damnable party. And you can't seriously believe that I'm even remotely interested in either one of them. I could have had them years ago if I'd wanted them. They wanted to marry me but I didn't want to marry either of them," he added with a trace of his usual Kane-like bluntness.

His voice lowered. "I didn't want to marry Missy or Robin Sue or any other woman, Carly. Just you. Only you. It's always been you and always will be. But I'm not going to force you to stay with me any longer. Your father's political career doesn't depend on whether you go or stay, not anymore. You're free to choose."

She clutched the portfolio. Her mind had cleared. She could see everything so clearly now. And what she saw made her heart pound with joy. "So this is my own personal Emancipation Proclamation?" An intense burst of love exploded within her. "You're saying I'm free to go if I please. You won't stand in my way or try to influence my decision in any way." Her mouth curved into a wickedly seductive smile and her blue eyes shone as brightly as twin stars. "You'll do or say nothing to try to make me stay."

"For godsake's, don't make it any harder for me to let you go," he said hoarsely. Carling stared at him in surprise. She'd been teasing him and he'd taken her seriously. It astonished her that he didn't realize what she was trying to tell him. Kane was usually so fast to catch on, so quick-witted.

But the pain, which shadowed his face, had obviously dulled his perceptive powers. "What I did was wrong. Using my hold over your father to force you into marrying me was *wrong,* Carly." His voice was low and deep and filled with remorse.

Carling gripped the back of a chair and hung on. She was stunned. Kane McClellan admitting he was wrong? She thought back to their wedding day when he had informed her—with his customary blend of unshakable confidence and maddening arrogance—that marrying her against her will was a perfectly acceptable thing for him to do because he knew they were right for each other.

There had been a time when it would have galled her to admit that he'd been right all along. They *were* perfect for each other. And there was a time when she would have positively reveled in his admission of wrongdoing. But that time was past. They had both come a long, long way in a relatively short period of time. Love had reformed and redeemed them both.

"Are you telling me that you regret marrying me?" she asked quietly, knowing the answer, yet wanting to hear him say it.

"No!" he exclaimed fiercely. "Marrying you is the best thing I've ever done. I love you, Carly. I love you so much I..." His voice trailed off and he stared moodily into space. "I want you to love me, to stay with me and live with me as my wife because you want to, not because you—"

"Were bought and paid for?" Carling filled in, trying but not quite succeeding in stifling a mischievous grin.

He gave her a long, penetrating stare. She could almost see *his* mind clearing. She could feel the relief and the happiness that he was feeling as he realized the truth. That she was free to choose and that she'd chosen to love him.

He pulled her into his arms for a long, hungry kiss, holding her, loving her with a passion that would never be extinguished.

"I love you," Carling whispered when he lifted his mouth from hers. "Oh, Kane, I love you so much." Tears began to trickle down her cheeks, and she wiped them away with an apologetic smile. "I'm sorry. Lately, I seem to cry all the time, whether I'm happy or sad or mad."

He smiled down at her. "Mmm, and why is that, do you think?"

She drew back from him, linking her arms around his neck and gazing into the gray depths of his eyes. His hands moved over her waist, her belly, with loving possession. "You know about the baby!" she exclaimed.

"I wasn't sure if you did. I've been waiting for you to tell me."

She sighed happily and snuggled closer to him. This had to be one of the sweetest moments of her life, she thought, and was not at all surprised when her eyes filled up again. "I'm pregnant, Kane. I bought two of those kits at the drugstore to be absolutely sure." She hugged him tight. "And don't you dare mention anything about *breeding cycles*," she added, looking up at him with laughing, loving blue eyes.

"Not a word, I promise." He leaned down to kiss her again, and then asked seriously, "Are you happy about the baby, Carly? I wanted a child right away, but I never asked you. It's something we should have discussed before I made you pregnant, I realize that now."

"Next time we will," she resolved. "But I'm thrilled about having this baby, Kane. There is something I'd like you to promise me, though."

"Anything, darling. Name it."

"I want you to help me be the kind of parent I want to be. You know, give our kids plenty of love but also the freedom to be themselves. If I ever get the urge to mold our children into perfect little campaigners for Grandpa, please remind me of this conversation. Likewise, if they try something once and it doesn't work out and they feel scared and nervous about trying again, help me to convince them that it might not be such a bad idea, after all."

"You're going to be a wonderful mother, Carly, the best. And I promise to be the best father I can be."

"The kind of dad who would be supportive and not angry if we have a musically talented son who decides he'd like to be a rock star instead of, oh, working in a bank?"

"Hmm." Kane considered it. "If he was young and had already completed his education and didn't have a wife or family to support, I guess I might be—" he cleared his throat "—can we leave it at, not totally aghast?"

"That'll do for now. And if we have a daughter who gets involved with the wrong man, you wouldn't lecture her, you'd do everything to ease her heartbreak, wouldn't you? And if we have a young neighbor who falls in love with an Apache and his family hates Indians, you'd do your best to convince them otherwise. And you'd succeed, too," she added lovingly. "Because Kane McClellan always does."

His brows narrowed. "Exactly how hypothetical are those situations and those kids?" But then she smiled at him and nothing else mattered except that she loved him, that she wanted to stay married to him of her own free will and that she was going to have their child.

"What the hell, together we can face anything," he said in a lighthearted tone far removed from his usual responsible, serious mode. "Here, open the present I bought you in Dallas."

He handed her a big gift-wrapped box which she quickly opened. "Rabbits!" she exclaimed in delight, removing each individually wrapped piece of porcelain. She set them on his desk, one by one. "A rabbit wedding!" She was thrilled. "A bride and a groom, bridesmaids and a best man, and even a little flower girl and ring bearer." She threw her arms around him. "Oh, Kane, they're wonderful. I've never seen anything like them!"

"Believe me, neither have I," he said dryly. "I saw them in a gift shop window in Dallas this afternoon. Normally, I avoid gift shops the way you avoid horses, but I had to go in and buy them." His eyes gleamed with laughter. "A bunny rabbit wedding set somehow seemed—symbolic."

"You're right," she said breathlessly.

His fingers were already tackling the long zipper in the back of her dress.

"Of course. I'm always right." He swept her up in his arms.

"Except when you're wrong," she said, kissing the firm, strong line of his jaw. "But don't worry, I'll be here to tell you when you are. I love you, Kane. I love being married to you and I'm going to love raising our family."

"I was right about that," he said with satisfaction. "We belong together, Carly. I knew it would work out."

She began to unbutton his shirt. "Are you going to take me to bed or stand here gloating?"

They were in the bedroom within thirty seconds flat.

* * * * *

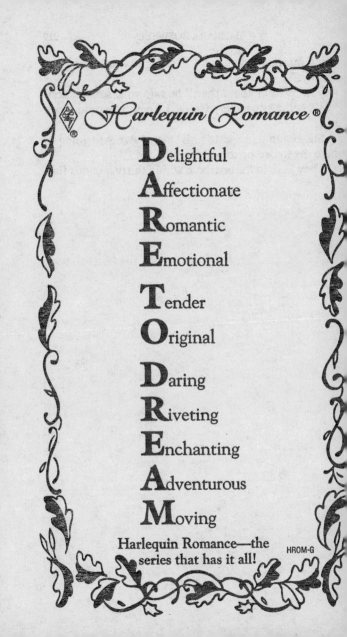

Harlequin Romance ®

Delightful
Affectionate
Romantic
Emotional

Tender
Original

Daring
Riveting
Enchanting
Adventurous
Moving

Harlequin Romance—the
series that has it all!

HROM-G

HARLEQUIN  PRESENTS®

HARLEQUIN PRESENTS
men you won't be able to resist falling in love with...

HARLEQUIN PRESENTS
women who have feelings just like your own...

HARLEQUIN PRESENTS
powerful passion in exotic international settings...

HARLEQUIN PRESENTS
intense, dramatic stories that will keep you turning
to the very last page...

HARLEQUIN PRESENTS
The world's bestselling romance series!

Harlequin® Historical

If you're a serious fan of historical romance,
then you're in luck!

Harlequin Historicals brings you
stories by bestselling authors, rising new stars
and talented first-timers.

Ruth Langan & Theresa Michaels
Mary McBride & Cheryl St. John
Margaret Moore & Merline Lovelace
Julie Tetel & Nina Beaumont
Susan Amarillas & Ana Seymour
Deborah Simmons & Linda Castle
Cassandra Austin & Emily French
Miranda Jarrett & Suzanne Barclay
DeLoras Scott & Laurie Grant...

You'll never run out of favorites.

Harlequin Historicals...they're too good to miss!

HH-GEN

SPECIAL EDITION

Stories of love and life, these powerful
novels are tales that you can identify with—
romances with "something special" added in!

Fall in love with the stories of authors such
as **Nora Roberts, Diana Palmer, Ginna Gray**
and many more of your special favorites—as
well as wonderful new voices!

Special Edition brings you
entertainment for the heart!

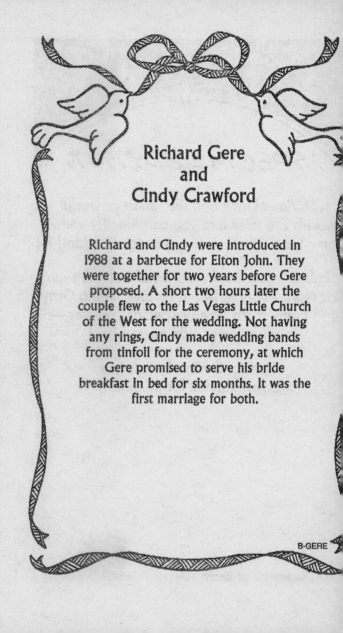

Richard Gere
and
Cindy Crawford

Richard and Cindy were introduced in
1988 at a barbecue for Elton John. They
were together for two years before Gere
proposed. A short two hours later the
couple flew to the Las Vegas Little Church
of the West for the wedding. Not having
any rings, Cindy made wedding bands
from tinfoil for the ceremony, at which
Gere promised to serve his bride
breakfast in bed for six months. It was the
first marriage for both.

B-GERE